The changing past

The changing past

Trends in
South African historical writing

Ken Smith

Ohio University Press
Athens

Copyright © 1988 by Ken Smith

Originally published by Southern Book Publishers.

Ohio University Press edition published 1989.
Printed in the United States of America.
All rights reserved.

Ohio University Press books are printed on acid-free paper. ∞

Library of Congress Cataloging-in-Publication Data

Smith, Ken.
　The changing past: trends in South African historical writing/
Ken Smith.
　　p.　c.m.
　Reprint. Originally published: Southern Book Publishers, 1988.
　Includes index.
　ISBN 0-8214-0926-3.—ISBN 0-8214-0927-1 (pbk.)
　1. South Africa—Historiography. 2. South Africa—Race relations—
Historiography. 3. Social classes—South Africa—Historiography.
4. Marxian historiography—South Africa. I. Title.
DT769.S63　1989
968'.0072—dc19
　　　　　　　　　　　　　　　　　　　　　　　88-39277
　　　　　　　　　　　　　　　　　　　　　　　CIP

To my parents, and especially to my father who taught me to enjoy reading.

Acknowledgements

For permission to reproduce the photographs in the text I gratefully acknowledge the following: The Standard Encyclopaedia of Southern Africa for those of E.A. Walker, D.W. Krüger, G.E. Cory and A.J. Boëseken; the Transvaal Archives depot for that of G.S. Preller; the South African Library for the portrait of G.M. Theal; the Public Relations Division of Rhodes University for the photo of T.R.H. Davenport; the Archives of the University of the Witwatersrand for that of W.M. Macmillan; the University of Stellenbosch for the photo of H.B. Thom. The photograph of P.J. van der Merwe, also in the possession of the University of Stellenbosch, comes from the frontispiece of the Archives Year Book for S.A. History, 1986 (II). The photograph of S. Marks is taken from *Natalia* 6, published by the Natal Society of Pietermaritzburg. The photograph of C.W. de Kiewiet was made available to me by the Department of Rare Books and Special Collections, Rush Rhees Library, the University of Rochester. The likeness of M. Wilson comes from the University of Cape Town Libraries.

Photographs

Contents

Preface

In reviewing Harrison M. Wright's book *The burden of the present: Liberal-radical controversy over Southern African history* (Cape Town, 1977), that incisive observer and commentator, the University of Cape Town mathematician, K. R. Hughes, wrote as follows: "The history of historiography is a strongly intellectual discipline, a branch of the history of ideas. I think it is fair to say that no South African historian has attempted it with success: it is a discipline which calls for very special qualities of heart and mind and, perhaps more important, also of intellectual training . . . What is needed is skill in hermeneutics – the art of interpretation and close reading of texts, and empathy – the ability to feel one's way into the mind of the writer and read between the lines. It is thus I think auspicious that this first essay in South African historiography is written by a Harvard graduate, no South African would have been as well equipped."[1]

Had I read this before I started, the formidable list of attributes that a successful historiographer had to number among his intellectual baggage and skills of craftmanship, would probably have warned me off the subject. But as it was, when I chanced upon his review I had already done enough reading to be fully committed and compromised. I was in fact already experiencing serious pangs of doubt about what I had embarked upon. Hughes's words merely confirmed my own uncomfortable feeling that I had let myself in for more than I had originally intended.

* * *

There are a few things that should be stressed right at the outset: this is not an exhaustive study of historical literature pertaining to South Africa, it is a highly selective one, concentrating on *trends*; it aims to provide students with an overall view of the main trends in South African historical writing.

My original intention was to concentrate on the so-called liberal-radical controversy that had dominated the scene in the 1970s. This was because my starting point was Harrison Wright's book. The first thing that struck me in studying the history produced by the so-called "new left", neo-Marxist or radical historians, was that whether Harrison Wright's essay, written in Cape Town in the second half of 1975, was at *that* time a good or bad guide to what was happening in historical writing, there could be no question that by 1986 it was hardly an adequate source for the study of the development of the controversy. In fact, the battlelines themselves in some respects were not even clear in 1975, the debate had hardly been fully developed. By 1986 it appeared as if the heat had been taken off the exchanges between liberals and radicals, and that even to divide historians into such categories had become somewhat artificial and arbitrary. From the perspective of 1986, the controversy was no longer a controversy. In the space of some 15 years the fire had come and gone. Historians were moving on to fresh horizons.

Wright, in any event, had largely failed to challenge the new interpretations presented, concentrating his criticism at one end of the scale on minor, mainly technical points, and on the other, on broad charges of excessive presentism. Presentism, in the sense used by Wright, has always been an interesting point of debate among historians, but to suddenly link it in an accusatory way to the liberal and radical schools of historical writing seemed very much like an attempt to distract attention from the real issues. Although Wright confined his case to these two schools, charges of presentism could equally well be brought against all the schools of history discussed in this book. In the South African context, it would be difficult to find a tradition of historical writing that was more preoccupied with the contemporary situation than Afrikaner nationalist historiography.

But in spite of the limitations of his book, Wright had performed a useful function. Knowledge of the differences between liberal and radical historians, sociologists and others who had focused attention on the past, had been confined to a relatively small number of people, so that even the broader academic world was largely ignorant of them before Wright published his essay. Besides making the debate known to a wider public, his work was also important as the first book-length survey of South African historiography in English.[2]

* * *

I started out with the limited aim of saying something about the liberal-radical history scene. But on suddenly finding myself in the position of having to teach South African historiography to a postgraduate class, the majority of whom were studying through the medium of English, I was made painfully aware of the lack of a suitable textbook – there was no book-length survey covering the whole field of South African historical writing. I therefore decided to broaden my aim and make good that lack.

Afrikaans-speaking students are not as badly off as their English-speaking counterparts, for there are numerous books by that prolific historian Professor

F. A. van Jaarsveld. His most recent contribution is freely available. *Omstrede Suid-Afrikaanse verlede: Geskiedenisideologie en die historiese skuldvraagstuk* (Johannesburg and Cape Town, 1984) deals not only with the liberal-radical controversy, but with the full sweep of South African historiography, albeit from the narrow angle of "guilt" and the laying of blame for the mistakes made and wrong directions taken in the past. It was also, unfortunately, written from an emotional and very subjective viewpoint, particularly with regard to historical writing over the past 15 or so years.

Most of the work delineating a South African historiography has been in Afrikaans. Among early attempts in this direction were I.D. Bosman's *Dr George McCall Theal as die geskiedskrywer van Suid-Afrika*, published in Amsterdam in 1932; J. S. du Plessis's *Gustav Preller as historikus van die Groot Trek* of 1944;[3] and G. D. Scholtz's 1946 article "Die ontwikkeling en huidige stand van die Afrikaanse historiografie".[4] More recently Grietjie Verhoef has written on the radical school.[5] But above all, when one thinks of Afrikaner historiography, one thinks of Professor F. A. van Jaarsveld. Throughout this book there are references to his many works on South African historiography, from his inaugural lecture at the University of South Africa in 1961 to his latest book on the guilt question.[6]

Van Jaarsveld has also made an important contribution to English literature on South African history, with his *The Afrikaner's interpretation of South African history* (Cape Town, 1964) which includes chapters on other strands in historical writing besides the Afrikaner tradition.

Until recently there was very little in English on South African historiography. In 1962 Merle Babrow wrote an M.A. thesis on Dr George McCall Theal. In an article published in 1987 the Canadian-born historian was the subject of inquiry by Deryck Schreuder who analysed him in the context of "colonial nationalism"; parts of Theal's early career in South Africa have been dealt with by Christopher Saunders.[7]

Saunders has published a number of other articles on aspects of South African historiography, as well as a more substantial study on the liberal historian, C. W. de Kiewiet.[8] Another liberal historian, W. M. Macmillan, has been the subject of an M. A. dissertation by Jayaraman Naidoo.[9]

On more general themes, in 1962 Leonard Thompson published an article on Afrikaner historiography; he followed this in the latter 1960s with a chapter on South African historical writing in general in Robin Winks's book on the writing of history in the British Empire-Commonwealth.[10] Some of the points raised by Thompson in 1962 with regard to myths in the Afrikaner's vision of his past, have been amplified by him in a book published in 1985.[11]

The above works deal mainly with historical writing before the Second World War. On developments since then, besides Wright's slim volume, there have been a number of articles. Shula Marks of London University, formerly of the School of Oriental and African Studies, and more recently director of the Institute of Commonwealth Studies, who played a major role in giving direction to historical writing in the 1970s, has published three articles on the state of historiography in South Africa.[12] Frederick Johnstone has written an article that has been widely recognised as a succinct and penetrating analysis of recent trends,[13] and there have been a number of other contributions in journals, each of which illuminates a particular point, but does not provide an overall survey.[14]

One other feature of South African historiography requires some comment. The great majority of South Africa's people is black, but the great majority of studies discussed in this book have been written by whites. Informed black input has been minimal. There are several reasons for this. Foremost among these is that blacks do not have the same sort of access to education as do whites. What is taught in black schools and colleges is tightly controlled by the state, and the syllabi are drawn up under white control. And whites, to a large extent, have seen South African history as the march and triumph of white "civilisation", so that blacks were denied their history. Denied political rights, the majority of blacks in the country experience dispossession, forced resettlement, discrimination in urban areas, exploitation and poverty. That is their present and also, for the most part, their past. For the majority of blacks in the urban situation the past cannot perform a stabilising role and give them a sense of direction. Having been severed from their indigenous roots, the past is not seen as something that they can look back on with a sense of satisfaction – it represents only more of the same kind of struggle as they experience in the present. The history that they learn in school does not give them a sense of pride in past black achievement, for the whites have colonised this past. In the 1970s the Black Consciousness Movement said that the rulers of South Africa were "not satisfied merely with holding a people in their grip and emptying the Native's brain of all form and content, they turned to the past of the oppressed people and distorted, disfigured and destroyed it . . . No wonder the African child learns to hate his heritage in his days at school."[15] The same point was made by "Majeke" in 1952: "If the rulers can make the people believe that they are inferior, wipe out their past history or present it in such a way that they feel, not pride but shame, then they create the conditions that make it easy to dominate the people."[16]

It is not easy for blacks to reconcile black traditions of oral history with the history they were taught in schools and colleges. In the early 1950s, Z. K. Matthews expressed concern about the way history was taught to blacks. "Our history," he wrote, recalling his days as a student at Fort Hare from 1918, "as we had absorbed it from the tales and talk of our elders, bore no resemblance to South African history as it has been written by European scholars, or as it is taught in South African schools, and as it was taught to us at Fort Hare. The European insisted that we accept his version of the past . . . It was one thing to accept willingly and even eagerly the white man's world of literature and science. It was quite another to accept his picture of how we all came to occupy the places in life now assigned to us ... If it was difficult for us to accept the white man's account of his own past doings, it was utterly impossible to accept his judgements on the actions and behaviour of Africans, of our own grandfathers in our own lands."[17]

In 1970, Sir Seretse Khama, who had studied at Fort Hare, recalled that they were taught, "sometimes in a very positive way, to despise ourselves and our ways of life. We were made to believe that we had no past to speak of, no history to boast of. The past, so far as we were concerned, was just a blank and nothing more. Only the present mattered, and we had very little control over it."[18] Chief Mangosuthu Buthelezi said on 18 June 1983 on the occasion of the unveiling of a plaque where Dingane was killed by the Swazis, "it was difficult for black people to regard King Dingane as a villain because of his assassination of Piet Retief and his voortrekkers".[19] History books from which blacks have to learn and absorb if they wish to pass examinations, may still represent Dingane as the cruel, treacherous murderer of the unsuspecting and peaceful band of Voortrekkers, but it is not a version with which blacks will be satisfied.

In a reappraisal of Dingane in 1969, Felix Okoye wrote that because he had Piet Retief and his men murdered, Dingane had incurred "the seemingly undying hatred of historians. Almost every commentator on this period of Zulu history has portrayed him as a man with hardly a redeeming quality: blood-thirsty, capricious, treacherous, self-indulgent, an absolute despot, an ingrate and an inveterate liar. What is remarkable about this consensus among historians is that Dingane ... lacked all these unflattering attributes. Many reasons could be given for this grievous error on the part of scholars. Among these must be included ... an inability to understand the dynamics of an alien society."[20]

Although black scholars and students did not relate to South African history as it was presented to them, the situation was different when it came to European and American history. "We drank in, like thirsty wanderers in the desert," Professor Z. K. Matthews recalled, "the stories of the American and French revolutions, and the much more recent struggles of Italy to become a nation under the leadership of Mazzini and Garibaldi. We saw all this as foreshadowing an experience we were yet to have. Struggles such as these lay ahead for Africans, we felt, although we did not know when, and hardly dared to think they might come in our own lifetime. These too were forbidden thoughts which we scarcely dared to conceive, much less utter, even among ourselves."[21]

In his presidential address to the tenth biennial conference of the South African Historical Society in January 1985, Professor B. A. le Cordeur said that the Africans as well as the so-called "Coloured" people "have been indoctrinated by the negative cultural stereotypes which the whites have created of their ancestors to believe that they are not important enough to have a history at all."[22] In the mid-1970s a survey of the teaching of history in black secondary schools, principally in Soweto, revealed that in the textbooks "Blacks are depicted as useful labour, dishonest bargainers, foolish farmers, or homeland citizens".[23] Although it is dangerous to cite the way the past has been represented by whites and forced upon black scholars and students as a prime reason why blacks do not feel drawn to the study of history, it is obviously a contributory factor.

* * *

Five broad trends in historical writing have been chosen for study (British imperial, settler, Afrikaans, liberal and radical). I am not so confident of the categorisation that I am prepared to argue that this division is the only one and, in writing this book, I have been constantly aware of the fact that few historians fitted snugly into the pigeonholes I had made for them. I did not intend creating a separate section for Afrikaans historical literature, but when it came to structuring the book, this was the most convenient way of doing it. I do not want to suggest that English-speaking historians write history in one particular way, and that the histories written by Afrikaners are all of a kind. Afrikaners are to be found among most of the other schools. Thus, in what I have called the British school, two of the most important writers dealt with are Afrikaners. This is also true of the liberal school, and an Afrikaner like J. S. Marais is classified as belonging to it. For the most part, these historians did not write in Afrikaans. There is one trend in South African historical writing that is peculiarly the preserve of Afrikaans, and that is the Afrikaner nationalist or republican school of writing, which is the main focus of the chapter on Afrikaans historical literature.

The treatment is not even. The chapters dealing with early trends contain more detail than those outlining more recent trends. There are more quotes from fewer works. This could be justified on the grounds that many of these early books are not so freely available to students, but there is another reason that weighed more heavily with me. In following the pattern of historical "schools" as outlined by van Jaarsveld and Thompson, I found myself disagreeing with van Jaarsveld's conclusions at many points. It seemed to me, for example, when discussing the anti-Afrikaner or pro-British viewpoint of various writers, that it was necessary to reproduce the language in which they couched their prejudices. In many cases their views did not appear as extreme as a reading of van Jaarsveld had led me to expect.

It is broad *trends* I have been interested in outlining. I have not discussed all the important works in every school, I have deliberately ignored many of the subtle nuances within schools in order to present a *bold* statement. Rather than arguing abstractedly about the various "schools", I have concentrated throughout on specific themes that seem to me to be saying something unique about one or other aspect of the past. Despite the initial stimulus given to this study by Harrison Wright's book, I have attempted to move

6

away from seeing the liberal-radical controversy in the terms framed by Wright. Although I do focus on the "debate" between liberals and radicals, I regard this as of secondary importance to my principal aim of delineating a number of areas in which new insights have been responsible for a change in the way we view the past. In adopting this approach, I fully share the sentiments expressed by Rodney Davenport in the preface to the third edition of his *South Africa: A modern history*. He writes: "It no longer seemed necessary or desirable to highlight the confrontation between liberal and Marxist approaches. That confrontation has already produced such stimulating debate that it seems better to look at it reflectively in the context of particular historical crises, than to set it out, as it were, in battle array."[24]

As will be clear from this book, very often what a historian is saying tells us far more about his own times than it does about the times he is trying to illuminate. In this book the discussion of the authors chosen to illustrate a particular trend is somewhat leisurely, in the sense that more attention is devoted to their lives and work than may be regarded as strictly necessary to make the point. This has been done to familiarise readers with the *people* who have been responsible for the creation of our historical traditions. It is important not to lose sight of the *person* behind the historical portrayal presented, to keep in mind the link between the writers and the historical tradition they helped to create, to see the writers in their social context. But in this respect too the treatment is selective, and details are not given of all our major historians.

Some parts of this book have been easier to write than others. It has proceeded most fluently in such areas where as a result of my own researches or teaching I have had some familiarity with the subject and the sources. It has been most difficult in those large areas where I have little more than a passing acquaintance with historical developments.

Throughout the writing I have been confronted by a dilemma: to what extent should the reader be told what he ought to think of this or that book or school of historical writing. At the risk of presenting a rather bland and colourless account I have preferred to limit explicit judgments to a minimum, and rather provide an introductory study to what South African historical writing has been all about.

* * *

I have unashamedly picked the brains of many of my colleagues in preparing this work, buttonholing them in corridors and appropriating the thoughts they have expressed at seminars. Their names are too numerous to mention. I am sure that most of them are totally unaware that as I stood quietly listening to them, or challenging them in the role of devil's advocate, they were helping to clarify my own thoughts or leading me to explore fresh avenues, thus contributing to this study.

There are however a few people whose assistance in particular I should like to acknowledge. I am greatly indebted to Ben Liebenberg and Johannes du Bruyn for their detailed attention, suggestions and advice on the entire manuscript. I was also fortunate in being able to avail myself of the comments of Albert Grundlingh, Burridge Spies, Arthur Davey and Rodney Davenport. To all of them, my grateful thanks.

NOTES

1 K. R. Hughes, "Challenges from the past: Reflections on liberalism and radicalism in the writing of Southern African History", *Social Dynamics*, 3(1), 1977, p. 50.

2 Ibid.

3 Unpublished M.A. at the Pctchefstroom University for Christian Higher Education.

4 *Tydskrif vir Wetenskap en Kuns*, November 1946, pp. 30–40.

5 G. Verhoef, "Die Neo-Marxistiese historiografie oor Suid-Afrika", *Historia*, 30(1), 1985, pp. 13–25.

6 His inaugural lecture was *Ou en nuwe weë in die Suid-Afrikaanse geskied-skrywing*, Communications of the University of South Africa, A16, Pretoria, 1961. Some of his most recent publications of interest in the historiographical sphere include *Geskiedkundige verkenninge*, Pretoria, 1974, *Die evolusie van apartheid*, Cape Town, 1979, *Wie en wat is die Afrikaner?*, Cape Town, 1981. These are compilations of addresses and journal articles. A recent full-length book is *Moderne geskiedskrywing: Opstelle oor 'n nuwe benadering tot geskiedenis*, Durban and Pretoria, 1982.

7 Merle Babrow, *A critical assessment of Dr George McCall Theal*, University of Cape Town. She later married, and it was as Merle Lipton that she published *Capitalism and apartheid: South Africa, 1910–1986* (This first appeared in 1985 in London; a South African edition with an epilogue entitled "January 1986" was published in 1986 by David Philip; Cape Town); Deryck Schreuder, "The imperial historian as colonial nationalist: George McCall Theal and the making of South African history" in G. Martel (ed.), *Studies in British imperial history: Essays in honour of A. P. Thornton*, New York, 1986, pp. 95–158; Christopher Saunders. "The missing link in Theal's career: The historian as labour agent in the Western Cape", *History in Africa*, 7, 1980, pp. 273–280; "George McCall Theal and Lovedale", *History in Africa*, 8, 1981, pp. 155–164; "The making of an historian: The early years of George McCall Theal", *South African Historical Journal*, 13, 1981, pp. 3–11.

8 "The writing of C. W. de Kiewiet's 'A history of South Africa social and economic' ", *History in Africa*, 13, 1986, pp. 323–330; *C. W. de Kiewiet; Historian of South Africa*, Centre for African Studies, Communications of the University of Cape Town, no. 10, 1986; "Our past as literature: Notes on style in South African history in English", *Kleio*, 18, 1986, pp. 46–55; " 'Mnguni' and 'Three Hundred Years' revisited' ", *Kronos*, 11, 1986, pp. 74–80; in its catalogue for 1986–1987, David Philip announced the forthcoming publication of a book by Christopher Saunders entitled *The making of the South African past: Historians on race and class*.

9 Jayaraman Naidoo, *W. M. Macmillan: South African historian*, M. A., Unisa, 1983.

10 L. M. Thompson, "Afrikaner nationalist historiography and the policy of apartheid", *Journal of African History*, 3 (1), 1962, pp. 125–141; "South Africa" in R. W. Winks (ed.), *The historiography of the British Empire-Commonwealth: Trends, interpretations, and resources*, Durham, N. C., 1966, pp. 212–232.

11 *The political mythology of apartheid*, New Haven, 1985.

12 "South African studies since World War Two" in C. Fyfe (ed.), *African studies since 1945: A tribute to Basil Davidson*, London, 1976, pp. 186–199; "Towards a people's history of South Africa? Recent developments in the historiography of South Africa" in R. Samuel (ed.), *People's history and socialist theory*, London, 1981, pp. 297–308; "The historiography of South Africa: Recent developments" in Bogumil Jewsiewicki and David Newbury (eds),

African historiographies: What history for which Africa?, Beverly Hills, London and New Delhi, 1986, pp. 165–176.

13 " 'Most painful to our hearts': South Africa through the eyes of the new school", *Canadian Journal of African Studies*, 16(1), 1982.

14 Examples are Stanley Trapido, "South Africa and the historians", *African Affairs*, 71 (1972); Donald Denoon, "Synthesising South African history", *Transafrican Journal of History*, 2(1), 1972; B.S. Kantor and H. F. Kenny, "The poverty of Neo-Marxism: The case of South Africa", *Journal of Southern African Studies*, 3(1), 1976; Gary Minkley, "Re-examining experience: The new South African historiography", *History in Africa*, 13, 1986; M. Lipton, "The debate about South Africa: Neo-Marxists and Neo-Liberals", *African Affairs*, 79(310), 1979.

15 R. Fatton, jr, *Class and nationalism in South Africa: A study in the radicalization of black politics (1952-1976)*, University of Notre Dame, 1981, p. 223. My analysis of black attitudes to history owes much to A. M. Grundlingh, "George Orwell's 'Nineteen Eighty-Four': Some reflections on its relevance to the study of history in South Africa", *Kleio*, 16, 1984.

16 N. Majeke, *The role of the missionaries in conquest*, Cape Town, 1952, Introduction.

17 Z. K. Matthews, *Freedom for my people: The autobiography of Z. K. Matthews: Southern Africa 1901 to 1968*, Cape Town, 1981, pp. 58–59. Matthews's reminiscences were recorded in 1952–1953, but were only published in 1981 under the guidance of Professor Monica Wilson.

18 Quoted by Neil Parsons, *A new history of Southern Africa*, London, 1982, p.v.

19 Quoted by F. A. van Jaarsveld, *Omstrede verlede*, p. 160.

20 Felix N. C. Okoye, "Dingane: A reappraisal", *Journal of African History*, 10(2), 1969, p. 221.

21 Matthews, *Freedom for my people*, pp. 58–59.

22 Basil A. le Cordeur, "The reconstruction of South African history", *South African Historical Journal*, 17, 1985, p. 3.

23 Lynn Maree, "The hearts and minds of the people" in Peter Kallaway (ed.), *Apartheid and education: The education of black South Africans*, Johannesburg, 1984, p. 152.

24 T. R. H. Davenport, *South Africa: A modern history*, 3rd ed., Johannesburg, 1987, p. xxii.

1 Introduction: the first documents and histories

Until well after World War II those who wrote about the history of Africa based their accounts almost entirely on written material. The reasons for this are twofold. They were mostly concerned with the activities of Europeans in Africa. The study of African societies was regarded as belonging to the fields of archaeology and anthropology. African societies were seen as static and unchanging, they had no history. In the second place there were few documents about these societies, and history had to be based on documents, not on archaeological artefacts or oral evidence.

In the nineteenth century, when the values of Europe seemed to contemporaries to be so superior to those in other parts of the world, only European history was judged to be worth studying, and even the history of Europeans in far-flung regions was for the most part neglected. The conviction took root that Africa did not have a history. This attitude persisted in certain circles at least until the 1960s, and in that decade the Regius Professor of Modern History at Oxford University, Hugh Trevor-Roper, wrote "perhaps, in the future, there will be some African history to teach. But at present there is none or very little: there is only the history of the Europeans in Africa. The rest is largely darkness . . . And darkness is not a subject for history. Please do not misunderstand me. I do not deny that men existed even in dark countries and dark centuries, nor that they had political life and culture, interesting to sociologists and anthropologists; but history, I believe, is essentially a form of movement, and purposive movement too. It is not a mere phantasmagoria of changing shapes and costumes, of battles and conquests, dynasties and usurpations, social forms and social disintegration." He argued that only European history counted, because the world was dominated by Western European ideas, values and techniques. There was not time to "amuse ourselves with the unrewarding gyrations of barbarous tribes in picturesque but irrelevant corners of the globe".[1]

Even amongst those who rejected Trevor-Roper's views, there was a feeling that if African societies did indeed have a history, it could not be discovered because there were no written records. There was something sacrosanct about the written word. Europeans firmly shared the Rankean concept of history as a science based on the closest critical analysis of written sources. The rigorous examination of documentary archival material was the hallmark of all good history, and the fact that Africa seemed to have few such sources reinforced the view that it had no history.

Civilisation was equated with literacy, which also seemed to put pre-colonial Africa, which had been for the most part non-literate, into the primitive category. But Africa was not really non-literate, for in a number of areas there were scribes who could read and write, but, of course, there was no mass literacy – this was everywhere a post-industrial phenomenon, in Europe no less than in Africa. Jan Vansina has pointed out that many African civilisations "were to a great extent civilisations of the spoken word" in which the "written word was often marginal to the essential preoccupations of a society". He warns that "it would be wrong to reduce the civilisation of the spoken word to a merely negative absence of writing and to perpetuate the inborn contempt of the literate for the illiterate which is found in so many sayings, such as the Chinese proverb, 'the palest ink is to be preferred to the strongest word.' "[2]

Very few people today would argue as Hugh Trevor-Roper did. Studies of the internal dynamism of African societies have rescued them from those who would portray them as timeless, static entities, that were in some way not subject to historical processes of change. It is also widely recognised that written records are not the sole evidences of the past. However, it is only in the last couple of decades that the artefacts that have long interested archaeologists have been brought into the historian's fold. The same applies to oral evidence.

So by and large the histories concerned with Africa rested on a foundation of written sources. As far as archival material is concerned, Africa has the oldest archival documents in the world. The oldest archival records preserved in Europe are the Ravenna papyri dating from the sixth century A.D., whereas the earliest Egyptian ones go back some 2 000 years before that. North Africa in the Classical era was part of the Roman Empire, and the African lands fringing the Mediterranean Sea had a long and close contact with Europe. From the seventeenth century, North Africa became part of the Muslim world and for this region the volume of documentary sources compares favourably with that in European countries. From the sixteenth century this was supplemented by material from the period of Turkish dominance in North Africa.

The strong Muslim influence in West Africa and the Western Sudan, where an intellectual elite of scribes and government officials held high office, meant a continuous written record of events here from the eleventh century; in Ethiopia too there were written records that went back many hundreds of years. The East African coast came under Muslim influence from the thirteenth century, and when the Muslims were driven out by the Portuguese, Arab documents gave way to Portuguese records and accounts.[3]

Southern Africa by contrast is poorly off as far as written material is concerned. Portuguese records having reference to the Cape littoral date from the time that the Portuguese rounded the southern tip of Africa and began calling in at Table Bay from the end of the fifteenth century. Numerous Portuguese ships were wrecked along the treacherous south-eastern coast, and records resulted from this.[4] There are even fewer documents for the interior. There is very little documentary evidence for most of the inland areas south of the Limpopo before the nineteenth century. There is none at all for the Bantu-speaking peoples.

* * *

Apart from the occasional Portuguese, English or Dutch document regarding the Cape, the first continuous documentary record began when the Dutch East India Company established a refreshment station in 1652, and the commander of the settlement, Jan van Riebeeck, made the first entry in his journal (Daghregister). A steady stream of visiting officials, missionaries, and various categories of travellers, left accounts of their experiences at the Cape. There was thus a continuous and growing body of archival material.

The settlement had not been established for very long before the first expeditions were sent out to explore the interior. Official parties that went out kept a record of their activities, but few of these were published before the twentieth century. In many cases the original manuscripts lay unremarked among the unordered and unclassified papers in the archives until rescued from oblivion by George McCall Theal who published a number of them in his three-volume *Belangrijke historische dokumenten over Zuid-Afrika* (London, 1896-1911). Others were published in E. C. Godeë Molsbergen's four-volume *Reizen in Zuid-Afrika in de Hollandse tijd* (The Hague, 1916-1932).

If the diary or journal was private it was usually retained by its author, to eventually pass on to his family. Many of these documents were only rediscovered much later by historians. Thus, although there was a wealth of written material about the interior and its inhabitants, most of this was either not available or easily accessible to historians in the nineteenth century.

The journals of the expeditions of Olof Bergh and Isaq Schrijver, written in the 1680s, were not published before the twentieth century.[5] The journal of Simon van der Stel's travels to Namaqualand in 1685-1686, was only rediscovered in Europe in the twentieth century and published in 1932,[6] although another version had earlier appeared in part five of Francois Valentyn's *Oud en nieuw Oost-Indiën* published in 1726. The record of ensign A. F. Beutler's 1752 expedition which was sponsored by the Cape governor, Rijk Tulbagh, and which went beyond the Kei River, was not published until 1896.[7] Hendrik Swellengrebel's description of life among the Boers of Camdebo in 1776 only became available to a wider audience in 1932.[8] Dirk Gysbert van Reenen's journal of 1803 was rediscovered in 1932 and published in 1937.[9] W. B. E. Paravicini di Capelli's record of journeys made during the period of Batavian rule (1803-1806) was likewise only recovered much later in the twentieth century and published in 1965.[10]

Although few accounts of *official* expeditions were easily accessible to nineteenth century historians, there were several other works, written mostly by travellers from abroad, that were published soon after the return of the authors from the Cape. The number of visitors who left accounts of their journeys increased markedly in the last quarter of the eighteenth century. Between 1772 and 1774 the young Swedish botanist, C. P. Thunberg, ventured into the interior on four occasions. English translations of the two volumes relating to his travels in Southern Africa were published in 1795.[11] Anders Sparrman, another Swede, was a zoologist, and between 1772 and 1776 he travelled as far east as modern Somerset East, describing his travels in two substantial volumes published in 1786.[12] In the late 1770s William Paterson, who later became Lieutenant-Governor of New South Wales in Australia, made four journeys into the interior, covering some 8 000 kilometres in the process. His records of his travels were published in 1790.[13] François le Vaillant, a young bird-collector from France, in the 1780s travelled extensively in the country and left five volumes (1790-1796) of colourful descriptions of his experiences. Doubt has been cast on the authenticity of many of the events he recounts.[14]

Some records resulted from the wreck of the Grosvenor on the Transkei coast in 1782. Expeditions that were mounted to search for survivors left accounts of their experiences.[15] One of the best-known and most controversial accounts of life on the eastern frontier at the turn of the century, was the two volumes of John Barrow's *Travels into the interior of Southern Africa*, containing details of his sojourn at the Cape between 1797 and 1799. These were published in 1801 and 1804.

A number of ventures into the interior were undertaken during the period of Batavian rule (1803-1806). One of the fullest and best descriptions of the Cape at this time is H. Lichtenstein's *Travels in Southern Africa in the years 1803, 1804, 1805 and 1806.*[16] First published in Berlin in two volumes in 1810 and 1812, the two volumes of the English translation appeared in 1812 and 1815. In the early years of the Second British Occupation of the Cape after 1806, noteworthy accounts of the far interior were the two volumes of W. J. Burchell's *Travels in the interior of Southern Africa*, published in the 1820s, and the three volumes of John Campbell's travels, published between 1815 and 1822.[17]

The first actual research foray into the archives, and which resulted in the publication of a collection of documents, was undertaken by Donald Moodie in the 1830s. The British naval officer's post of Protector of Slaves at the Cape became redundant when the slaves were set free on 1 December 1834. This roughly coincided with a crisis in the affairs of the Cape. Dr John Philip, the head of the London Missionary Society at the Cape, had published his *Researches in South Africa* in 1828,[18] in which the Cape government and the colonists were held responsible for the troubles in the colony. The indigenous inhabitants were described by him as the "wretched victims of European avarice and cruelty". According to Philip, they had been forcibly subjected, dispossessed of their land and turned into virtual slaves.[19]

Hearing that Moodie was interested in history, the Cape governor, Sir Benjamin D'Urban, instructed him to collect material in the archives that would refute Philip's allegations about the supposed ill-treatment of the Khoi and Xhosa by the colonists. Moodie entered into his task with enthusiasm; he learnt Dutch, and in the words of his son, "also acquired the peculiar power which enabled him to decipher the enigmatically written quaint old Dutch Documents".[20] He intended collecting all relevant documents up to 1834, but was forced by lack of public interest and official support to stop short at 1819.

Moodie's *The Record* was used extensively by writers like E. B. Watermeyer and A. Wilmot in the histories they wrote, and also by the anthropologist Dr Bleek. The latter was full of praise for the collection of documents and said that: "I never met with a book that appeared to me of so much value for imparting an accurate knowledge of the ethnography of Southern Africa, and none so rich in facts".[21] But the collection, in truth, was a jumble of disconnected items, many of them appearing only in translation. Unfortunately, Moodie treated the material in his charge rather carelessly, so that a number of records were lost.

An early work that was both a collection of documents and a chronicle, was J. C. Chase's two-volume, *The Natal Papers*, published in 1843. Chase initially intended the publication to consist entirely of copies of documents relevant to Natal that he had collected in the Cape archives, but he changed his mind and linked the documents together with comments of his own, so that it was not a source publication pure and simple. It was a particularly valuable collection for the study of the Great Trek and Natal, throwing light especially on Piet Retief.[22]

The archives were in a very disorganised state, and in July 1876 the Cape government named a commission "to collect, examine, classify and index the archives of the Colony".[23] The documents were removed from the Court of Justice premises to a more suitable location in the office of the Surveyor-General. Although the commission did valuable work in preventing the further deterioration and loss of material, it confined its activities to documents having reference to the period before 1806, and it did not concern itself with what was held in the government offices outside Cape Town in such places as Stellenbosch, Swellendam, Graaff-Reinet and Grahamstown. Although the government had been brought to see the need for action, it could not be persuaded that there was any urgency, and archivists like George McCall Theal and the Rev. H. C. V. Leibbrandt had to combine their activities as archivists with their other duties as public servants.[24]

* * *

When we come to historical writing, as opposed to the publication of collections of documents, the earliest known history of the Cape was J. Suasso de Lima's *Geschiedenis van de Kaap de Goede Hoop*, published in 1825. De Lima was not a historian, and was, *inter alia*, an interpreter and translator, teacher and poet, printer, publisher and journalist. In January 1826 he started the first Dutch newspaper at the Cape, *De Verzamelaar*, and he also published almanacs like the *Kaapsche almanak en naamboek* and *Kaapsche zak almanak*. He intended his history as a textbook for pupils in Cape schools, and it was divided into 20 lessons, using the question and answer technique. The book was full of errors, and virtually every page had several. One of the more obvious of these was the statement that Jan van Riebeeck died at the Cape![25] De Lima's book has no influence on the course of development of South African historiography, and Theal's judgement of it in the late nineteenth century, that it was "of more value now as a curiosity than as containing information", was probably also true of the book even in de Lima's time.[26]

In the years after the appearance of de Lima's book there was no great stampede of writers wishing to emulate or improve upon his efforts. W. B. Boyce's *Notes on South African affairs from 1834 to 1838*, published in 1838,[27] was not so much a history as a defence by the Wesleyan missionary and Xhosa linquist of the 1820 British Settlers and a refutation of the charges brought by British humanitarians against the settlers at the time of the Sixth Frontier War.

J. C. Chase's *The Cape of Good Hope and the Eastern Province of Algoa Bay*, was published in 1843, the same year as his *Natal Papers*. It aimed at attracting immigrants and providing them with detailed information about the Cape. It did contain two short sections on past events but these could hardly be described as a serious attempt to delineate Cape history. Van Riebeeck's first visit to the Cape on his way back to the Netherlands from Batavia was described thus: " 'In the fulness of time', Van Riebeeck, a surgeon and a botanist, touched at Table Bay in his homeward passage, in 1648. The excursions he made into the country, in the prosecution of a delightful and bewitching science, probably inspired him with the first desire to revisit this richest and most splendidly adorned temple of Flora; some lovely flower, perhaps . . . may have been the trivial cause of this important settlement".[28]

U. G. Lauts, professor of maritime history at Medemblick in the Netherlands, and who in fact never visited South Africa, in 1847 wrote *De Kaapsche landverhuizers of Nederlands afstammelingen in Zuid-Afrika*, which dealt with the Great Trek of the previous decade. The book was not based on any archival research and aimed at awakening interest in the Netherlands in the fate of the Voortrekkers so that ministers and teachers would be encouraged to come out and serve them. He also wrote *Geschiedenis van de Kaap de Goede Hoop, Nederlandsche Volksplanting, 1652-1806*. It came to the notice of very few people in South Africa. A similar fate befell his biography of Andries Pretorius, published in 1854, a year after the Voortrekker leader's death.[29] Another work in Dutch and which also aimed at making the Boers better known in the Netherlands was Jacobus Stuart's *De Hollandsche Afrikanen en hunne republiek* (1854). Stuart had had a hand in framing the 1855 constitution of the Transvaal. Much of the book was based on earlier accounts. The best parts of the book were where he narrated the history of the Transvaal after the arrival there of the Voortrekkers from Natal, and also the friction between the Voortrekker leaders Andries Pretorius and Hendrik Potgieter. The last part of the work was not historical, but an attempt to persuade the Transvaal government to encourage immigration from the Netherlands by instituting an attractive colonisation scheme, and to awaken interest and support for his plan in the Netherlands.[30]

NOTES

1 H. R. Trevor-Roper, *The rise of Christian Europe*, 2nd ed., London, 1966, p. 9.

2 Vansina, "Oral tradition and its methodology" in J. Ki-Zerbo (ed.), Unesco *General History of Africa*, vol. 1, *Methodology and African prehistory*, London, 1981, p. 142.

3 See bibliographical essays in R. Oliver (ed.), *The Cambridge history of Africa*, vol. 3, *from c. 1050 to c. 1600*, Cambridge, 1977.

4 These were collected and translated by G. M. Theal and published as *Records of South-Eastern Africa*, 9 vols, Cape Town, 1898-1903.

5 E. E. Mossop (ed.), *Journals of the expeditions of the honourable ensign Olof Bergh (1682 and 1683) and the ensign Isaq Schrijver (1689)*, Van Riebeeck Society no. 12, Cape Town, 1931.

6 G. Waterhouse (ed.), *Simon van der Stel's journal of his expedition to Namaqualand, 1685-6*, London, 1932.

7 It was first published in G. M. Theal, *Belangrijke historische dokumenten*, vol. 2, Cape Town, 1896 and was published again a few years later in E. C. Godeë Molsbergen, *Reizen in Zuid-Afrika*, Linschoten Vereeniging, vol. 3, The Hague, 1922. See also Vernon S. Forbes, *Beutler's expedition into the Eastern Cape, 1752*, Archives Year Book for S. A. History, 1953, vol. 1 and *Pioneer travellers of South Africa*, Cape Town, 1965.

8 Molsbergen, *Reizen in Zuid-Afrika*, vol. 4, The Hague, 1932. See also Forbes, *Pioneer travellers*, pp. 59-80.

9 W. Blommaert and J. A. Wiid (eds), *Die joernaal van Dirk Gysbert van Reenen: 1803*, Van Riebeeck Society no. 18, Cape Town, 1937.

10 W. J. de Kock (ed.), *W. B. E. Paravicini di Capelli: Reize in de binnelanden van Zuid-Afrika*, Van Riebeeck Society no. 46, Cape Town, 1965.

11 C. P. Thunberg, *Travels in Europe, Africa, and Asia, made between the years 1770 and 1779*, 4 vols, London, 1795.

12 A. Sparrman, *A voyage to the Cape of Good Hope towards the antarctic polar circle, and round the world, but chiefly into the country of the Hottentots and Caffres from the year 1772 to 1776*, 2 vols, 2nd ed., London, 1786.

13 W. Paterson, *A narrative of four journeys into the country of the Hottentots, and Caffraria in the years 1777, 1778, 1779*, 2nd ed., London, 1790.

14 M. le Vaillant, *Travels into the interior parts of Africa by the way of the Cape of Good Hope, in the years 1780, 81, 82, 83, 84 and 85*, 2 vols, London, 1790 and *New travels into the interior parts of Africa by the way of the Cape of Good Hope, in the years 1783, 84 and 85*, 3 vols, London, 1796.

15 C. G. Botha (ed.), *The wreck of the Grosvenor*, Van Riebeeck Society no. 8, Cape Town, 1927; P. R. Kirby (ed.), *A source book on the wreck of the Grosvenor East Indiaman*, Van Riebeeck Society no. 34, Cape Town, 1953.

16 Van Riebeeck Society nos. 10 and 11, Cape Town, 1928, 1930.

17 W. J. Burchell, *Travels in the interior of Southern Africa*, 2 vols, reprint of the original 1822-1824 ed., London, 1953; J. Campbell, *Travels in South Africa, undertaken at the request of the Missionary Society*, London, 1815 and *Travels in South Africa, undertaken at the request of the London Missionary Society, being a narrative of a second journey in the interior of that country*, 2 vols, London, 1822.

18 The full title of this is *Researches in South Africa illustrating the civil, moral and religious conditions of the Native tribes*, 2 vols, London, 1828.

19 Philip, pp. xii, 46-47.

20 D. C. F. Moodie, *The history of the battles and adventures of the British, the Boers, and the Zulus, & c., in Southern Africa*, vol. 2, Cape Town, 1888, p. 552.

21 Ibid., quoted by Moodie, p. 553.

22 I. D. Bosman, *Dr George McCall Theal as die geskiedskrywer van Suid-Afrika*, Amsterdam, 1932. The full title is *The Natal Papers; a reprint of all notices and public documents connected with that territory, including a description of that country, and a history of events from its discovery in 1498 to the mission of the Hon. H. Cloete. LL.D. etc. in 1843.* The subtitle is *Natal, a reprint of all the authentic notices – descriptions – public acts and documents – petitions – manifestoes – correspondence – government advertisements and proclamations – bulletins and military despatches relative to Natal; with a narrative of events at that settlement*, Grahamstown, 1843.

23 Quoted by Bosman, p. 6.

24 Ibid., pp. 6–8.

25 J. Suasso de Lima, *Geschiedenis van de Kaap de Goede Hoop*, Cape Town, 1825 and reprinted in the South African Library Reprint Series, no. 5, Cape Town, 1975. Referring on p. 9 to the year 1662, de Lima wrote that "ook was dit jaar zeer rampspoedig voor de volkplanting, daar de brave van Riebeek den 4den Mei overleed na dat hy tien jaren en eene maand de Kolonie tot nut en genoegen bestierd had".

26 G. M. Theal, *History of South Africa since September 1795*, London, 1908, vol. 3, p. 402. References to Theal's *History of South Africa*, with the above exception, are taken from the Struik 1964 facsimile reprint of the 11-volume "Star" edition.

27 It was published in Grahamstown in 1838 and reissued in London in 1839.

28 Chase, p. 5.

29 *Andries Wilhelmus Pretorius, de held van Zuid-Afrika.*

30 Bosman, pp. 13, 19–20.

2 The British and settler schools of historical writing

Much of the writing on South African history in English in the nineteenth and early twentieth centuries may for the sake of convenience be divided into two categories or schools. Leonard Thompson has named these the British and settler schools.[1] Professor F. A. van Jaarsveld has made a similar classification, seeing the schools as representing "a colonial-imperial point of view" and a "colonial South African view".[2] This division is a useful one, and will be employed here, although with variations.

In the category of "colonial South African" historical writing, van Jaarsveld included work by Alexander Wilmot and John Chase, William Holden, John Noble, Henry Cloete and E. B. Watermeyer. Van Jaarsveld correctly noted that this body of work, although written from the colonial viewpoint, also contained within it "the realisation that the colony was dependent on and formed a subordinate part of the colonising motherland, Britain".[3] It is for this reason that I have preferred to place this work within the classification of the British school, and to make a clear distinction between early and late works in this category. As van Jaarsveld saw it, what he called the "imperial direction" differed from the settler school in that its central theme was the *expansion* of the British empire and the achievements and benefits of empire.[4] I have no quarrel with this. In the history written by English writers around the middle of the nineteenth century, however, it was accepted without question that British predominance should prevail in the Cape and Natal, and the Boers beyond British control were dismissed with a few uncomplimentary remarks. For this reason, I do not see this work as being in line with what was being done by George McCall Theal and George Cory. It had far

18

more in common with the work of English writers later in the century, who were trying to ensure that the Boers in the republics did not succeed in eliminating the imperial factor from South Africa.

THE BRITISH SCHOOL
The mid-nineteenth century

English writers prior to G. M. Theal were apologists for the British takeover of the Cape. Their focus of attention was the British colonies seen as part of the British empire. The Cape Colony in this work was thus denied an independent identity. The writers concentrated on events after the First British Occupation of the Cape in 1795: the activities of British governors, the coming to the Cape of British settlers, and their activities in the eastern districts, their struggle against the Xhosa on the eastern frontier, the fate of the British settlers in Natal – this was the focus of their attention. They took little note of developments at the Cape during the period 1652-1795 when it was under the control of the Dutch East India Company (D.E.I.C.). They were generally scathing about Company rule, comparing it unfavourably to the British rule that followed it. Although they generally acknowledged that the Boers who departed on the Great Trek had legitimate grievances, and they had sympathy for their position, they could not but feel that the prospects of the Voortrekkers in the "wild untamed" interior were dismal – they were not slow in detecting signs that the Boers in the interior were degenerating as far as their adherence to "civilisation" was concerned. The interior was compared unfavourably with the "progress" and "civilisation" in the British colonies. The Great Trek was thus an unfortunate aberration and it remained on the periphery as far as the English writers before the 1880s were concerned. But these writers were for the most part not hostile to the Dutch or Afrikaner elements as such, and the Dutch who had not gone on the Great Trek of the 1830s, but who had remained in the Cape and could thus be counted as "loyal" British subjects, were treated sympathetically in their accounts. Their distaste was reserved for the Afrikaners beyond the frontiers of the British colonies.

Although some of this historical writing had an anti-Afrikaner bias, in the same way as much historical writing in Dutch and Afrikaans had an anti-English bias, both English and Afrikaans writers shared an anti-black image of the past. They saw the frontier from the white point of view, they were uncomplimentary about the Xhosa.

Although these writers shared a firm belief in the superiority of British rule and British values, this did not mean that they saw no wrong in British actions. They were critical of the "arbitrary" rule of Lord Charles Somerset. They also condemned the British government in London for the attention that it gave to the philanthropists and British humanitarians to the detriment of the views of the colonists about the true state of affairs on the eastern frontier. John Centlivres Chase, himself an 1820 Settler, in 1831 wrote a pamphlet on the slave question at the Cape, defending the slave owners against charges that they mistreated their slaves. In 1836 he was at pains to refute the charges brought by the head of the London Missionary Society at the Cape, Dr John Philip, in *Some reasons for opposing the author of the South African Researches, the Rev. John Philip.*[5]

Two writers who may be classified as belonging to the British school, although their work also contained elements more in keeping with the settler school, did not neglect the Dutch East India Company's period of rule, or the Voortrekkers. Significantly, both of them were of Afrikaner extraction. Henry Cloete was a member of one of the oldest and most respected Cape families. He was born in Cape Town in 1792 and in 1803 was sent to school in the Netherlands. He went on to study law in England, and returned to the Cape in 1813, where he practised as an advocate and became a member of the Legislative Council. In 1843 he was sent as Commissioner to effect the annexation of Natal. He remained on in the newly proclaimed British colony and in 1845 was appointed Recorder of Natal, a position he held for some 10 years.

In 1852 he gave three lectures to the Literary Society in Pietermaritzburg in which he dealt with the Great Trek up to 1840. They were published in the same year. Having himself been involved in the events surrounding the course of the Great Trek in Natal after 1843, Cloete became aware of the incorrect versions that were doing the rounds. He thus regarded it as his duty before he left for the Cape in 1855 "to commemorate the circumstances under which the leading men of that country co-operated in the year 1843 to bring about a peaceful and satisfactory submission to Her Majesty's authority". This he did in two further lectures.[6] His *Five lectures on the emigration of the Dutch farmers* appeared in 1856.[7] They were not based on archival material. Cloete relied on his prodigious memory and existing accounts, and his work contains many errors, such as getting his figures regarding the number of Boers involved in the Slagtersnek rebellion wrong. Although the Rev. Francis Owen, the missionary at Dingane's capital, had in fact had no part at all in the treaty between Retief and the Zulu chief, Cloete recorded that Owen "was requested to draw out and witness the instrument, which he accordingly did in English, and to this document Dingaan and some of his principal councillors affixed their marks, after the tenor thereof had been fully interpreted to them by the Rev. Mr. Owen". This version of events became widely accepted and was partly responsible for Sir George Cory's later announcement that he considered the treaty a forgery.[8]

Cloete's account of the Great Trek was a fairly objective one, and by tracing the causes of the movement his work is in fact a broad history of the Cape under British rule. He dealt with the events leading up to the Trek in a sympathetic manner, seeing the withdrawal of the Voortrekkers as a great loss for the Cape.[9] But his values were British ones. He was thus sceptical about the prospects of the Voortrekkers cut off as they were from the protection, "civilising" influence and other advantages of British rule.[10] His sense of values may also be seen in his verdict on Slagtersnek, that it was "the most insane attempt ever made by a set of men to wage war against their Sovereign . . . it originated entirely in the wild unruly passions of a few clans of persons who could not suffer themselves to be brought under the authority of the law".[11] This was a very different description from that presented by most Afrikaner writers of the time and later. Certain recent Afrikaner research demythologising Slagtersnek, however, has tended to agree with Cloete.[12]

Another writer who may be classified as belonging to the British school, but who, unlike most others, devoted his attention to Company rule, was Egidius Benedictus Watermeyer. He was also of Afrikaner stock. Born in Cape Town in 1824, like Cloete he obtained a training in law in Leiden and London, and then practised as an advocate at the Cape. He represented Worcester in the Cape parliament in 1854, and in 1855 he became a judge in the Cape Supreme Court. He died in 1867 in London at the comparatively young age of 43.[13]

He differed from virtually all the other writers of the British school in that he consulted the archives in the preparation of his three lectures on the Cape in the days of the D.E.I.C. The lectures were delivered at the Mechanics' Institute and published in 1857 as *Three lectures on the Cape of Good Hope under the government of the Dutch East India Company*. A Dutch translation appeared in 1858.

Watermeyer believed that "the Dutch colonial system as exemplified at the Cape of Good Hope . . . was almost without one redeeming feature, and was a dishonour to the Netherland national name". Like Cloete, he was a great admirer of British rule, and roundly condemned Company rule. His final assessment of the Company era, with which he ended his third lecture, was a damning condemnation: "Thus, at the end of the last century, after 143 years of existence, the domination of the East India Company fell at the Cape of Good Hope. At the commencement of the period, the energy of these traders of a small commonwealth, who founded empires, and divided the command of the seas, merits admiration. But their principles were false, and the seeds of corruption were early sown in·their colonial administration. For the last fifty years, at least, of their rule here, there is little to which the examiner of our records can point with satisfaction. The effects of this pseudo colonization were that the Dutch, as a commercial nation, destroyed commerce. The most industrious race of Europe, they repressed industry. One of the freest states in the world, they encouraged a despotic misrule, in which falsely called free citizens were enslaved. These men, in their turn, became tyrants. Utter anarchy was the result. Some national feeling may have lingered; but, substantially, every man in the country, of every hue, was benefited when the incubus of the tyranny of the Dutch East India Company was removed. Since then, the advancement of the colony, both under an

English and a brief Dutch administration, has been as rapid as that of any in the world. So great has been the progress, – so utterly different is the condition of the inhabitants, – so much has in the intermediate sixty years been effected, – that it is with incredulity, and with some effort, that we are compelled to accept the fact, that affairs within so short a period were in the state which our history describes".[14]

The lectures found ready acceptance and until Theal's work began appearing, Watermeyer was considered the authority on the subject of Company rule. Both Cloete and Watermeyer were the authorities upon which all English writers based what they had to say about either the Cape under the D.E.I.C or the Voortrekkers.

W. C. Holden of the Wesleyan Missionary Society, in 1855 had his *History of the Colony of Natal, South Africa* published. It contained a supplement on the history of the Orange River Sovereignty, because part of his aim was to lend support to the deputation that had gone to England in an effort to persuade the British government not to withdraw its authority north of the Orange. "I subjoin, as an APPENDIX," he wrote, "a brief History of the Orange River Sovereignty, and an exposition of the opinions and feelings of English settlers and others respecting the desirableness of that fine frontier remaining under the mild and fostering care of the British government, and their gloomy apprehensions of the disastrous consequences of its abandonment to the sway of incompetent and discordant rulers".[15] But the book appeared too late for this purpose.

His work did not make for good history and his propagandistic aim reduced even further what little historical value the book had. It was not based on archival research and he used the work of others before him; but he had a mind of his own and did not simply take over their conclusions uncritically. To delineate the trends in early Natal history, he used Chase's *Natal Papers,* and the Voortrekker era is described by extensive reference to Cloete. The causes of the Great Trek were the loss by the Boers "of their slaves, and the unsatisfactory manner in which the Kafir war of 1835 was settled, with other matters of minor importance; which so chafed and irritated their prejudiced (and often ignorant) minds, that they left the old Colony in vast numbers".[16] He also drew attention to the possibilities of the region for immigration.

Although looking for a fairer dispensation for the blacks his attitude was strictly paternalistic. "The Kafirs must be treated like children", he wrote. They "are children of a larger growth and must be treated accordingly . . . But they are men in physical and mental powers . . . and the great difficulty in governing them is to treat them as men-children, teaching them that to submit and to obey are essential to their own welfare, as well as to that of others . . . Who, I would ask, is their best friend, – the man who would save them by apparent severity, or the man who would destroy them by mistaken kindness? . . . The result of too mild a policy is, that in a few years they are changed from crouching, terror-stricken vassals, to bold, lawless, independent barbarians".[17]

The *History of the Colony of the Cape of Good Hope* by Alexander Wilmot and John Chase was published in 1869. Wilmot took the tale up to 1819, and Chase was persuaded to tackle the period from 1820 to 1868. Wilmot's section was written in a moderate tone, and contained some good history, although he did not consult the archives. Like Watermeyer he did not have a high opinion of the Dutch East India Company's rule. In common with most of the other writers in this school, Wilmot did not paint a flattering picture of life among the Boers in the interior: "At the remote farms bread was a luxury rarely attainable, and although the scattered colonists paid some outward attention to religious worship, we cannot wonder that semi-barbarism soon began to prevail among them, and that its effects were too often perceptible in their conduct towards natives and slaves".[18] Such descriptions were, however, not peculiar to English writers, and they did not differ very much from those given by Dutch visitors to the interior.[19]

Chase's section, entitled *Annals of the Cape of Good Hope* was centred on the Eastern Province, in line with his 1843 book. Chase was deeply involved in the agitation for a separate government for the eastern Cape, or at least for the removal of the seat of government from Cape Town to Grahamstown. He was elected in 1864 to represent Port Elizabeth in the Cape House of Assembly, but illness prevented him from taking his seat; he later served in the Legislative Council from 1866 to 1875. As a dedicated separationist, his account was coloured by his unshakable conviction that the eastern Cape was more important than the western Cape; he thus neglected the latter. But despite this lack of balance in his account, for a while it became the standard work on the Cape because it was the first one to present the past as a continuous tale.[20]

Although a number of these writers were in favour of the benefits of British rule and rather unflattering in some of their comments on the Boers, particularly those outside the Cape or in the outlying regions of the Cape, this did not mean that they saw no wrong in British rule. On the contrary, they were on occasions highly critical of it. For example, Chase in his section of the above book had this to say about the position of Governor: "The Governor of the Cape Colony is always a bird of passage, and not always selected for his peculiar aptitude for the situation to which he is appointed. He generally accepts office with the crudest of notions – often with some favourite crochet of his own; crams, before leaving England, for information out of works on the Colony, many of them obsolete; reads up in ponderous Blue-books containing correspondence of his predecessors, and then, furnished with 'instructions' from Home, where the best information, political, geographical, & c., does not exist in perfection, arrives in Cape Town, dons the purple, issues a proclamation on the assumption of the new dignity, and lingers in that seductive metropolis until some thunderclap of disaster on the Border calls him to the front. Such has been the usual role for more than forty years. As soon as he has, by personal experience, mastered the difficulties of his position, or differs in opinion with his employers at the Colonial Office at home, or they get weary and impatient because certain objects are not soon enough attained, he is relieved by another gentleman as uninformed as he was on his arrival."[21]

The above history was superseded as the best work on the Cape by John Noble's *South Africa, past and present*, which appeared in 1877. It was not, however, based on archival sources, and he relied heavily on Watermeyer for the Company period.[22] Although he has been portrayed by van Jaarsveld[23] as being hostile to the Boers in the far interior of the Cape, as in the case of Wilmot his opinion of the situation was very similar to that of visiting Company officials. Part of the following statement he made about these Boers has been quoted by van Jaarsveld to show that he had an antipathy towards the Afrikaners: "Happily the pioneers were remarkable for their religious character and attention to the simple teaching of the Bible and the observances of the Dutch Reformed Church. In the absence of any regular government, these served to maintain good order and morality amongst them. But the condition of the rising generation was by no means satisfactory. Growing up in comparative ignorance, or with little or no education beyond the elementary truths conveyed to them by their parents, their moral condition was scarcely higher than the Hottentots or slaves who were their household companions."[24]

While not directly hostile towards the Voortrekkers in the Transvaal, he spoke of them in somewhat uncomplimentary terms. Thus the Boer government established in the Transvaal "was of a ruder and less enlightened character than that of the Free State". This was a feature of much of the writing of members of the British school, that while they had little good to say of the Boers in the Transvaal, they were generally well disposed towards the people of the Orange Free State. Many Transvalers "viewed with ignorant alarm and hostile feeling the civilization of the natives by Christian missionaries". Hendrik Potgieter's brother Hermanus is described as "a rough borderer, who had no compunction about forcibly carrying off anything he found in the possession of natives, and even occasionally made a raid amongst them, capturing their children for barter with the traders from Delagoa Bay and elsewhere."[25]

Like other writers of this school, and also the settler school, blacks were seen as barbarians. Thus Dingane's reception of Piet Retief and his party of Voortrekkers in 1838 "was characteristic of a savage barbarian. Base and treacherous, suspicious of his visitors, jealous of their power, and dreading the neighbourhood of their arms, yet unwilling to attack them openly – he massacred them clandestinely".[26]

24

The period of the Anglo-Boer wars

John Noble's book was published in 1877. By the time that Rider Haggard's *Cetewayo and his white neighbours* appeared in 1882, the situation in South Africa had changed dramatically. In fact the position had altered by 1877, although this was not reflected in Noble's history. The changes in South Africa were part of the new scenario that was developing in the world at large. In mid-century the European powers were not consciously seeking to extend their empires, in fact they were more interested in limiting their imperial responsibilities. This was no longer true of the last two decades of the century. The concept of empire had become more important in these years, it was the era of the New Imperialism, of the so-called "Scramble for Africa," where the tensions and rivalries of Europe were spilling over into Africa, where the quest for empire was inextricably linked to the nation's prestige among the concert of European powers. And this was all tied up with Europe's civilising and Christianising mission. Rudyard Kipling was to write of the "White Man's Burden," the French were to speak of a *mission civilisatrice*.

That was the wider European background to a new chauvinistic and jingoistic expansionist mood. Apart from this wider backdrop, there were strong local imperatives that drew the imperial factor deeper into the South African interior. In its specific South African context, a new expansionist era in South African politics was ushered in when the imperial factor once more began to make its influence felt north of the Cape Colony. In terms of the Sand River and Bloemfontein Conventions of 1852-1854, Britain had left the two inland Boer republics to their own devices and, by implication, had decided to limit her responsibilities in Southern Africa. But in 1868 Basutoland was taken under British protection, in 1871 the diamond fields were annexed as Griqualand West, in 1877 the Transvaal itself became a British colony. This step led, at the end of 1880, to the First Anglo-Boer War, which left a legacy of ill-feeling that was to gradually grow in the years that followed. South Africa became increasingly divided into two camps. The Jameson Raid of 1896 heightened Anglo-Boer tensions, and the final breach came with the Second Anglo-Boer War of 1899-1902.

The above factors are also of relevance to the growth of Afrikaner nationalism and the development by the Afrikaners of a specific historical consciousness. And if a threatened Afrikanerdom at the end of the nineteenth century searched the past for other grievances, rediscovering Slagtersnek and the Great Trek, English writers who turned to South African history became more attached to the ideal of empire. The fact that the expansion of British control northwards was being contested by the Boers, and that this seemed to threaten the entire British position in South Africa, caused the English writers who had complacently accepted the fact of British dominance in the colonial south in the 1850s and 1860s, as also the "obvious" benefits of such dominance, to react to imagined or real Afrikaner attempts to eliminate the imperial factor in South Africa. They now actively defended and justified Britain's role in South Africa, and launched bitter attacks on those who would seek to diminish it. They even began to adopt a hostile attitude to the "loyal" Afrikaners in the Cape because of the support that they gave the Transvaal. Writers of the settler school like George McCall Theal were accused of glorifying the Boers and denigrating British achievements in South Africa.

This new situation resulted in a significant shift in the approach of those writing about South African history. But there was also a measure of continuity between the early histories these men wrote and what came from their pens, or those of their colleagues, at the height of Anglo-Boer tension. Much of what was now more explicitly stated had been there before the dawning of the new age of imperialism: the basic assumption that British institutions and ideals were superior to the home (South African) grown product, the fact that the British presence in South Africa represented the spread of beneficial influences – "culture", "civilisation" and "progress". They had always stressed the empire connection – they now did so rather more heavily, but that was because that link was being threatened and they shared the desire to see the British empire expand. They adopted a stronger line towards the Afrikaners in the Transvaal, but the antipathy had been there much earlier. They may have begun stressing equal rights for all men as a British ideal more than they had done earlier and, although they made some vague noises about this signifying a better deal for blacks, they were really thinking of equal rights for all *white* men, to posit this as a superior policy to that followed by Paul Kruger, who had denied equal rights to the Uitlanders. Their attitude towards the country's blacks had not in general changed significantly. They were still largely ignored.

*   *   *

The new attitude of this British school emerged at the time of the First Anglo-Boer War, in the wake of the British defeat at Majuba and the withdrawal from the Transvaal. British writers felt that humiliation deeply and roundly condemned Gladstone's policy. They adopted a hostile attitude towards the Transvaal. Early books in this category include H. Rider Haggard's *Cetewayo and his white neighbours* (1882) and John Nixon's *The complete story of the Transvaal from the Great Trek to the Convention of London* (1885).

Rider Haggard, a British author of note, and better known for his novels, *She, King Solomon's mines* and *Allan Quatermain*, was a member of the British administration in the Transvaal at the time of the annexation in April 1877, and was in fact a member of the British commission that went to Sekhukhune's capital in March 1877 to hear the Pedi chief's version of the controversial peace treaty he had signed with the Boer government.[27]

The British author did not have a high opinion of the Boers in the Transvaal. "They are very religious," he wrote, "but their religion takes its colour from the darkest portions of the Old Testament; lessons of mercy and gentleness are not at all to their liking, and they seldom care to read the Gospels. What they delight in are the stories of wholesale butchery by the Israelites of old; and in their own position they find a reproduction of that of the first settlers in the Holy Land. Like them they think they are entrusted by the Almighty with the task of exterminating the heathen native tribes around them, and are always ready with a scriptural precedent for slaughter and robbery. The name of the Divinity is continually on their lips, sometimes in connection with very doubtful statements." According to Haggard, the Boers did not have many good characteristics. Their homes were "too frequently squalid and filthy to an extraordinary degree", the Boer had "no romance in him, nor any of the higher feelings and aspirations that are found in almost every other race".[28]

The annexation of the Transvaal was greatly approved: "And thus the Transvaal Territory passed for a while into the great family of the English Colonies"; the annexation itself had been carried out with "very remarkable ability". The birthday celebrations of Queen Victoria on 24 May 1877 and the raising of the Union Jack were, for Haggard, "one of the proudest moments of my life. Could I have foreseen that I should live to see that same flag, then hoisted with so much joyous ceremony, within a few years shamefully and dishonourably hauled down and buried, I think it would have been the most miserable." The British withdrawal from the Transvaal in 1881 was "an act of treachery to those to whom we were bound with double chains – by the strong ties of a common citizenship, and by those claims to England's protection from violence and wrong". Haggard was able to give his grudging admiration to the way the Boers had "managed their revolt". He believed that it demonstrated that "they have good stuff in them somewhere, which, under the firm but just rule of Her Majesty, might have been much developed, and it makes it the more sad that they should have been led to throw off that rule, and have been allowed to do so by an English Government".[29]

Alexander Wilmot's *The story of the expansion of Southern Africa* was published in 1895, before the Jameson Raid and the height of Anglo-Boer tensions. A major difference between Haggard and this work of Wilmot's is that the latter shows no animosity towards the Afrikaners as such. In Wilmot's view the Voortrekkers had had very good grounds for leaving the Cape, and they had "been the powerful means of opening up to civilisation most of that vast territory which will yet form one of the greatest confederation of states in the southern hemisphere". As with other writers of the British school he was well-disposed towards the Free State, where there was "a happy, well-governed people"; there had been "no doubt that the great dry diggings at Kimberley were all really within the Free State boundary". The annexation of the Transvaal had been "a blunder" which had been brought about because "the ignorance of our representatives was simply phenomenal".[30]

It was not the Boers he disliked, but the Transvaal government for having failed to accord the Uitlanders fair treatment. He did not approve of Paul Kruger's Transvaal government; the Uitlanders who did not have the vote were "justly discontented people ... exposed to oppressive exactions and unjust monopolies".[31]

He is anything but flattering about traditional African society where "concubinage is permitted, while the vilest and most degrading immorality prevails". He agreed with the view that "marriage among the Kafirs has degenerated into slavery, and that among them not only is seduction not punishable, but no disgrace whatever attaches to it".[32]

Wilmot adopted a stronger anti-Transvaal stand in the three-volume *History of our own times in South Africa* (1897-1899) and his *The History of South Africa* (1901). This last work was virtually the same as *The story of the expansion of Southern Africa*, with the exception of two chapters that were added, dealing with the build-up to the outbreak of war in 1899, and a description of the military campaigns of the war up to the end of 1900. So the growing enmity in South Africa did not cause Wilmot to change his mind about what he had said earlier – the British blunders were still blunders, the Voortrekkers had had genuine grievances, the Free State was wisely ruled. The difference comes in what he had to say about the Transvaal.

In *The story of the expansion of Southern Africa* his disapproval of the Transvaal Afrikaners was quite open. This opposition had, if anything, become more extreme in *The history of South Africa*. President Kruger "fitly represented the mass of the people of Dutch extraction by entertaining an undying hatred of England, the firm idea that he and his followers were the people of the Lord ... Ignorance with prejudice reigned supreme, and in its wake followed corruption". The Uitlander population "was a hated enemy to be plundered and persecuted. Plunder was amply secured by means of unequal taxation and systematic bribery ... At the same time the foulest hypocrisy was added to injustice, and Krugerism posed as a saintly system, whose principles and practice were based on the teachings of the Bible. While quoting scripture and preaching on hell, the President was at the same time robbing and oppressing the people". The Jameson Raid had been justified, and the Raiders were "condemned to extortionate fines for committing the heinous crime of endeavouring to throw off the yoke of one of the most corrupt and arbitrary oligarchies whose rule ever covered the name of Republic with disgrace".[33]

Although his earlier book appeared in 1895 and could thus have contained details of political developments in the Cape, it did not. This is remedied in the *History of South Africa* and his dislike for the Transvaal is now extended to Afrikaners in the Cape. This was because of the sympathy of the latter for their fellow Afrikaners in the republics. Since at least 1882, Wilmot declared, certain Afrikaners had made it known that their ultimate aim "was the overthrow of the British power and the expulsion of the British flag from

South Africa". There was a plan afoot "to establish in South Africa an Afrikander nation or confederation totally independent of Great Britain".[34] The Afrikaners in the Cape had demonstrated "gross ingratitude" to the imperial government. "They not only received the gift of managing their own affairs under a responsible system of government, but Britain has poured forth the blood of her soldiers and the treasures of her people in conquering the numerous savage foes who successively threatened not merely the independence but the existence of the white people of South Africa". Wilmot concludes thus: "Let us trust that reason will soon assert its sway, and that people of all nationalities will, for mutual interests, endeavour to accept the inevitable, promote amity among themselves, and thus pave the way for a successful South African federated Dominion under the British Crown".[35]

James Cappon was another member of the British school. As he saw it, the struggle between Boer and Briton was basically "a conflict between the standard of civilisation and progress which the British authorities felt bound to maintain, and the somewhat different one to which the Boers had accustomed themselves, especially in matters relating to the treatment of the native races". He saw the future of South Africa as one in which British values would prevail. "I think it can be made clear," he stated, "even to the Dutch of the Transvaal and Orange River colonies, that in general the policy of Great Britain has been based on large conceptions of justice towards all the races in South Africa, and has represented a standard of civilisation which in the end it will be better for them to conform to than to fight against".[36]

The British school was at its height at the time of the Anglo-Boer War and in the aftermath of the war, when all the states in South Africa were British colonies, and it seemed as if South Africa had been won as a permanent part of the British Empire. Arthur Conan Doyle, better known as the creator of Sherlock Holmes and the inimitable Dr Watson, wrote *The Great Boer War* which was printed for the first time in October 1900; by the end of 1902, 18 impressions had appeared, 16 of them new editions, each "a little more full and accurate than that which preceded it".[37]

His message throughout was that the British government may have made mistakes at times, but their motives could not be called into question, they had always acted from the highest ideals. In his opinion, the Second Anglo-Boer War had brought in its train "at last, we hope, a South Africa of peace and prosperity, with equal rights and equal duties for all men". South Africa had been a troublesome area for the empire: "But surely the most arduous is the most honourable, and, looking back from the end of their journey, our descendants may see that our long record of struggle, with its mixture of disaster and success, its outpouring of blood and of treasure, has always tended to some great and enduring goal."[38]

In common with others of the British school, the Transvaal comes in for the most criticism. Arthur Conan Doyle was critical of the withholding of the franchise from the Uitlanders. As he saw the situation, the British government had treated the Cape, which had a majority of Dutch people within its borders, very generously by giving them responsible government in 1872 so that the Dutch "could, and did, put their own representatives into power and run the government upon Dutch lines. Already Dutch law had been restored, and Dutch put on the same footing as English as the official language of the country. The extreme liberality of such measures, and the uncompromising way in which they have been carried out, however distasteful the legislation might seem to English ideas, are among the chief reasons which made the illiberal treatment of British settlers in the Transvaal so keenly resented at the Cape. A Dutch Government was ruling the British in a British colony, at a moment when the Boers would not give an Englishman a vote upon a municipal council in a city which he had built himself".[39]

But the British are not absolved from all blame. The punishment meted out at Slagtersnek "was unduly severe and exceedingly injudicious. A brave race can forget the victims of the field of battle, but never those of the scaffold. The making of political martyrs is the last insanity of statesmanship". Although British mistakes are pointed out, British actions were always seen in the best possible light. The annexation of the Transvaal in 1877 had not worked out well. "But the empire has always had poor luck in South Africa, and never worse than on that occasion", Conan Doyle reflected. In annexing the Transvaal, "Great Britain, however mistaken she may have been, had no obvious selfish interest in view. There were no Rand mines in those days, nor was there anything in the country to tempt the most covetous . . . There was nothing sordid in our action, though it may have been both injudicious and high-handed."[40]

According to Conan Doyle, the Second Anglo-Boer War had been good for the empire. "We had hoped that we were a solid empire when we engaged in the struggle, but we knew that we were when we emerged from it. In that change lies an ample recompense for all the blood and treasure spent . . . That the heavy losses caused us by the war were borne without a murmur is surely evidence enough how deep was the conviction of the nation that the war was not only just but essential – that the possession of South Africa and the unity of the empire were at stake . . . The deepest instincts of the nation told it that it must fight and win, or for ever abdicate its position in the world. Through dark days which brought out the virtues of our race as nothing has done in our generation, we struggled grimly on until the light had fully broken once again. And of all the gifts that God has given to Britain there is none to compare with those days of sorrow, for it was in them that the nation was assured of its unity, and learned for all time that blood is stronger to bind than salt water is to part . . . On the plains of South Africa, in common danger and in common privation, the blood brotherhood of the Empire was sealed."[41] In such ringing and dramatic, heroic terms, did Conan Doyle see Britain's mission in South Africa.

Another writer who may be classified as belonging to the British school was E. B. Iwan-Müller. His *Lord Milner and South Africa* (London, 1902) was also written at the time of the Second Anglo-Boer War. Iwan-Müller was extremely critical of Theal. Others who wrote about Milner and also adopted an anti-Afrikaner stance included W. Basil Worsfold and Cecil Headlam.[42]

Although the British school was at its height at the time of the war, and tended to disappear as the passions aroused subsided after the end of the conflict, elements of this British school persisted until at least the middle of the 20th century. This may be seen in attempts that continued to be made to vindicate Milner's role in South Africa, as in the works of Edward Crankshaw and Sir Evelyn Wrench.[43]

THE SETTLER SCHOOL

George McCall Theal

No other historian has stamped his authority on the study of South African history to the same extent as George McCall Theal. In volume 4 of his *The rise of South Africa*, published in 1926, Sir George Cory expressed the opinion that "no one can write upon the history of this country, without having recourse to the work of the late Dr. Theal".[44] Two years earlier Edgar Brookes had said much the same thing: "No book on any aspect or period of South African history can fitly close without a tribute of thanks to that Master of research . . . Dr. Theal. It is due to his extraordinarily indefatigable and discriminating labours that it is possible to-day to prosecute historical research under conditions, which, if not perfect, are at least infinitely better than when he undertook his great life-work."[45]

Since these statements were made in the 1920s, much historical research has been undertaken, and there are large areas of the past where thorough and detailed research and the setting of new questions about the past has rendered the views of Theal as of only passing interest, a matter of historical curiosity. But in other areas his imprint on the study of South African history has been a particularly enduring one. That it was still dominant in the 1940s may be adduced from the fact that Professor J. S. Marais, concerned at how much people's image of the past had simply been taken over uncritically from Theal, conducted intensive research into the documents relating to events on the eastern frontier of the Cape between 1778 and 1802.[46]

In 1962 Merle Babrow wrote as follows: "Theal's continuing importance and influence are illustrated by the fact that not only are school textbooks (the only history that most people read) largely based on him, but that there are still historians who rely on and consult him. Indeed his importance is underscored by the use which even his severest critics continue to make of him. He is not only listed in their bibliographies, but cited as source and authority in their footnotes. Moreover, even historians who reject Theal's interpretation and facts, usually continue to work largely within the framework erected by him – his selection and choice of themes and events. His work, even where it is rejected, is the starting-point of our enquiries, and the main props of the structure of our history are still those erected and established by him. We may agree or disagree, but our thoughts tend to centre around his interpretation; his work determines our selection of what is important and relevant . . . The mere fact that someone has organised the material and phrased the questions and answers in a particular way, predisposes us to do the same. Theal is still used as a textbook at the universities. He is recommended to students, whose previous education, background and feelings predispose them to accept his interpretation. When they leave, what will most of them be likely to remember: the detailed scholarship of Marais and Reyburn,[47] or the generalities of Theal, which they have heard since they were children?"[48] Merle Babrow may possibly have overstated the position somewhat, but there can be no doubt about Theal's significance in South African historiography.

His life and work

Who was this man who has had such an important influence on our study of history? George McCall Theal, the son of a medical doctor, was born in New Brunswick in Canada on 11 April 1837, and was the eldest of a large family of nine children. To avoid becoming a minister, a vocation his father wished him to follow, Theal ran away from home when he was 17. He spent some time in the United States and also two years in Sierra Leone, working in his uncle's trading post. In 1861, en route to Australia, he stopped off at the Cape and decided to remain there. In the next 17 years he held various posts, starting off as a teacher at a farm school in the neighbourhood of Knysna. This was followed by positions as a bookkeeper in King William's Town, as editor in Maclear, the owner of a newspaper in East London, and a teacher at Dale College, King William's Town. After a brief and unsuccessful attempt to make his fortune on the diamond fields at Kimberley in 1870, he became a teacher at the Lovedale Missionary Institution. While he was there the Ninth Frontier War broke out in 1877, and Theal, who had in the course of his wanderings about the eastern Cape, added Xhosa to the English, French and Dutch languages he already spoke, spent five months as a resident government agent with a chief whom the government wished to keep out of the war. From May 1878 to early 1879 he acted as labour agent in the Western Cape rural districts, trying to find employment for Africans sent there from the eastern frontier in the aftermath of the frontier war. On being offered a post in the public service he moved to Cape Town.

His interest in South African history had by this time already borne fruit in print. While at Lovedale, in 1871 he published *South Africa as it is*. This pamphlet was followed in 1874 by the more ambitious project, *A compendium of South African history and geography.* This was based on existing works, Watermeyer, Cloete and Moodie in particular, as well as travellers' accounts like those of Kolbe, Mentzel, Barrow, Lichtenstein and Burchell. As the first comprehensive history of South Africa it was an immediate success, and was widely used in schools. By 1877 it had gone into a third edition.

Theal was a prodigious worker, and although he had a full-time position that kept him busy until four o'clock in the afternoons, he requested that he be allowed to spend his sparetime sorting out and classifying the mass of archival records, which were then housed in the Surveyor's office. His wish was granted and from the middle of March 1879 he had control of the archives; over and above his salary as a civil servant he was paid at the rate of £100 per annum for his labours in the archives. He devoted himself to the task with enthusiasm and was deeply hurt when the Cape parliament in January 1881, for reasons which still remain obscure, announced that the Rev. H. C. V. Leibbrandt, hitherto Free Church minister at Graaff-Reinet, had been appointed to the post and would combine it with his position as librarian of the Cape parliament. Theal's supporters raised the question in parliament, but were unable to obtain a reversal of the decision.

The severely disillusioned Theal was transferred to the Department of Native Affairs, and in 1881 spent a few months as acting magistrate at Tamacha near King William's Town. However, he soon obtained an opportunity of once more indulging in the history he had come to love so much. His request for leave so that he could go to The Hague and continue his historical research, was granted and he went to the Netherlands to search for and copy documents relating to South Africa which were not in the Cape archives. Theal spent some 10 months thus engaged, and returned to South Africa in 1882.

From this time onwards the number of publications that appeared under his name increased rapidly. In 1881 a collection of documents came out entitled *Abstracts of the debates and resolutions of the Council of Policy at the Cape, 1651-1687.* His return to the Cape coincided with a tense and difficult period in the Cape's administration of Basutoland, and Theal was given the assistance of a number of clerks and instructed to collect, copy and translate all the documents he could find on Basutoland. This resulted in the publication in 1883 of three volumes of *Basutoland Records.* A fourth, unpublished volume, is in the Cape archives. *A fragment of Basuto history, Boers and Bantu,* and *The republic of Natal,* all appeared in 1886. These were followed in 1887 by *The history of the Boers in South Africa* and a year later by the first volume of *History of South Africa.* By 1893, five volumes of this series, which took events up to 1884, had seen the light of day. In preparing new editions, he added to the work so that it eventually consisted of 11 volumes. His habit of publishing old works under new titles, and drastically revising works for new editions, makes it difficult to establish precisely the number of works he published – but it was in excess of 70. He was indefatigable, often working 12 hours a day, 7 days a week.

A school textbook, *A short history of South Africa for schools* (1890), was translated into Dutch in the same year by President F. W. Reitz of the Orange Free State. A second edition of *Korte geschiedenis van Zuid-Afrika* appeared in 1891. In 1892 another schoolbook, *Primer of South African history*, was also translated into Dutch, and by 1896 had gone into a third edition.

By the early 1890s Theal was widely recognised as South Africa's foremost historian. In 1891 he was appointed Colonial Historiographer by the Cape government with an annual allowance of £150 over and above his salary from the Department of Native Affairs. In 1895 Queen's University in Kingston, Ontario, Canada, conferred an Honorary LL.D. degree on him, and in 1899 the University of the Cape of Good Hope followed suit, conferring the D. Litt. degree on Theal.

From 1896 he spent nine years abroad, mainly in London, Paris and Rome having documents copied. He added Portuguese to the other languages he knew so that he could translate early records copied for him in Lisbon. In these nine years he published some 45 volumes of documents, the cost of which was borne by the Cape government. In 1896 his *History and ethnography of South Africa* (in nine volumes) appeared, as did *The Portuguese in South Africa*, and two volumes of *Belangrijke Historische Dokumenten*, being collections of documents obtained in The Hague. A third volume of this followed in 1911. Between 1897 and 1905 the 36 volumes of *Records of the Cape Colony* were published, at the rate of some four volumes per annum, including two index volumes. The nine volumes of his *Records of South-Eastern Africa* were published between 1898 and 1903.

The above-mentioned publications do not include all his works. The author of *Geslacht-register der oude Kaapsche familiën*, C.C. de Villiers, died suddenly, and with the assistance of W.J. Vlok, Theal completed the work, which was published in three volumes by the Cape government in 1893-1894. In 1894 his *South Africa*, which was part of the *Story of the Nations* series, appeared. By 1916 it had gone into 16 editions. Among his other works were *Kaffir folklore; or a selection from the traditional tales current among the people living on the eastern border of the Cape Colony* (completed while he was at Lovedale, but only published five years later in 1882), *History and ethnography of Africa south of the Zambesi, 1505-1795* (three volumes, 1907), *Documents relating to the Kaffir War of 1835* (1911), *Willem Adriaan van der Stel and other historical sketches* (1913), *Catalogue of South African books and pamphlets* (1912).

As part of an economy drive by the Cape government, Theal was pensioned off from the Department of Native Affairs in 1904, but he was allowed to retain the post of Colonial Historiographer and the allowance attached to it. He returned to the colony in 1906, and until his death in 1919 he lived at Wynberg, working on new editions of his books.[49]

34

An evaluation of his source publications

From the above it is clear that Theal's contribution to the study of South African history was considerable. His source publications made available to researchers a vast body of material from archives all over Europe. Immelman writes that: "In connection with Theal's phenomenal output, his achievement is all the more amazing when the fact is taken into account that he laboured in the days before photocopying or microfilming, while dictaphones and tape recorders were as yet unknown. Every document he had personally to copy by hand, not even having the use of a typewriter or a shorthand-typist to whom he could dictate. Except for such help as his wife gave him in matters like proofreading and indexing, Theal worked, to all intents and purposes, alone and unaided. Then, too, it must be remembered that in his early days there were no properly organised archives, and he had to cull what he could from chaotic masses of records. When these factors are taken into consideration, his tremendous number of publications becomes all the more incredible."[50]

In evaluating his source publications it should be noted that his technique improved with time. His *Abstracts of the debates of the Council of Policy*, consisted, as the title indicates, of extracts or summaries of the documents, but Theal soon came to realise that this was inadequate as a historical source for serious research. Leibbrandt, however, with his *Précis of the archives* continued to publish summaries of documents, although Theal was critical of this and came to believe that such summaries were useless to researchers.[51]

His *Basutoland Records* were an improvement, but there were also weak points in this as a source publication, and some of the documents were given only in translation, nor did he indicate where the original documents were to be found. Material in these documents that did not have relevance to Basutoland was omitted, without any indication that this had been done.

Theal later came to realise that some of his methods were inadequate and in his 1895 report as Colonial Historiographer he said that: "In Europe whole series of ancient papers are continually being printed, and if that should be done in South Africa each paper should appear *verbatim et literatim*, and no translation should be given without the original at its side."[52] By the time that he came to do the *Records of the Cape Colony* his technique had improved. He writes of the documents presented there that they "have been copied as carefully as possible, and no changes have been made in either the spelling, the punctuation, or the use of capital letters".[53] In the *Records* he gave information on the location of the document copied, whether the document had been taken from an original document or was itself a duplicate or a copy, and whether it was a translation.

In the preface to *Records of South-Eastern Africa* he put his position even more strongly: "I give these documents without the alteration of a letter or a point, as only in that form can they be of value for reference."[54]

Judged by the more rigorous standards that apply to modern collections of documentary material, it is easy to find fault with Theal's publications. He did not check the accuracy of his text closely enough, nor did he as editor ensure that omissions in the text were always indicated. But if one takes into consideration the time and the circumstances under which he worked, his documentary publications were well done. They still remain a valuable and usable source in the 1980s.[55]

An evaluation of his historical works

It is difficult to evaluate Theal's historical writing. He was and remains a controversial figure. His influence on the study of South African history is not in doubt, and the controversy is about the nature and quality of his work. In 1915 Theal declared that: "To the utmost of human ability I have striven to write without fear, favour, or prejudice, to do equal justice to all with whom I had to deal. I can, therefore, without laying myself open to the accusation of vanity, place my work confidently before the public as not alone the only detailed history of South Africa yet prepared, but as a true and absolutely unbiased narrative."[56] The arrogance of this statement is in line with another statement he made to the effect that he did not need to give his sources because no-one had made such a detailed study of the sources as he had.[57] Marais refers to Theal's claim as "somewhat naive".[58] Much of the debate surrounding Theal is concerned with his claim to have written "without fear or favour".

Theal was much beloved by Afrikaner historians, and his history books were translated into Dutch and used in schools in the republics. For many years Afrikaners regarded Theal's history as *the* history of South Africa. Afrikaner historiographers have made much of the fact that Theal was at first hostile towards the Afrikaners but that after he came to know the "true" situation he altered his opinion. In his first comprehensive history, *A compendium of South African history and geography* (1874), which was based on existing secondary accounts, Theal adopted a liberal point of view, praising the British government for the freedom it had brought to Coloureds and slaves, seeing the Afrikaners as oppressors of the blacks. But once he had studied the archives, particularly when he compiled the *Basutoland Records*, he changed his opinion, becoming the great champion of the Afrikaners. He now adopted a conservative, pro-white and in particular pro-Boer, anti-missionary and anti-black standpoint.[59]

In the preface to his *History of the Boers* he acknowledged his change of direction as follows: "Regarding the acts of various missionaries, there is certainly a difference in the tone of this volume and of my 'Compendium of South African History' written sixteen years ago. I had not then read the mass of missionary correspondence in the colonial records nor the comments upon their complaints and the refutations of many of their statements made by officers of the Colonial Government."[60]

He was the first English historian to comprehend the striving and struggles of the republican Afrikaners, and as such they welcomed his work. From the appearance of his *History of the Boers* in 1887 to about 1927, he dominated the historical scene. This book made a considerable impact as it was the first comprehensive study on the Voortrekker era,[61] far broader in its scope than either Cloete or Watermeyer, nor did it have their pessimism regarding the decline of "civilised" standards in the country beyond the limits of "progressive" British influence.

By giving the Great Trek a prominent place in his 11-volume *History of South Africa*, for the first time the whole story of the Great Trek was placed against the broad background of the history of South Africa. Although he was sympathetic towards the Voortrekkers, he was not blind to their faults. His contribution to the study of the Great Trek lay in providing a relatively loosely linked, chronological battery of facts on the Great Trek that could later be used by trained historians to make important reinterpretations.[62]

Theal's treatment of the Boers in the Cape, on the eastern frontier of the colony, and in the republics, is sympathetic and warm. In the late 1870s and early 1880s there was a growing identity of interests between the rural Cape Afrikaners and the English-speaking business community, as epitomised in the political alliance between "Onze Jan" Hofmeyr and Cecil Rhodes. Hofmeyr included in his definition of Afrikaner all whites who regarded Africa as their home, while Rhodes projected a colonial nationalism, a Cape-based identity and imperialism, which sought to limit the British imperial factor. Theal came to identify very strongly with this "colonial nationalist" attitude, and adopted a hostile stance towards the interference of British imperialists. In his writing he extended the idea of the Cape alliance between English and Afrikaner northwards across the Orange and Vaal Rivers, developing the theme of the formation of a new white South African society, ruled by whites of both Anglo-Saxon and Dutch heritage. In this sense it was Theal who was responsible for the invention of the concept of a "white South Africa" in historical writing.[63]

Although Theal also gave considerable attention to tracing the history of African societies, and used oral sources in an attempt at preciseness, he did not see a role for blacks in his white South Africa, except as a labour supply. To him the coloured races of South Africa were "fickle barbarians, prone to robbery and unscrupulous in shedding blood".[64] Manumitted slaves had become so much of a drain on the resources of the poor fund at the Cape, he indicated, that in 1708 the government had been obliged to take steps to prevent slaves from being manumitted unless they could prove that they would be able to maintain themselves and would not become a public burden. He explained that: "As time wore on, it became apparent that in most instances emancipation meant the conversion of a useful individual into an indolent pauper and a pest to society. Habits of industry, which in Europeans are the result of pressure of circumstances operating upon the race through hundreds of generations, were found to be opposed to the disposition of Africans. Experience showed that a freed slave usually chose to live in a filthy hovel upon coarse and scanty food rather than toil for something better. Decent clothing was not a necessity of life to him, neither did he need other furniture in his hovel than a few cooking utensils. He put nothing by, and when sickness came he was a burden upon the public. Such in general was the negro when left to himself in a country where sufficient food to keep life in his body was to be had without much exertion."[65]

Blacks did not play a major role in the history of South Africa as seen by Theal. The history of South Africa was the history of the whites and their efforts to open up and bring civilisation and Christianity to a wild untamed country. Blacks were part of the background, and the British philanthropic missionaries, Philip in particular, who took up the case of blacks, were enemies of the whites. In the difficulties on the eastern frontier it was blacks and these missionaries who were responsible for the situation that developed.

One should note, however, that such an unashamedly "white view" of the past was not unique to Theal, and that in the era of European dominance over virtually the whole of Africa and large parts of Asia, European values and ideas were regarded as being far superior to any indigenous values. Theal's attitudes towards blacks were shared by the overwhelming majority of Europeans.

Theal was criticised for portraying blacks in a poor light, for taking up an anti-imperial stance and playing down British achievements in South Africa, and for glorifying the Boers. But he was also criticised for other shortcomings connected with his workmanship. His work was largely a chronicle, he was mainly concerned to establish a continuous chronological series of events, so he *described* rather than *interpreted*. His facts are often given without any distinction being made between what is important and what is trivial. He took very little note of the influence of events in Europe on South African affairs; he gave scant attention to geographical features that may possibly have had a bearing on the course of history, his economic history consisted of little more than dry statistics, dished up with no reworking or interpretation.[66] He was very good at summarising archival material, but less adept at analysing or giving perspective to this material.[67]

The main criticism levelled against Theal's workmanship was his failure to cite his sources. Except in certain select instances, where his sources were contradictory and the issues controversial or sensitive, he failed to say where his data came from. In certain instances where doubt was cast upon his statements he did give his sources, as with the attitude of the Cape colonists towards the first missionaries: "As my account of the Moravian mission differs", he wrote "from the general statements of English writers, I have given in a previous chapter the documents relating to George Schmit [sic] upon which it is based."[68] When he dealt with the sensitive issue of the

British annexation of the diamond fields in 1871, he likewise reproduced many of the documents in his text.

There can be no question that Theal's failure to provide evidence of the way he had reached his conclusions was poor historical practice. Why did he not cite his sources? He gave at least two answers to this question. In his preface to *The Portuguese in South Africa*, referring to African peoples in South Africa, he said: "I need not give my authorities for what I have now written concerning these people, for I think I can say with truth that no one else has ever made such a study of this subject as I have."[69] Apart from the great, and at times overweening, confidence he had in his own work, there was another reason, and one which is undoubtedly more satisfactory. In volume 3 of his *History*, he said that he "was deterred from giving extracts from these records throughout the volumes by the great expense which would thereby be occasioned and the bulk to which the work would have extended".[70] The Cape government was by no means flush with money, and it was bearing the cost of publishing his work; he was on occasion exhorted to keep his expenses down, so that this reason was probably decisive.

The fact that he so seldom cited his sources was a major criticism, and one which has led many people to question Theal's interpretations as well as his facts. One of his contemporaries to do so was Leibbrandt, who contested the accuracy of Theal's account of the Slagtersnek rebellion and his condemnation of Wilhelm Adriaen van der Stel. In order to prove his point, Leibbrandt published collections of documents on these two issues.[71] Theal later went to much trouble locating his sources, in an attempt to prove that they did exist and that they did indeed prove what he said they did.[72]

Another contemporary , E. B. Iwan-Müller, in his *Lord Milner and South Africa* (1902) declared that he "had regarded Dr. Theal's 'History of South Africa' as dependable, so far as facts and the more obvious inferences to be drawn from facts were concerned. Unfortunately, a careful study of his later volumes" had led him "to the conclusion that it was impossible to accept Dr. Theal as an authority without the most vigilant scrutiny, not only of his narrative itself, but of the official documents upon which it is professed to be based . . . It is one of the peculiarities of Dr. Theal's historical methods that, unless he has some very distinct object to serve, he rarely supplies the data for forming a judgment on the incident he chronicles."[73]

* * *

From the 1920s the emerging liberal school took Theal to task for neglecting the role of blacks and for his unflattering portrayal of them. The first attacks on Theal, however, did not come from the liberals but from members of the British school who objected to his anti-imperial stand. As South Africa became ever more divided into a republican and a British camp in the years leading up to the Anglo-Boer War of 1899-1902, particularly in the years after the abortive Jameson Raid of 1896, so these writers regarded Theal with growing distaste.

Among those contemporaries who attacked him was James Cappon, Professor of English at Queen's University in Kingston, Canada, the university which had a few years earlier conferred an honorary doctorate on Theal. *Britain's title in South Africa, or The story of the Cape Colony to the days of the Great Trek* appeared in 1902. Cappon declared that Theal was "by no means the safest of guides in this part of the Empire's history; it even seems to me that he has laboured to darken the British side of it; he has passed lightly or in silence over the characteristic merits of British rule, especially when tried by the standards of the times of which he is speaking; he has misunderstood or misrepresented its highest traditions, he has unfairly emphasised its defects and made as little as possible even of the economic and industrial advantages which it undoubtedly conferred on South Africa. And he has done this for the sake of setting the history of a special class of Boers in the best light, and of building up traditions of Boer history, which are certainly at variance both with these records[74] and a common-sense analysis of the facts. The problem of ruling and developing South Africa has had various phases, all of them difficult enough, but Dr. Theal has saved himself all trouble of seeking for the moral or economic principles involved in it by the easy application of one principle, namely, that the Briton was always in the wrong and the Boer always in the right. I have really been unable to discover any other organising principle in his work."[75]

With some justice it could be claimed that Iwan-Müller and James Cappon, to whom Theal's condemnation of British imperialism was anathema, objected to Theal's account on political grounds. But this did not apply to Professor Edgar's criticism in 1909 that he had examined the documents relating to Wilhelm Adriaen van der Stel but could find no support for Theal's "sweeping assertions". He asked Theal to give his sources as it was unreasonable to expect that his "mere personal assurance on an important matter of this kind" would be accepted uncritically.[76]

Opposition to Theal on political grounds could certainly not be applied to Professor P.J. van der Merwe of Stellenbosch University. He obviously had great respect for Theal, and prefaced the areas where he had found Theal wanting with statements such as: "If I may with the utmost respect, differ from such a great authority on our history".[77]

A most thorough researcher, Professor van der Merwe examined the first clash on the Cape's eastern frontier between Boer and Bantu in 1779 in his book *Die trekboer in die geskiedenis van die Kaapkolonie (1657-1842)* (1938), and he had "considerable criticism of Dr Theal's representation of matters".[78] Van der Merwe found it strange that in his account Theal omitted certain matters that were clearly documented but that he made other statements about the situation for which van der Merwe, despite the most exhaustive search into all possible sources, could find no documentary support. Most

40

of van der Merwe's differences from Theal concern the extent of cattle thieving by Xhosa on the frontier. Thus Theal stated that when Governor van Plettenberg visited the frontier in 1778, the Boers living in the area complained to him that the Xhosa had been stealing their stock. Van der Merwe could find no evidence that the Boers had in fact made such a complaint. He thus rejected Theal's implication that it was because of cattle theft that the Governor had proclaimed the Fish River as the border and told the Xhosa to move east of the river. Van der Merwe's conclusion, based on his careful research, was that the Boers had complained of the fact that the Xhosa cattle were destroying the grazing on the west side of the Fish River, and that the number of Xhosa and their stock had increased to such an extent that the Boers were experiencing pangs of insecurity.[79]

The failure of the Xhosa to remain east of the Fish River is seen by Theal as an "invasion" of the colony in March 1789, but van der Merwe's research led him to the conclusion that it was nothing of the sort, that the Xhosa, without hostile intentions, had been gradually entering the colony over a period of time – not a sudden invasion as Theal would have it.[80] Theal states that the Boers suffered "ruinous losses", but van der Merwe was unable to find the documents that refer to stock losses following on this "invasion". He did not believe that stock losses played an important role in difficulties on the frontier in 1789.[81] But it is Theal's account of "invasions" and large-scale cattle rustling that have found their way into textbooks and "standard" accounts, rather than the carefully researched and cautious conclusions of van der Merwe. In this sense, Theal's influence has been tremendous – he has been responsible for the creation of myths that have become accepted "facts" of South African history.

Professor van der Merwe did not set out to "debunk" Theal. But having found him wanting in his representation of the first clash between white and black on the eastern frontier, he decided to make a detailed study of the circumstances surrounding the frontier war of 1793. In this instance, van der Merwe declared that he substantially agreed with Theal's account.[82]

Professor J. S. Marais, also an Afrikaner, had been brought up on Theal's interpretation of South African history, and initially it came as quite a shock to him to hear Theal's descriptions queried.[83] By the time that Marais completed his *Maynier and the first Boer republic* in 1944, numbers of historians had questioned Theal's comments on his facts. But they had "tended to accept the facts themselves as reliable". One of the aims of Marais's work was "to question Theal's competence as a finder of facts". Like van der Merwe, Marais turned his attention to the Cape's eastern frontier, concentrating on the turbulent years between 1778 and 1802.

Unlike van der Merwe in *Die Kafferoorlog van 1793*, Marais did not agree with Theal's conclusions at all, and he went into some considerable detail unravelling the tangled skein of events on the frontier, believing that "only by a detailed appeal to the documents was it possible to convict Theal of bad workmanship". His conclusion was that "almost all Theal's errors, whether of fact or of interpretation, tend to one result: to tilt the balance in favour of the European colonists and against the non-Europeans as well as those Europeans who, like Maynier, were critical of the colonists' point of view and behaviour". Professor Marais concluded that "if a man's errors tend overwhelmingly in one direction, there is reasonable ground for concluding that his inability to find the facts is largely due to prejudice."[84]

Marais's study, however, had a wider aim than the eastern frontier in the late eighteenth century. "If a man's prejudices have spoilt his work on the period 1778-1802", he asked, "might they not have done the same in respect of other periods, and more particularly in respect of the relations between Europeans and non-Europeans during such periods?" Since so much of what was believed of the past in South Africa was based on Theal, to find Theal guilty of bad workmanship was an exhortation to people to go to the records and study them themselves rather than rely on Theal.[85]

Marais's study, although impressive, did not find universal acceptance, and Afrikaner historians, particularly those of the republican school, tended to ignore his reappraisal of Maynier and to repeat the stereotypes formulated by Theal. Marais's work was dismissed as a liberal production, and as such did not merit serious attention. This was the fate too of the work of another member of the liberal school, W. M. Macmillan. In *The Cape Colour Question* (1927) and *Bantu, Boer, and Briton, the making of the South African Native problem* (1929) he challenged Theal's view of the frontier and defended Dr Philip against the charges levelled by Theal.[86]

Theal has had numerous detractors, but, on the other side, there has been no shortage of people willing to step in and defend him. Dr A. J. Böeseken has decried attempts to reduce Theal's status as a historian, saying that it was not Theal who had misread the documents, but Marais.[87] However, when Hermann Giliomee re-examined the evidence some 30 years after Marais, he came to very much the same conclusions as Marais concerning events on the frontier.[88]

Of course, Theal did make mistakes. It would have been impossible not to have done so in a work that covered 11 volumes and dealt with some 400 years of South African history, and those who have later concentrated on this aspect have perhaps been a little harsh. What is really remarkable about his work is that he made so few errors in his facts.

He remains a controversial figure, and there is no consensus on his work.[89] Merle Babrow, who in the early 1960s undertook a study of Theal for her M.A. degree at the University of Cape Town,[90] confirmed his great influence on the study of history in South Africa, saying that even Eric Walker's *History of South Africa* (1928) "relied very heavily, in truth, was largely based, upon him". She went on to write that "many South African historians would probably be surprised to know how much of their work derives from Theal. They probably did not get it *directly* from him, nor do they cite him as the source. But it comes from him, and is often in his very phraseology. . . . I do not think it is sufficiently recognised, how great a part of that area of 'generally accepted' and 'known' facts in South African history, derives from the work of Theal."[91]

Merle Babrow was clearly unhappy at what she considered was Theal's overwhelming and enduring influence over the writing of history. He enjoyed a reputation she felt he had not deserved. "Indeed his pioneering role as a South African historian is usually somewhat exaggerated", she wrote. "Theal, and his admirers, give the impression that South African history before Theal was an unexplored, uncharted mass residing in unorganised archives scattered all over the country, out of which he, alone and unaided, carved his great history of South Africa and compiled his documentary collections. This view underrates the value and number of the secondary sources available and his considerable reliance on them. He is ungenerous and arrogant towards other writers. His assessment of their books as 'worthless' and his denial that he has made much use of them is misleading and untrue. . . Theal, not an original thinker, relied frequently and heavily upon them, filling out his account with (often) undigested and indiscriminate chunks from documents by providing more details on for example commandos, museums, clergymen, shipwrecks, regulations and proclamations."[92]

Theal's work was generally very descriptive. It did not make for colourful writing, but there are exceptions. Thus, in referring to travellers who believed the Boers in the interior were taciturn and ignorant, Theal writes that these same travellers "would probably have been surprised if an aged grazier had spoken about the lives of any of the old testament heroes or had compared a storm on the lofty inland plains with that grand description of one given in the twenty-ninth psalm. On subjects like these the grazier could talk freely enough, because they came within the range of his experience. He was living under such skies as those which Abraham lived, his occupation was the same, he understood the imagery of the Hebrew writers more perfectly than any one in Europe could understand it for it spoke to him of his daily life. He had heard the continuous roll of thunder which was the voice of the Lord upon many waters, and had seen the affrighted antelopes drop their young as they fled before the storm, when the great trees came down with a crash and the lightning divided like flames of fire. He knew too of skies like brass and of earth like iron, of little clouds seemingly no larger than a man's hand presaging a deluge of rain, and of swarms of locusts before whose track was the garden of the Lord, while behind was a naked desert. When he spoke of these things he could be eloquent enough, but they were not subjects for conversation with casual visitors."[93]

In the final analysis, however much Theal relied on other works, however heavily he quoted from documents, however much he failed to give his sources, however much his work is filled with descriptions rather than interpretations, and however much of his work has had to be redone, there is no escaping the fact that a man who had no formal training as an academic or historian, who wrote an 11-volume history of South Africa, deserves the status of a pioneer of the first order. No one man or even teams of historians have as yet produced anything that can remotely compare with the scope and volume of Theal's work. The extensive field covered by him means that research workers on a wide variety of topics have to begin their studies by looking at what Theal had to say. Thus his work remains useful, and will probably be so for some time to come.

In 1964 Immelman wrote that it should "be remembered that he was a pioneer in his particular field, and like all pioneers in whatever sphere, his work suffers to some extent on that account. . . The Cape Colony, all said and done, was in those days a poor, struggling country where every penny had to be counted. References, notes regarding location and other data for lack of which we criticise him today, were probably omitted by him in order to get anything published at all. Between 1874 and 1919 South Africa experienced many momentous events and passed through tremendous crises. Inevitably Theal was to some extent a product of his age, however much he consciously tried to overcome this disability in himself. He was a controversial figure during his lifetime, but if anything, he is today more so than ever."[94]

George Cory

Next to Theal, the best-known historian of the settler school was George Edward Cory. Like Theal, he was not a trained historian. He was born in England on 3 June 1862, and studied at King's College, Cambridge, graduating in 1888 with a B.A. tripos in the Natural Sciences. In 1891 he obtained his M.A. in chemistry at Cambridge, and later that year went to South Africa as vice-principal of the Grahamstown Public School. He became a lecturer in physics and chemistry at St. Andrews College in 1894. When Rhodes University College was established in 1904, the four professors at St. Andrews became the foundation professors of the new university college. Cory was one of them.[95] He remained at Rhodes as professor of chemistry until he retired in 1925.

If this had been the sum of his career his name would today not be known outside the Drostdy Gate of Grahamstown. He is remembered not for the way he earned his keep, but for the way he spent his leisure hours. Cory became interested in history soon after his arrival in South Africa. He later said that it had begun "as a recreation".[96] Ronald Currey related a tale of how Cory's interest in history was quickened. He said that Cory caught one of the infectious diseases usually associated with childhood and was quarantined in the old Drostdy building. There he discovered "overlooked, forgotten and awaiting destruction – a collection of papers, mainly letters to and from the original Settlers". This find fired his imagination and his forced incarceration in the Drostdy became a joy as he pored over the old documents.

As Currey would have it, when Cory's period of quarantine was over and "he came back to the ways of men the idea of *The rise of South Africa* had taken firm shape in his mind".[97] It is likely that this account is apocryphal, and Cory himself said that he had discovered in the record room of the civil commissioner's office in Grahamstown many hundreds of letters "dating back almost to the foundation of Grahamstown". In any event, however he came upon these letters, to copy and summarise them occupied a good deal of his leisure time over a period of ten years.[98]

Cory was a man with wide interests and boundless enthusiasm for life. He liked meeting people. "Genial and kindly and a vivacious talker from a great fund of experience and knowledge, he was a man with a host of friends and popular with all manner of men."[99] His interest in his fellow-man undoubtedly played a large role in his growing concern with history, and in Grahamstown he met and talked to some of the original 1820 Settlers, realising that if their fascinating stories of pioneering in Albany were to be preserved it had better be done soon or this priceless first-hand testimony would be lost for ever. He collected and wrote down what they had to say, and he did so not only in Grahamstown itself, but used his university holidays to travel around the border districts and also the African areas, talking to all sorts of people, Settlers and African chiefs in particular, collecting their narratives. With his knapsack on his back and an umbrella to protect him from the sun and rain, he travelled hundreds of miles on foot, alone, interviewing people, collecting oral evidence and transcribing it later. He explained that he had tried to make his travels on horseback but that as his few attempts to ride a horse had "been fraught with consequences which give me no pleasure to recall to mind, I have therefore preferred walking".[100] Besides this, during his vacations he searched the government offices in Uitenhage and Graaff-Reinet for material; he visited, too, the archives depot in Cape Town.

Dr L. S. Jameson, who was at the time prime minister of the Cape, was instrumental in securing a grant from an educational bequest of Sir Alfred Beit for Cory to pursue historical research that would lead to a publication. This resulted in the appearance in 1910 of the first volume of *The rise of South Africa*. Grants from the Rhodes Trustees allowed him to continue with the series. Cory initially planned a four-volume work, that would follow the course of events up to 1846, but he later changed his mind and decided to take his history up to 1857, expanding it to six volumes. Volumes 2 and 3 appeared in 1913 and 1919 respectively. Volume 4 followed in 1926, the year after Cory retired from Rhodes, and volume 5 in 1930. Volume 6 was to have contained 12 chapters, but he only completed six of them. He was busy with the seventh chapter when failing health caught up with him. He died on 28 April 1935. The completed part of volume 6 was published posthumously in the 1939 Archives Year Book for S.A. History.[101]

*   *   *

The above was his major, but not his only historical work. In 1922, in the Church Missionary Society archives in London, he discovered the diary of the Rev. Francis Owen, who had been the missionary at Dingane's capital when Piet Retief and his fellow Voortrekkers were murdered in February 1838. Cory secured the diary and edited it for the Van Riebeeck Society. [102]

In 1923 he caused something of a stir in historical circles when in the course of reading a paper on the Retief-Dingane treaty at the congress of the South African Association for the Advancement of Science in Bloemfontein, he declared that "his research had led him to believe that there was no such thing as a Retief-Dingaan Treaty, and that the document believed all these years to be a Treaty was nothing more than a fake of some ten months later."[103] The implication that the Voortrekker hero Andries Pretorius, or members of his commando, had manufactured the treaty which they claimed to have found on Retief's body when the commando entered Dingane's capital after defeating the Zulu at the battle of Blood River in December 1838, brought down on Cory the opprobrium of many Afrikaners, who felt that he was attacking the good name of the Voortrekkers. Cory denied this, saying that "in my investigations I have been actuated by nothing else than a desire to arrive at the truth". He went on to declare that "if in making my views public I have in any measure given offence to any, who, like myself, hold the memory of the old Voortrekkers in veneration, I wish now to express my regret". Something of Cory's integrity emerges as he continued by saying: "But I do not see how one can work impartially at historical matters without, at times, running the risk of going counter to some sentiment or other. This is not the first time, metaphorically speaking, that my blood has been sought. In other cases it has been the British settler and missionary folk who have expressed hostile surprise at statements of mine which I believe to be the truth."[104]

Gustav Preller and Professor W. Blommaert, among others, made a careful examination of the documentary evidence. There were only copies of the treaty. The original was thought to have been among a shipment of state papers sent to Dr Leyds in the Netherlands after the occupation of Pretoria by British forces in June 1900. The papers never reached their destination. In spite of this, Preller and Blommaert succeeded in substantially refuting Cory's allegations by subjecting tracings of the document to intensive internal and external criticism. Cory, who had made the allegations in a spirit of furthering historical criticism, accepted their findings with good grace, later admitting that he had been overhasty in his judgment.[105]

For his historical research, in 1921 the University of Cambridge bestowed the degree of Doctor of Letters, *honoris causa*, on Cory. In the following year he was awarded a knighthood. When he retired from Rhodes in 1925 the government granted him an honorarium to continue his research. He settled in Cape Town and spent the remaining years of his life engaged in historical research. All his books, and the documents he had collected and digested, were left to Rhodes University and became the basis of the Cory Library for Historical Research.

* * *

Cory was a man of extremely wide interests. One of these was church music and he was a chorister at the cathedral. He served on a number of public bodies, was a Grahamstown city councillor for two years, organised the 1912 Grahamstown centenary celebrations, and helped substantially with the 1921 celebration of the arrival of the 1820 Settlers. As an authority on the 1820 Settlers, he was much in demand as a public speaker.

In his younger days, in fact while he was still at St. Andrews, he had distinguished himself in another sphere. When the clock faces on the cathedral tower needed repainting, no-one could be found to do the job, despite a substantial financial inducement being offered. In "a spirit of bravado", Cory said that for "two pins" he would do it. His offer was accepted with alacrity, and the work was duly done. The city council presented him with a silver model of a painter's palette and brushes.[106]

Cory had great respect for Theal, as is evident from the quotation at the beginning of this discussion on the settler school, and he leaned heavily on Theal's historical works and source publications. But he also consulted other archival material and worked systematically through the files of *The Graham's Town Journal*. Although he called his work a history of South Africa, it was very much a history of the eastern districts of the Cape, with the British settlers at the centre. Like Theal, he saw the history he described from the point of view of the white colonists, and he was critical of missionaries who had "interfered" in South African affairs. He was not particularly sympathetic towards blacks, as may be gauged from the caption accompanying a photograph of an armed Xhosa warrior in volume 3 of *The rise of South Africa*, that the man was "meditating mischief". The warrior in the picture in fact is sitting with his spears, knobkerrie and oxhide shield, quietly smoking a pipe.[107]

He had great sympathy for the Afrikaners and wrote as follows about them: "In reading through the many documents relating to the numerous and continued inroads of Bushmen and Kaffirs, which took place before the influx of the British into the Eastern Provinces, one cannot but be impressed with the patient heroism of the Dutch inhabitants in their incessant struggles to preserve their homes and properties. So much has been written and said in high official quarters concerning the cruelty and oppression of the Dutch towards the native races, and so little on the aggressions of the latter on the former . . . that one feels constrained to pause and say *audi alteram partem*. That there have been bad characters among the Dutch, as among all nationalities, no one for a moment will deny, but to regard all the sufferings which have befallen the whole of the frontier inhabitants as the result of their own wickedness, and the Kaffirs as harmless and inoffensive neighbours . . . is either to acknowledge oneself ignorant of the facts, or deliberately to refuse to be actuated by a sense of justice. Surely a people who lived in constant fear of being murdered by savages, or having their homes destroyed by fire and robbed of their means of subsistence, deserve some consideration and sympathy."[108]

He was full of praise for the Voortrekkers, referring to their "dogged determination in overcoming difficulties and a bravery in the face of imminent dangers probably unparalleled in the history of any other community".[109] In dealing with the Great Trek he corrected both Theal and Preller, building on what they had done. Because Cory was focusing on a smaller period and area, he was able to provide a more detailed picture of the Great Trek than Theal. But in his handling of the Trek, as indeed in all his work, he had trouble eliminating lesser detail, so that the main points of his exposition often do not stand out very clearly. His work is closely packed with detail, so that it is all too easy for the reader to get the feeling that he is being bludgeoned by facts, detail packed upon detail. But in general, Cory is easier to read than Theal. His work, like that of Theal, was very much a chronicle, but he left behind him a mass of carefully arranged information that would later be of great use to other researchers.[110]

Frank Cana

Another writer who may be classified as falling broadly into the settler school is Frank R. Cana, whose *South Africa from the Great Trek to the Union* was published in 1909. In his preface he stated that "the narrative is written without bias, and an endeavour has been made to do full justice to both the great races – British and Dutch – whose past struggles are here recorded." These were not mere idle words and Frank Cana did indeed make an attempt to give both sides of the story. He is not anti-imperial or anti-Afrikaner, but is prepared to criticise both when he feels it necessary.

In connection with the Sixth Frontier War and Glenelg's role in events there, like most other writers, of both the settler and British schools, he is critical of Lord Glenelg's policy on the eastern frontier, describing his administration as "a lamentable failure". He goes on to say that although he "lacked neither courage nor ability . . . he was as misguided as he was high minded, and let his sympathies with the grievances of the Kaffirs entirely blind him to the wrongs of the Cape settlers".

Similarly, with reference to the period 1868-1871 and the British handling of the diamond fields dispute, he writes that "a statesman endowed with greater insight than Lord Kimberley possessed might have not only recognized the errors committed in 1852-59 by his predecessors at the Colonial Office, but have repaired them". Unlike most of the British school, he condemned the Jameson Raid as a blunder, but saw the "evil wrought" by the raid as resulting from the fact that it was Rhodes as prime minister of the Cape who was seen to have "stimulated, subsidized, and organized an armed insurrection against the Government of a neighbouring State". Had the "rising been a purely internal movement, its success would not have shocked public opinion in the other States of South Africa", he declared, for the "*uitlanders* had sufficient grounds for rebellion, and would have been justified in overthrowing the Kruger *regime*".[111] So even in this message of reconciliation, Cana comes close to the views of the British school, which was that the Transvaal government had acted badly towards the English people on the Rand.

Prominence is given throughout the book to the movements towards a closer union. The establishment of a union would not have been possible without the Second Anglo-Boer War. "Unification", he wrote, "has at length been attained only by the abandonment by both white races of the struggle for racial supremacy. The leaders of the South African Dutch, as a direct outcome of the war, understood that there was no longer any possibility of realizing the old, and legitimate, dreams of an independent Dutch republic which should include the British as well as the Dutch States. On their part the British elements in the Cape, Natal and the Transvaal became convinced that in the frank recognition of equal rights for all white men they had the security needed to assure for themselves their full share in the development of the country and the evolution of the coming Afrikander race – which, one may venture to believe, will be formed by the fusion of the British and Dutch peoples of South Africa."[112]

As with most settler history, scant attention is given to the Africans. They are hardly noticed at all in this history which is the history of how the whites resolved their differences to establish a white-dominated Union of South Africa.

* * *

Historical writers writing on South Africa before World War I had not received any academic training in history. It could be argued that some of the books discussed here should not be categorised as historical works at all, that they were really contemporary writing on current affairs. But virtually all the authors discussed in this chapter felt the need to explain the current position in terms of the country's past, and as such warrant inclusion. They did not all feel that the whole of that past was relevant to their explanations, but there is nothing new in this, for historians have always been called upon to exercise a choice as to what in the past is material to them in explaining the world in which they live.

NOTES

1 R. W. Winks (ed.), *The historiography of the British Empire – Commonwealth: Trends, interpretations, and resources*, Durham, N.C., 1966, pp. 212–213.
2 *Standard Encyclopaedia of Southern Africa (SESA)*, vol. 5, (Historiography), pp. 529–530. See also F. A. van Jaarsveld, *The Afrikaner's interpretation of South African history*, Cape Town, 1964, pp. 117–121.

3 Van Jaarsveld, *The Afrikaner's interpretation*, p. 117.

4 Ibid., pp. 121–122.

5 Ibid., p. 157, n. 10.

6 I. D. Bosman, *Dr. George McCall Theal as die geskiedskrywer van Suid-Afrika*, Amsterdam, 1932, pp. 16–17.

7 The full title was *Five lectures on the emigration of the Dutch farmers from the Colony of the Cape of Good Hope, and their settlement in the district of Natal until their formal submission to Her Majesty's authority in the year 1843*. In 1899 two further editions were published under the title *The history of the Great Boer Trek and the origin of the South African republics*, and it was reprinted twice in 1900.

8 Cloete, *The Great Boer Trek*, p. 99. For the controversy concerning Cory and the Retief-Dingane treaty see p. 46.

9 Cloete, *The Great Boer Trek*, p. 3.

10 Van Jaarsveld, *The Afrikaner's interpretation*, p. 118.

11 Cloete, *The Great Boer Trek*, p. 28.

12 See for example J. A. Heese, *Slagtersnek en sy mense*, Cape Town, 1973.

13 E. B. Watermeyer, *Selections from the writings of the late E. B. Watermeyer with a brief sketch of his life*, Cape Town, 1877, pp. vii–xxiv.

14 Ibid., pp. 54,95.

15 Holden, p. 334.

16 Ibid., p. 346.

17 Ibid., p. 215.

18 Wilmot and Chase, p. 157.

19 See, for example, Hendrik Swellengrebel's description of a Boer house in the interior in 1776, quoted by V. S. Forbes, *Pioneer travellers of South Africa*, Cape Town, 1965, p. 68 and also K. W. Smith, *From frontier to midlands: A history of the Graaff-Reinet district, 1786-1910*, Grahamstown, 1976, pp. 10–11.

20 Bosman, pp. 28-30.

21 Wilmot and Chase, p. 369.

22 Bosman, p. 24.

23 F. A. van Jaarsveld, *Omstrede Suid-Afrikaanse verlede: Geskiedenisideologie en die historiese skuldvraagstuk*, Johannesburg and Cape Town, 1984, p. 34.

24 Noble, p. 15; van Jaarsveld, *Omstrede verlede*, p. 34.

25 Noble, pp. 168–170, 173.

26 Ibid., p. 87.

27 See K. W. Smith, *The campaigns against the Bapedi of Sekhukhune, 1877-1879*, Archives Year Book for S.A. History, 1967, vol. 2.

23 Haggard, fifth ed., 1893, pp. 96, 98–99.

29 Ibid., pp. 167, 174-175, 287–288.

30 Wilmot, *The story of the expansion of Southern Africa*, pp. 116, 162, 173, 236.

31 Ibid., p. 236.

32 Ibid., pp. 14–15.

33 Wilmot, *The history of South Africa*, pp. 203, 205-206.

34 Ibid., p. 198.

35 Ibid., pp. 232–233.

36 James Cappon, *Britain's title in South Africa or the story of Cape Colony to the days of the Great Trek*, London,1902, pp. viiia, viiic, preface to 2nd ed.

37 Conan Doyle, *The Great Boer War*, preface to the final edition, p. vii.

38 Ibid., p. 5.

39 Ibid., p. 15.

40 Ibid., pp. 7, 17–18.

41 Ibid., pp. 740–743.

42 W. B. Worsfold, *Lord Milner's work in South Africa from its commencement in 1897 to the Peace of Vereeniging in 1902*, London, 1906 and *The reconstruction of the new colonies under Lord Milner*, 2 vols, London, 1913; C. Headlam (ed.), *The Milner Papers, 1897-1905*, 2 vols, London, 1931-1933.

43 E. Crankshaw, *The forsaken idea: A study of Viscount Milner*, London,1952; J. E. Wrench, *Alfred Lord Milner: The man of no illusions, 1854-1925*, London, 1958.

44 G. E. Cory, *The rise of South Africa*, vol. 4, pp. vii–viii.

45 E. H. Brookes, *The history of native policy in South Africa from 1830 to the present day*, Cape Town, 1924, p. 11.

46 J. S. Marais, *Maynier and the first Boer republic*, Cape Town, 1944, pp. v–vii.

47 For Reyburn see Chapter 5 on the liberal school.

48 Merle Babrow, "Theal: Conflicting opinions of him" in B. J. Liebenberg, (comp.), *Trends in the South African historiography*, Unisa, Pretoria, 1986, pp. 18–19. This article is a revised version of pp. 1–11 and 189-195 of Merle Babrow's unpublished M.A. thesis, *A critical assessment of Dr George McCall Theal*, U.C.T., 1962.

49 This sketch of Theal's life is based on the following sources: R. F. M. Immelman, "George McCall Theal: A biographical sketch", in C. Struik's 1964 reprint of Theal's *Basutoland Records*; see also Bosman's work and *SESA*, vol. 5 (Historiography) and vol. 10 (Theal); Deryck Schreuder, "The imperial historian as colonial nationalist: George McCall Theal and the making of South African history" in G. Martel (ed.), *Studies in British imperial history: Essays in honour of A. P. Thornton*, New York, 1986, pp. 95–158; Christopher Saunders, "The missing link in Theal's career: The historian as labour agent in the Western Cape", *History in Africa*, 7, 1980, pp. 273–280; Saunders, "George McCall Theal and Lovedale", *History in Africa*, 8, 1981, pp. 155–164; Saunders, "The making of an historian: The early years of George McCall Theal", *South African Historical Journal*, 13, 1981, pp. 3–11.

50 Immelman, pp. 9–10.

51 A. J. Böeseken, "Theal as baanbreker (1837–1919)", *Suid-Afrikaanse Argiefblad*, no. 1, 1959, reprinted in Liebenberg, *Trends*, p. 27.

52 Quoted in Liebenberg, *Trends*, p. 27.

53 Theal, *Records of the Cape Colony from February 1793 to December 1796*, London, 1897, preface.

54 Theal, *Records of South-Eastern Africa*, vol. 1 , London, 1898, p. vi.

55 See also C. F. J. Muller's article on Theal in *SESA*, vol. 10.

56 G. M. Theal, *History of South Africa*, (Struik reprint), vol. 5, preface.

57 Theal, *The Portuguese in South Africa*, London, n.d., p. 7.

58 Marais, *Maynier*, p.v.

59 See for example, van Jaarsveld, *Omstrede verlede*, pp. 35–36.

60 Theal, *History of the Boers in South Africa* (Struik reprint), Cape Town, 1973, p. xiii.

61 Van Jaarsveld, *Omstrede verlede*, pp. 13, 37-38.

62 See C. F. J. Muller "Die Groot Trek", in Liebenberg, *Trends*, p. 63.

63 Schreuder, "The imperial historian as colonial nationalist."

64 Theal, *History of South Africa* (Struik reprint), vol. 6, p. 121.

65 Ibid., vol. 3, pp. 464–465.

66 Bosman, pp. 155,158.

67 See also Leonard Thompson in Winks, *The historiography of the British Empire*, p. 216.

68 Theal, *History of South Africa* (Struik reprint), vol. 4, p. 300n.

69 *The Portuguese in South Africa*, London, n. d., p. 7.

70 Theal, *History of South Africa* (Struik reprint), vol. 4, p. 411.

71 *The defence of William Adriaan van der Stel* (1897) and *The rebellion of 1815: Generally known as Slagters Nek* (1902).

72 Bosman, pp. 67–68.

73 E. B. Iwan-Müller, *Lord Milner and South Africa*, London, 1902, pp. 1,482.

74 Theal had sent as many volumes as had up to then been published of his *Records of the Cape Colony* to the Queen's University library, and ironically it was these documents that Cappon used to attack Theal's *History of South Africa*, which was at that stage a five-volume work.

75 James Cappon, *Britain's title in South Africa*, preface to first edition, p.vii.

76 Quoted by Babrow in Liebenberg, *Trends*, pp. 14–15.

77 "As ek met die grootste beskeidenheid van so 'n groot kenner van ons geskiedenis mag verskil" – *Die trekboer*, p. 265.

78 ". . . en heelwat kritiek op dr. Theal se voorstelling van sake uitgeoefen" – Preface to his work *Die Kafferoorlog van 1793*, Cape Town, 1940.

79 See *Die trekboer*, pp. 263–266.

80 *Die trekboer*, p. 313; *History of South Africa* (Struik reprint), vol. 4, p. 242.

81 *Die trekboer*, pp. 313–315.

82 *Die Kafferoorlog van 1793.*

83 See *The Cape Coloured People* (1939), 1957 reprint, p. viii.

84 Marais, *Maynier*, pp. v–vi.

85 Ibid., pp. vi–vii.

86 See discussion on Macmillan in Chapter 4.

87 A. J. Böeseken, "Theal en sy bronne," *Historia*, 9(1), 1964.

88 *Die Kaap tydens die Eerste Britse Bewind*, Cape Town, 1975. See also review of Giliomee by K. W. Smith in *Kleio*, 8(1 and 2), 1976, pp. 88–89.

89 See the following articles: Böeseken, "Theal en sy bronne", *Historia*, 9(1) 1964, pp. 48–52; Merle Babrow, "A reply to Dr. Boeseken", *Historia*, 9(4), 1964, pp. 256–260; Boeseken, "In defence of Dr. George McCall Theal: A reply to Miss Merle Babrow", *Historia*, 10(1), 1965, pp. 16–21.

90 *A critical assessment of Dr George McCall Theal.*

91 Liebenberg, *Trends*, pp. 16,19.

92 Ibid., p. 21.

93 Theal, *History of South Africa* (Struik reprint), vol. 4, pp. 369–370.

94 Immelman, pp. 18–19.

95 R. F. Currey, *Rhodes University 1904-1970: A chronicle*, Grahamstown, 1970, p. 20; *SESA*, vol. 3 (Cory), pp. 445–446.

96 *The rise of South Africa*, vol. 1 p. vi.

97 Currey, pp. 20–21.

98 *The rise of South Africa* vol. 1 p. v.

99 *SESA*, vol. 3 (Cory), p. 446.

100 *The rise of South Africa*, vol. 1 p. vi; *Die Huisgenoot*, 10 May 1935.

101 *SESA* vol. 3 (Cory) p. 446; Archives Year Book for S.A. History, 1939, vol. 1, foreword.

102 *The diary of the Rev. Francis Owen*, Van Riebeeck Society no. 27, Cape Town, 1926.

103 These were his words as reported in the *Cape Times* of 12 July 1923 – quoted in *Annale van die Universiteit van Stellenbosch*, Serie B, No. 1, May 1924 p. I (G. Cory, G. Preller and W. Blommaert, "Die Retief-Dingaan ooreenkoms").

104 *Annale van die Universiteit van Stellenbosch*, pp. 1,12.

105 *Annale van die Universiteit van Stellenbosch.*

106 *SESA*, (Cory).

107 *The rise of South Africa*, vol. 3, opposite title page.

108 Ibid., vol. 1, pp. vii–viii.

109 Ibid., vol. 4, p. 1.

110 Muller, "Die Groot Trek", in Liebenberg, *Trends*, pp. 65-66; *Die Huisgenoot*, 10 May 1935; van Jaarsveld, *The Afrikaner's interpretation*, pp. 120-121.

111 Frank R. Cana, *South Africa from the Great Trek to the Union*, pp. 9,48,163.

112 Ibid., p. 2.

G.M. Theal

G.E. Cory

Sir George Cory in his study at Rhodes University

C.F.J. Muller

G.S. Preller

H.B. Thom

54

F.A. van Jaarsveld

B.J. Liebenberg

D.W. Krüger

G.D. Scholtz

P.J. van der Merwe

A.J. Boëseken

3 Afrikaans historiography

This chapter's primary concern is to examine historical works which represented a major trend in South African historical writing. The emphasis is on nationalist Afrikaner or republican writing, which has been the dominant trend in Afrikaans historical literature to date. But to focus exclusively on this would mean ignoring the work of some very good historians for no better reason than that they have not followed the mainstream of Afrikaner historical writing. So space will also be found for historians who do not readily fit into an Afrikaner nationalist mould but who wrote in Afrikaans. The question of those Afrikaners who for one or other reason had their work published in English is more problematical. It seemed preferable to include authors like J. S. Marais in the discussion of the liberal school up to the 1960s, but to mention the work of writers like Hermann Giliomee and André du Toit in this chapter although much of their recent work has been published in English. The reasons for doing so are that Giliomee and du Toit have concentrated largely on developing themes that directly challenge the assumptions of the Afrikaner nationalist school in a way that a historian like Marais did not. This chapter thus seemed the best place to locate their work.

THE PRE-ACADEMIC PHASE

The growth of a historical consciousness

As in America, South Africa's first writers of history, whether they wrote in English, Dutch or Afrikaans, were not professional historians. With a few notable exceptions, the academic or professional historian was strictly a post-World War I phenomenon. It was only then that the study of South African history at university level came into its own, although, of course, non-academics continue to write South African history up to the present, and some

57

of it is very good; by the same token, some of the work of so-called professional historians is very poor. There is no point in dividing historical works into those written by "amateurs" and "professionals". There are good and bad histories on both sides of the divide. But it is valid to point out that prior to the First World War, the historical works that appeared all came from the pens of men who had no formal training in history as a discipline.

Prior to the 1920s there were obstacles in the way of writing a balanced history based on primary sources. Archives were for the most part uncatalogued and unclassified, there was no official documentation. There were some source publications in English, such as D. Moodie's *The Record* (1838), John Chase's two-volume *The Natal Papers* (1843), and also the two-volume collection of documents on Natal compiled by J. Bird (*The annals of Natal*, 1888); the three volumes of George McCall Theal's *Basutoland Records* appeared in 1883; a few years later, between 1897 and 1905, the 36 volumes of his *Records of the Cape Colony between 1795 and 1831* were published; H. C. V. Leibbrandt's 16-volume *Précis of the archives of the Cape of Good Hope* was published in the decade between 1896 and 1906. But the subject matter of these collections of documents reflected British concentration on the Cape and Natal and was far removed from the interests and concerns of those who wrote in Afrikaans or Dutch. But this was not as big a disadvantage as might be imagined, for the majority of those who put pen to paper to depict the South African past, were in fact not so much interested in history as in using the past to make a point. In the case of the Dutch and Afrikaner writers, one of their primary aims was to mobilise Afrikaner nationalist sentiment and to see this employed in defining and achieving the Afrikaner's political aims.

The authors of the majority of nineteenth century accounts that fall into the category of Afrikaner national or republican history were Dutch. One of the aims of a number of Dutch and English writers in the nineteenth century was to depict South Africa, and its past, in a way that would be likely to attract immigrants. Dutch examples of this are the mid-nineteenth century works of U. G. Lauts, *De Kaapsche landverhuizers of Nederlands afstammelingen in Zuid-Afrika* (1847), Jacobus Stuart, *De Hollandsche Afrikanen en hunne Republiek in Zuid-Afrika* (1854), J. H. Hofstede, *Geschiedenis van den Oranje-Vrystaat* (1876). But the message of this last book went beyond an appeal to prospective immigrants, and it was among the first books to be written in what was to become the major characteristic of Afrikaner historical writing, which is a pro-Afrikaner nationalist and anti-British imperialist trend.

The Afrikaner interpreted his history as a bitter struggle for self-preservation and fulfilment in the face of the hostile forces of nature and the indigenous peoples that he found in the country. The Second British Occupation of the Cape in 1806 marked the start of an era of varying degrees of enmity between Boer and Briton which in many ways may be said to have continued until 1961 when South Africa became an independent republic outside the Commonwealth. In the course of this struggle to prevent themselves from being overwhelmed by British culture, the Afrikaners developed an anglophobia. The British were seen as oppressors and opponents, as sympathisers with blacks in their struggle against the Boers. By the late nineteenth century there was among Afrikaners a strong sense of history and a historically orientated nationalism with a virulent anti-colonial and anti-imperial image of the past. This image revolved around two poles. One was the Great Trek of the mid-1830s, when, according to the traditional version, large numbers of Boers left the British-controlled Cape to escape from the "liberal" British policy that favoured the blacks. They went into the interior to organise matters their own way, to establish "proper relations between master and servant", to look after their own defence without being hamstrung by "interfering" missionaries who could make life very awkward for them with the access that they had to the corridors of power in Whitehall.

The Voortrekkers secured Natal after making a "covenant" with God who gave them a great victory over Dingane's Zulu in 1838. When in 1843 the British followed them and annexed Natal as a British colony, many Voortrekkers moved on again. For some years the Boers were left more or less to their own devices on the highveld of the Orange Free State and the Transvaal. The discovery of minerals changed this. Diamonds were first found to the west of the Free State in 1867, and this discovery drew the English to the area. The British first of all took the Sotho under their protection in 1868. They then annexed the diamond fields in 1871, and in an attempt to bring about a federation of the whole of South Africa under the British flag, annexed the backward and bankrupt agricultural Boer republic in the Transvaal in 1877. At the end of 1880 the Transvalers took up arms to regain their independence and, after a British expeditionary force was routed at Majuba Hill, the British government restored independence to the Transvaal republic. Together with the Great Trek, the War of Independence (or in more neutral terminology, the First Anglo-Boer War) of 1880-1881 became the other pole of Afrikaner historiography, the symbols of which were Dingaan's Day, later renamed the Day of the Covenant, (and even more recently the Day of the Vow) and Majuba Day.

The growth of the Afrikaner's awareness of himself in terms of his national calling as an Afrikaner dates from the period 1868-1881 and did not always manifest itself in historical writing – it was often expressed in political pamphlets and speeches. But there was, nevertheless, a close relationship between this awakening and the development of a historical consciousness. The Great Trek had given the Afrikaners a sense of grievance against the British, but when in the 1850s the Boers were left to run their own affairs without British interference, the injustice felt at the time subsided. However, it again came to the fore with the assertion of the imperial factor in the period 1868-1881; a strong consciousness of belonging together and of sharing a common past was felt by the Afrikaners. They began to search history to throw light on their current plight. "New grievances resulted in the discovery of old ones. Grudges that had been latent at the time of the Great Trek were activated and given their place in a version of history that comprised little more than a tabulation of national grievances."[1]

* * *

The change came first in the Free State around 1868, as a reaction to the way in which the British had robbed the Boer republic of the fruits of victory against the Sotho. Thus it was no coincidence that the Free State government provided funds towards the publication of Hofstede's work in 1876.[2]

At the time of the Great Trek the events of Slagtersnek in the Eastern Cape, where five Boers had been hanged in 1815 for fomenting a rebellion and attempting to enlist the aid of the Xhosa in overthrowing their British rulers, had virtually been forgotten. However, around 1868 Slagtersnek was suddenly rediscovered, it came to symbolise the way the British treated the Afrikaners. Virtually all Afrikaans history books featured Slagtersnek prominently. The Boers hanged at Slagtersnek were not seen as rebels but as "martyrs" in the cause of Afrikaner freedom, victims of British "inhumanity" and "cruelty".

History was meant to serve a practical aim, and little distinction was made between history, the language struggle and politics. They were all part of the same striving for Afrikaner identity. Thus the activities of the Genootskap van Regte Afrikaners and *Di Patriot*, the first Afrikaans newspaper, were of relevance to the study of South African history. The first history written in Afrikaans was the Rev. S. J. du Toit's *Di geskiedenis van ons land in di taal van ons volk* which was published in 1877. Although it devoted some attention to the period of the Dutch East India Company prior to the assumption of British control, Company rule was glossed over somewhat blandly, and it is clear that du Toit wanted to make a statement about British rule after 1806, and to refute charges levelled against Afrikaners by English-speaking writers. In the foreword he wrote that his aim was to "tell the truth, correct the lie and again bring to notice the deeds and fortunes of our forefathers". His intention was "to acquaint our children from their childhood of the trials and sufferings of their fathers in this land where foreigners now seek to tread us under foot".

Du Toit writes of Slagtersnek as follows: "And while we sit and meditate for a moment among their friends by their grave, we feel that our heart says: 'Weep Afrikaners! – Here lie your flesh and blood! – martyred in the cruellest manner. Wrong was it to rebel against their government; but truly they did not do it without reason! Wrong was it to take up arms; but only because they were too weak! Guilty they were, says the earthly Judge! but what shall the Heavenly Judge say some time?

" 'But come! It is getting darker! – Come, – if we sit here too long, then we too shall be regarded as conspirators! – Come, – another day will dawn

– then we shall perhaps see the grave in another light! Come – we go home with a quiet sigh.' "

Even in their adversity God was on their side. Thus although the British emancipated the slaves, who were finally set free to follow their own designs on 1 December 1838, having served a four-year apprenticeship after the emancipation on 1 December 1834, the evils that the Boers had expected to follow the 1st of December did not materialise because of God's intervention with the weather: "Unexpected and out of time – in the heart of the summer – our dear Lord, who manages everything so wisely, allows eight consecutive days of rain, such as happened never before nor since that time in the Colony. Then the freed slaves could not wander around so much in troops; they had to go to work again to get food; most of them went back to their old bosses to hire themselves; that was better for boss and boy, and however much was wrong in the way in which the English government freed the slaves, today we thank the Lord that He arranged it all so wisely."

Of the Great Trek he writes: "What Afrikaner is there whose heart does not miss a beat when he reflects on the reason for the exodus? Anyone who remains cool after reading of the oppression, injustice and disasters suffered by the poor Boers is unworthy of the name of Afrikaner."[3]

The war of 1880-1881 broadened the basis of community feeling and this was expressed in C. P. Bezuidenhout's *De Geschiedenis van het Afrikaansche Geslacht van 1688 tot 1882* (1883), which focused on the Afrikaner's role in opening up the country for "civilisation". He made a close identification of the Afrikaners with the Jews of the Old Testament. The Afrikaners had been placed in the Cape as a separate people to go forth and bring light to the heathen. This was their calling. The sympathy of the Afrikaners in the Cape and Free State for the Transvalers in the First Anglo-Boer War of 1880-1881 helped to form the concept of one Afrikaner nation. Histories such as J. A. Roorda-Smit's *Het goed recht der Transvaalsche Boeren* (1883) and F. Lion Cachet's *De Worstelstrijd der Transvalers* (1882) consist of lists of grievances against the British, a story of injustice and oppression, with much attention given to Slagtersnek; British policy is attacked, British lies exposed. In *Geschiedenis van de Emigranten-Boeren en van den Vrijheidsoorlog* (1882) by J. D. Weilbach and C. N. J. du Plessis, the aim is to foster the growth of national sentiment, to show how "their forefathers had suffered and struggled for freedom and independence" – it could be summed up in the phrase "all that they had always had to endure at the hands of England and the English".[4]

The two small Afrikaner republics did not enjoy their independence for long, for in 1886 gold was discovered in the veld some 50 kilometres south of Pretoria, the Boer capital of the South African Republic. Tensions built up and in 1896 feelings ran high after the abortive Jameson Raid, an attempt by imperialists in South Africa like Cecil John Rhodes to overthrow the Transvaal government of Paul Kruger. The years between the Raid and the

Anglo-Boer War of 1899-1902, provided more grist to the mill of the Afrikaner nationalists. N. J. Hofmeyr wrote *De Afrikaner-Boer en de Jameson-inval* and from the pen of C. N. J. du Plessis came *Uit de geschiedenis van de Zuid-Afrikaansche Republiek en van de Afrikaanders* (1899). He saw Slagtersnek as the beginning of the Great Trek, a movement to free Afrikanerdom from the English yoke. The English had been guilty of "inhuman conduct" towards the Afrikaners. In 1897 the state historian of the South African Republic, Dr J. W.G. van Oordt, published *Slagtersnek*, which he saw as part of the "pre-history" of the Transvaal. Thus a direct line was drawn between Slagtersnek and the Afrikaner's struggle for his political ideals in the Transvaal.

At the beginning of the Second Anglo-Boer War, the well-known *A century of wrong* appeared. This was first published in Dutch in 1899 under the title *Eene eeuw van onrecht*. It was printed in the same format and type-face as the so-called "greenbooks", the official government publications, but there was no indication as to who was the author of the piece. Over the years there has been much speculation on this point, particularly as in the English editions that soon followed, the title page stated that the book was issued by F. W. Reitz, former president of the Orange Free State and State Secretary of the South African Republic. But the name of Jan Smuts, State Attorney for the embattled republic, was also frequently mentioned in connection with the publication. It appears that when *Eene eeuw van onrecht* came into the hands of publishers in the Netherlands, Britain and the United States, immediate plans were made to reprint and distribute it. But the publishers felt that the book would have more success if it could be coupled to a name, and although Reitz had had no hand in its composition, he allowed the book to be issued in his name. An American edition in English was published in Baltimore in 1900 with the title *A century of injustice;* the London edition, *A century of wrong* also appeared in 1900. Another name that was associated with the writing of this book has been that of Jacob de Villiers Roos, or Jimmy Roos as he was popularly known. Roos was a journalist and attorney, and later became Secretary for Justice, Director of Prisons, and Controller and Auditor-General in the Union government. Smuts never acknowledged his part in it, presumably because it would have been embarrassing for a politician who was striving for greater English – Afrikaner co-operation in South Africa and to draw closer to England, to have his sharp criticism of Britain brought forth publicly. Jimmy Roos however, later admitted that he had "supplied the body of it, Genl. Smuts wrote the introductory and the closing part."[5]

The tenor of the book makes it clear that it was written for overseas consumption, but the opening words of the introduction written by Smuts are a ringing call to "Brother Africanders". "Once more in the annals of our bloodstained history", he wrote, "has the day dawned when we are forced to grasp our weapons in order to resume the struggle for liberty and existence, entrusting our national cause to that Providence which has guided our people throughout South Africa in such a miraculous way... The hour has struck which will decide whether South Africa, in jealously guarding its liberty, will enter upon a new phase of its history, or whether our existence as a people will come to an end, whether we shall be exterminated in the deadly struggle for that liberty which we have prized above all earthly treasures, and whether South Africa will be dominated by capitalists without conscience, acting in the name and under the protection of an unjust and hated Government 7,000 miles from here." In this book, history was depicted as a struggle against the forces of nature, the Africans and the British. It is full of Old Testament imagery. The case of the republic is forcefully and effectively argued. Britain, of course, is the chief villain. Slagtersnek is represented as "a murderous tragedy", the philanthropically inclined missionaries had "slandered" the Boers with "libellous stories", the 1877 annexation of the Transvaal was "a crowning act in these deeds of shame" and "an enduring characteristic of British policy in South Africa" was "treacherous duplicity".[6]

Once more Afrikaner independence was threatened, and again it was fought for, in the much longer and more bitter struggle between the two Afrikaner republics and the British empire between 1899 and 1902. This time the Afrikaners lost their independence, and some eight years after the war, the four provinces, all of them now British colonies, were given independence in 1910 within the framework of the British Empire, later the Commonwealth. The war of 1899-1902 quickly replaced the first war of 1880-1881 as the pole of the Afrikaner's image of the past.

History was seen as a list of grievances against the British, a tale of suffering and struggle towards freedom, towards their own republican form of government. History became at the same time a source of solace and an inspiration – they could take comfort from their persecuted past, they could draw strength from it.[7]

There was a veritable flood of literature on the war. At the end of the conflict, Slagtersnek, while still a grievance, was pushed into the background as the new symbol of Boer suffering at the hands of the British became the concentration camps. The camps captured the imagination of the Afrikaners as few other occurrences had done. Here was a whole new breed of martyrs to British cruelty.

Typical of Boer nationalist literature after the war were the two works of Dr W. J. Leyds, *De eerste annexatie van de Transvaal* (1906) and *Het insluiten van de Boeren Republieken* (1914). Referring to the first of these books, Leyds in a letter to H. C. Bredell on 7 September 1906, wrote that "It is my intention to provide the Afrikaner people with a vademecum, with a collection of documentary items of evidence that have hitherto not been available. I have in mind those documentary items that have reference to the way in which the English always acted towards the Boers. And that is something the Boers should not forget or lose sight of if they wish to safeguard their existence in future and their own interests – They must not let themselves be taken in by friendly appearances!" Old grievances should not be forgotten. The present was gloomy, but he had a vision of the future that would give new meaning to the past – history would serve to promote the Afrikaner's political ideology.

The *Eerste annexatie* dealt with relations between the Afrikaner and English from 1795 to 1884 while *Het Insluiten* covered the period 1894-1895 and the British encirclement of the Transvaal. Leyds's work was not a straight-forward account of relations between Afrikaners and English – he was more concerned with showing the methods used by England to assume power over the Boers in the Transvaal. Britain was thus on trial, and it was clear from the outset that it was not to be an impartial hearing – guilt was a foregone conclusion. He saw everything in terms of friend and foe, black and white, he merely sought proof for his predetermined convictions.

Van Jaarsveld writes that: "He undoubtedly did the Afrikaners a service in shattering the impression of the past that had been created by English writers and in stripping the English and their representatives in South Africa of their pretensions. . . Dr Leyds achieved something that no Afrikaner could have done at that time; he searched the past and put useful information at their disposal. It was not only serviceable activistic material that was amassed; valuable knowledge of the nineteenth century was accumulated. It bore the stamp of the war and was compiled with the future in view." It interpreted the sentiments of the Afrikaner at that time and had a great impact; it set a standard for historical writing, and for a long time it "remained the ideal model of historical writing in some Afrikaner circles".[8]

The Afrikaners had lost their independence in 1902, but they were de-termined to regain it. The union of the four South African states in 1910 did not capture the imagination of the Afrikaners. They were totally involved in a struggle to safeguard their cultural and political identity. Their ideal future was a republican one, and they used the past to help accomplish this. They concentrated on the sense of grievance against the British, portraying them as the enemies of this republicanism. The Voortrekkers, and the Boers who had fought in the Anglo-Boer War to retain the independence of the re-publics, were the representatives of this republican tradition, the heroes of the past. The Afrikaners would keep this republican ideal alive until it was eventually fulfilled. In this fight for self-identity and self-fulfilment, with its heavy concentration upon the way the Afrikaners had overcome human and geographical obstacles to firmly establish "Christian civilisation" in South Africa and evolve the Afrikaner nation or "volk", important milestones were the coming to power of the Nationalist Party in 1948, and the final triumph of Afrikaner nationalism in 1961, when a republic was established and the link with England finally severed.

The Afrikaner's history has thus been very much coloured by an almost mystical belief in the development of the "volk" to complete independence. History written by Afrikaners reflected this intense preoccupation with the fate of the "volk" and history was seen as a justification for the Afrikaner's actions. This was an all-consuming history, and it left no time for consideration of the socio-economic implications of South Africa's rapid industrialisation. This passed the Afrikaners by, and it was left to English-speaking historians of the liberal school to take up this challenge. On the whole the Afrikaner establishment ignored such work.

Gustav Preller

The Great Trek and the Second Anglo-Boer War were the main foci of the Afrikaner's historical image, and this remained true until well into the third quarter of the 20th century. As late as 1980, van Jaarsveld told an international gathering of historians and other academics in Canada that Afrikaner historical writing revolved around these two themes, and that Afrikaners had devoted very little attention to events after 1902.[9] Although in this section of the chapter we are concentrating on Afrikaans historical writing before the First World War, in its pre-academic phase, it is clear that the academic historians did not differ all that much from the amateurs as far as subject matter was concerned.

In explaining why Afrikaans historical writers should have concentrated so heavily on these two themes, van Jaarsveld says that it was "a dynamic period and a peculiarly romantic one; it was the period of great epic achievements by the Afrikaner people. . . The Afrikaners saw the Great Trek as the central thread of their history; all events after 1806 led to it and the Anglo-Boer War was the Trek's ultimate sequel. A chain of casuality linked the Great Trek – the axis of Afrikaner history – with the war of 1899-1902. The Trek divided them and the war united them; in both cases the imperial factor was the determinant. The period 1836-1902 gave South Africa its present shape." The Voortrekkers were seen as heroes. The true republican spirit resided in them. They were superior to the Afrikaners who had remained at the Cape, those referred to somewhat contemptuously as Queen Victoria's Afrikaners. The Trekkers epitomised everything that was good and worthwhile in the Afrikaner existence. It was the Great Trek that had opened up the interior to civilisation. It was their love of freedom and independence that had driven the Afrikaners from the Cape. It is maintained that the Voortrekkers were fond of seeing themselves in Biblical terms. After the oppression in Egypt (the Cape) they had settled in Canaan (the Orange Free State and Transvaal) among the heathens (the Africans). It was God who had called them to open up the desert to civilisation and Christianity. The Voortrekkers, so it was said, often compared themselves to the children of Israel.[10] Hermann Giliomee and André du Toit were later to query this version, and deny that the Voortrekkers had seen themselves as a Chosen People.[11]

It was only the rediscovery of the Great Trek as the central feature of the Afrikaner's past in the generation after the Trek (about 1868-1881) that caused Afrikaners to begin looking for biographies of Trek leaders. Thus the 1854 biography of Andries Pretorius in Dutch by U. G. Lauts of the Netherlands (*Andries Wilhelmus Pretorius, de held van Zuid-Afrika*), came to the notice of few South Africans. The publication of C. W. H. van der Post's *Piet Uys* in 1898, on the other hand, received widespread publicity and was seen as an event of major importance in Afrikaner circles. Based on recollections of Voortrekkers, it is not really so much a biography as a tale woven around the events of the Great Trek.

The major work on the Great Trek prior to the Second World War was that of Gustav Schoeman Preller (1875-1943).[12] He has been widely seen in Afrikaner circles as one of the most important South African historical writers in the first four decades of the twentieth century, on account of the extent of his work, his sympathetic portrayal of the Afrikaner's past, the new light he shed on the past and his style of writing. Preller served in the artillery of the South African Republic during the Second Anglo-Boer War, and was captured towards the end of the conflict. He became a journalist, editing *De Volksstem* and later *Ons Vaderland*. He was thus not a professional historian. In 1905-1906 Preller wrote a regular feature on the Voortrekker leader Piet Retief in *De Volksstem*, and in 1906 these articles were published in book form under the title *Piet Retief, Lewensgeskiedenis van die grote Voortrekker*. Altogether, 11 impressions of the work appeared, seven of them by 1911, which is some indication of its popularity among Afrikaners. In the same way that S. J. Toit's *Geskiedenis van ons land*, was one of the first fruits of the Eerste Afrikaanse Taalbeweging (First Afrikaans Language Movement), the publication of Gustav Preller's book coincided with the Tweede Afrikaanse Taalbeweging (Second Afrikaans Language Movement). Next to J. H. H. de Waal's novel *Johannes van Wyk*, it is the first prose work of the second Taalbeweging.

In his book on Retief, which was important as the first full-length biography of an Afrikaner leader, he saw the Great Trek in terms of the destiny of the Afrikaner and Afrikaner nationalism. The Great Trek was a national movement. According to Preller, the Afrikaner people would not have come into being without the Great Trek. He saw Retief as the man who had given rise to a new nation, "the free Afrikaner nation of the future".

But his narrative covered only about three years of Retief's life, from the beginning of his trek to his death, and had very little on his early life in the Colony. Most of his sources were printed ones, which he used uncritically. More often than not he did not rework his sources, so that the biography in fact was almost a collection of sources, in which long letters of Retief were linked together with only a brief comment. He did not tell the story in his own words. Preller's great admiration for Retief blinded him to the positive qualities of other Voortrekker leaders, and Potgieter and Uys were dismissed lightly, while Maritz was portrayed as the leader responsible for dissension in Voortrekker ranks. In 1917 *Piet Retief* was followed by the *Dagboek van Louis Trichardt*.

The 1938 Great Trek centenary inspired many people to take up the subject of the Great Trek, and Preller, whose wife, incidentally, was a descendant of both Retief and Andries Pretorius, wrote *Andries Pretorius, 'n lewensbeskrywing van die Voortrekker-kommandantgeneraal*; a second edition appeared in 1940. As reflected in the title, the book dealt with the period 1838-1853. Preller had by this time come strongly under the influence of the racial theories of National Socialism and he tried to establish parallels between the Great Trek and the Teutonic tribal migrations in Europe. The issue of race came strongly to the fore, also undoubtedly influenced by the political question of segregation and by the Poor White issue that was such a feature of the 1930s. Signs of these contemporary influences were evident at many points in the book. In one of the chapters in *Andries Pretorius* he made use of current pseudo-scientific racial theories about basic differences between races as far as their intellectual capacity, moral outlook and other qualities were concerned. Some races, he alleged, like the Anglo-Saxons and Nordic people (that is, the Aryan races), had a creative type of intelligence, whereas other races had been born with only an imitative sort of intelligence. It was these differences that explained why whites had come to dominate so much of the world – the other races were unable to defend themselves against superior Aryans.

As in the case of his work on Retief, Preller used mainly printed sources, particularly memoirs and reminiscences, and he made little attempt to uncover Pretorius's life in the Cape Colony prior to the Great Trek. His research into the material in the Transvaal archives left much to be desired; although he complained in 1911 about the state of the archives, he almost never visited them. But, at the same time, he did consult an enormous amount of other material in his quest.

Many long documents are reproduced in the text, which makes the work somewhat tedious, repetitive and over-long. In the work on Pretorius there are quotations between three and seven pages long. Apart from this, he was often careless in quoting his documents, he changed the punctuation and spelling, inserted words and omitted paragraphs. Although the book was much praised when it appeared, Professor B. J. Liebenberg, the latest of Andries Pretorius's biographers, considers it a lesser book than the one on Retief. In the final analysis, his treatment of Pretorius is superficial and lacks insight. Preller was not easily moved to revise anything he had written, and he ignored criticism, repeating the errors in later editions, despite the fact that his mistakes were pointed out to him.

Preller made a notable contribution to the history of the Second Anglo-Boer War. Among his books on the subject were *Scheepers se dagboek en die stryd in Kaapland* (1938) and *Talana: Die drie Generaals-slag by Dundee* (1942). For the most part, these too were reworked memoirs and diaries. They are rather sources for the study of history than real historical narrative. Although his historical writings may thus be regarded as being, in part at least, primary source material, Preller also made a contribution to the study of South African history with his "consciously" collected source publications. In this connection, particular mention should be made of the 6-volume *Voortrekkermense*. Realising that the days of the last of those who had participated in the Great Trek were fast drawing to a close, in the early years of the twentieth century he either wrote up or caused to be written up the reminiscences of many of them. He also collected an enormous number of documents in the course of his life, as may be seen in the Preller Collection in the Pretoria archives where his material is deposited.

He wrote at a time when there was much despair in the air in the aftermath of the Anglo-Boer War. The intervention of foreigners had brought about the loss of freedom. Until then most history had been overwhelmingly in English, projecting an English image, concerned with dependent British colonies and the expansion of the British empire in South Africa. Preller wrote as an Afrikaner nationalist. It was his express aim to familiarise the Afrikaner with his own history, so that in the dark days after the Anglo-Boer War he could obtain encouragement from the past. He was able as a nationalist to give a sympathetic portrayal of his people's past. The weakness of his approach was that he closed his eyes to the mistakes of the Afrikaners, while he did not have a good word to say about the blacks or the British. He saw the history of South Africa as a clash between Afrikaner nationalism, British imperialism and black "barbarism". And throughout, the Afrikaners were the heroes and the English and blacks the villains. He was very subjective and one-sided politically, so that his contribution to the stimulation of Afrikaner nationalism was more noteworthy than his contribution to South African historical writing.

The view that a historian should adopt an objective stance towards the past was rejected with contempt by Preller as doctrinaire pedantry. He was not concerned very much with objectivity. He saw history as the fulfilment of a national calling, and events that did not accord with this view were ignored. As Preller saw it, if history were not for learning and guidance, then it was meaningless. He saw history as a means of teaching certain truths that were important in the present. For him, the past was a giant arsenal from which he could select weapons to defend Afrikaner nationalism and attack British imperialism and black "barbarism". Preller's importance lay in the manner in which he succeeded in arousing the Afrikaner's interest in history. Despite the deficiencies in his work, he contributed to our knowledge of the Great Trek but, writes van Jaarsveld, "more especially he gave it a place in our hearts".[13]

Preller often dramatised events in order to create an atmosphere and he is at his best where he can give colour to his writing, as with his description of the crossing of the Drakensberg by the Voortrekkers in *Piet Retief*. His work is readable. He could unravel past events in the finest detail, and make the characters live. His style has often been praised, and it has been said that it enriched Afrikaans literature. Others again have contested this, admitting that he had a very individual style and that his writing was expressive and had a robust vigorousness to it, but maintaining that it was too full of eccentric elements, which were irritating to the reader. The critics of his prose argue that it was burdened with numerous words that were, if not altogether foreign to Afrikaans, archaic survivals.

THE ACADEMIC PHASE

After the First World War historical writing by trained academics began to come into its own, although, of course, amateur historians both good and bad continued to produce historical works. It was not only Afrikaans works that entered a new phase but also English works. At the University of Cape Town, J. Edgar and E. A. Walker were laying the basis for a more professional approach to the writing of the past, while in Natal A. F. Hattersley was doing the same; W. M. Macmillan was at the University of the Witwatersrand. Afrikaans universities were only established after the First World War, and the foundations for scientific Afrikaner historiography were laid at Stellenbosch University by two Dutch historians, E. C. Godeë-Molsbergen and W. Blommaert, who both taught at the University of Stellenbosch. Their successors included men like Professors S. F.N. Gie, J. A. Wiid, H. B. Thom and P. J. van der Merwe. A. J. H. van der Walt, later rector of the University of South Africa, was one of the first Afrikaners to submit a dissertation for the M.A. *Die vroegste konstitusionele geskiedenis van die Suid-Afrikaanse Republiek (1836-1854)* was published in *Die Saaier* in 1923. D. W. Krüger (Potchefstroom) and I. D. Bosman of Pretoria, were two of many Afrikaner historians who received at least part of their training overseas at German, Dutch or French universities. Until 1939 a smattering of Afrikaner students thus went abroad to do postgraduate work, studying under men like J. Huizinga, H. Brugmans and F. Meinecke, and this resulted in history departments at Afrikaans universities acquiring continental flavour; when they returned to South Africa these students, now young professional historians, inculcated into their students the principles of scientific historical writing as established by Ranke. In line with this tradition, historical thematology invariably centred around "national" history – politics, the state and interstate relations, military history and the deeds of great men. They were not alone in the prominence they gave to national and political history, to biographies of the great men of the past, for this sort of Rankean history was predominant in Europe as well until after the Second World War. The periodisation and the division of their material was according to political highpoints of the Europeans in South Africa, and the Afrikaners in particular.

As far as academic history is concerned, the choice of themes was determined largely by the interests of the researchers and the availability of material in archives. The equating of history with "political" history was given its particular twist by the way that the Afrikaner perceived his own history and destiny. And there was not all that much difference between men like Preller and the topics researched by academic historians. As Afrikaners, the academic historians largely shared the same interests as the amateur historians. Political history was dominant, with the Transvaal as the centre of focus. In particular the Great Trek and the two Anglo-Boer wars received most of the attention. No broadly based monographs were undertaken, but attention was devoted to the heroes of the Trek period, and the period was romanticised.

Apart from the question of interest, periods or subjects for which material was difficult to come by, were left alone, such as the history of the twentieth century, where the archives were still closed by the 50-year statutory limitation on the accessibility of material, or pre-colonial history, where written material was scarce. The dissertations of students had to be based on archival research, and the Public Archives Act of 1922, which did much to put the organisation of archival material on a sound footing, provided them increasingly with a body of classified and organised material. The number of source publications was also steadily increasing. Between 1926 and 1935 volumes of the *Kaapse Archiefstukken* appeared, and between 1944 and 1951 the *Kaapse Plakkaatboek* series. *South African Archival Records* included the *Resolusies van die Politieke Raad*, the Natal *Records of the Executive Council* and the Orange Free State *Volksraadsnotule*. Historical publications began to appear, such as *Historiese studies* and *Historia* and in 1938 the *Archives Year Book*, an official publication that owed its initiative to Professor J. L. M. Franken, made available the masters' and doctoral dissertations of history students. By the time that volume 1 of the 1982 *Year Book* had appeared in 1984, some 150 theses had been published in the series.

The Great Trek

The Afrikaner continued to regard the Great Trek as one of the key events in South African history. As late as 1963, C. F. J. Muller, for many years Professor of History at the University of South Africa, stressed its importance as being largely responsible for the borders of the country; it had given direction to the country's racial policies and influenced its political thinking decisively. For the Afrikaner historian it was the first genuine republican period, in which the Afrikaner, through a series of heroic deeds, secured his own identity and laid down policy with regard to the blacks. Even to those who, like many English-speaking historians, did not see it in a positive light, it was an important landmark. Liberal historians tended to see the Great Trek as a disaster, sowing division, creating new problems, because it was a flight from old problems, not a solution of them. To the African it was seen as a period of conquest, in which whites with better organisation and superior weapons succeeded in taking over their cattle and land.

But although Muller in 1963 still saw the Great Trek as central to South African history, being a thoroughly professional historian, he admitted the possibility that the Great Trek might not always be seen as holding such an important place in the South African past. For example, he said that if white South Africa one day disappeared as a political factor, the Great Trek would be seen as merely a brief era of white imperialism that moved up from the Cape as far as the Limpopo or Zambezi Rivers. The emphasis would then fall on the pattern of resistance of blacks to white penetration.[14]

* * *

There was a great demand for books on the Great Trek. Professor G. B. A. Gerdener's *Sarel Cilliers die vader van Dingaansdag*, which appeared in 1919, had by 1925 gone into a third edition. The basis of this account was the journal compiled by Cilliers shortly before his death. Gerdener felt that Dingaan's Day should be seen in its proper context and celebrated as the victors of Blood River had intended it should be, which meant that a proper attitude of respect should be adopted towards the Voortrekker heroes, and that their experiences should be used to build up an Afrikaner national consciousness. His book contributed to this and in particular to the way in which Dingaan's Day came to be celebrated.[15]

The 1938 centenary celebrations, and the inauguration of the Voortrekker Monument in 1949, saw more attention given to various aspects of the Trek. Microscopic attention was focused on certain small details, source publications appeared. But the emotionally charged atmosphere did not further the scientific study of the Trek. In 1938 *Hendrik Potgieter* by Dr Carl Potgieter and N. H. Theunissen saw the light of day. The authors' starting point was the fact that hitherto Potgieter had been neglected by other writers on the Great Trek, and that he had not received the credit which was his due as a Voortrekker leader. But in correcting the picture and restoring Potgieter to a place of distinction, they went too far, regarding him rather uncritically.

J. L. M. Franken's *Piet Retief se lewe in die Kolonie* appeared in 1949. He did intensive research in the Cape archives and was a scholarly research worker. Franken saw the Great Trek as a "peaceable freedom movement" and coupled it to the Patriot movement and Slagtersnek episodes. Yet the book does not really add up to a genuine biography, it is more in the nature of extracts from documents linked together, with comments and interpretations by Franken thrown in.[16]

Franken's work, although scholarly, did not revolutionise the study of the Great Trek. But two historians who did change the study of the Trek were H.B. Thom and C. F. J. Muller. They did much to correct the picture of the

Great Trek that had been provided by Preller. Thom's *Die lewe van Gert Maritz*, published in 1947, was the work of a scholar. Until then Maritz had been neglected and underestimated; Thom, for many years head of the department of history at Stellenbosch University and later principal of the university, made a thorough study of the source material of the Great Trek and rehabilitated him, showing up Retief's weaknesses. Although Thom went about his task far more scientifically than Preller, he tended to see the Voortrekkers in nationalist terms as "racially pure Afrikaners" and "the first real Afrikaner nationalists". The book is written from an Afrikaner point of view, and condemnation of British policy is implied in the use of emotive words and phrases; Dingane's murder of the Voortrekkers is stigmatised as "barbarous murder and bestial blood-thirstiness".[17]

In 1949 Muller put the causes in a detailed framework of the attitude of the British government, taking material considerations into account as well as what he calls "spiritual" ones, not to condemn British policy but to explain it. Muller's *Die Britse owerheid en die Groot Trek* (1949) is a thesis obtained at the University of Stellenbosch in 1947, with Thom as promoter. The two basic questions he tried to answer were: Why did the Great Trek take place and why did the British government react to it as it did? In answering the first question he makes a distinction, at times somewhat forced, between material and spiritual causes. In analysing the former, he gives attention to shortage of land, capital and labour, and uncertainty of life on the border. As spiritual causes, he sees the equality granted on the frontier to the Khoi and slaves and the lack of self-government (though he deems this last aspect to be only a minor factor). To answer the question of the British reaction, Muller studied British financial and commercial policy, British perceptions of their empire and the need to defend it, and British philanthropism. By 1977 the book had gone into a 4th impression.[18]

Twenty-five years later Muller produced his next important book, *Die oorsprong van die Groot Trek* (1974) in which he tried to answer the question as to why the Great Trek took place in the 1830s. He thus returned to the causes, but did not remain there – he moved to look at the background against which the Trek occurred. Among other things, he went into the Trek idea and its propagation and made a proper study of the Uys Commission's visit to Natal. These were aspects about which very little was known. He also moved into hitherto unknown territory with his chapter on Louis Tregardt's career in the Cape Colony. What was also new was what he had to say about the role of black immigrants in the Cape Colony. On the basis of this work, in 1977 Muller was awarded the Stals prize for History by the Suid-Afrikaanse Akademie vir Wetenskap en Kuns.

Muller also made a number of smaller yet significant contributions to the historiography of the Great Trek. In *Leiers na die Noorde* (1976) he brought together several studies undertaken over a period of more than 30 years and which had appeared in journals. One dealt with Robert Scoon, the Scots trader who travelled north of the Vaal River long before the Voortrekkers. Parts of the study on Karel Landman first appeared in the 1940s. Another study dealt with a single event in the life of Piet Uys – the arrest of his wife in October 1835, which influenced his decision to leave the Colony. He also added snippets of information on Andries Pretorius, and pointed out a number of errors Preller had made.

Although Muller's style does not make for easy reading, and some of his work, in particular *Die Britse owerheid*, is overburdened with English quotations which tend to disrupt the flow of the work, more than anyone else Muller placed the writing of the history of the Great Trek on a scientific basis. He also did pioneering work in tracing sources on the Great Trek in South Africa, Britain, the Netherlands and the United States among others.

It is interesting however to note that his work is not entirely free of the sort of remarks that one might more readily associate with Preller. Thus he wrote that Landman was a typical Voortrekker, "upright, resolute, devout, deliberate and versatile" – a somewhat idealistic and romantic generalisation.[19]

Other writers have added their own perspectives to the Great Trek. As G. D. Scholtz saw it, the Trek created new issues which caused friction and eventually armed clashes between Boer and Brit. The Trek divided the small white population politically, and meant that the course of relations thereafter was one of friction.[20] In his treatment of the striving towards unity among the Trekkers, Scholtz focused attention on the anthropo-geographical influences, seeing the Great Trek as a deed of voluntary segregation that divided South Africa into a republican north and a colonial south.

People like J. A. Wiid, A .J. H. van der Walt and D. W. Krüger saw it as a flanking movement of Western civilisation that cut the southward-moving black stream into two, thus weakening the pressure on the Cape border. The Trekkers' native policy was one of territorial segregation and differentiation that set a precedent for the twentieth century. The Voortrekkers opened up three of the four provinces for Western civilisation.[21] Van der Walt concentrated on the importance of the Trek in maintaining a pure white race, on its role in stabilising a Dutch-Afrikaans culture, and in the idea of the existence of a separate, independent and free Afrikaner nation. Writers have found links between the Great Trek and the Patriot movement at the Cape in the late eighteenth century, with the so-called republics of Swellendam and Graaff-Reinet, and with Slagtersnek.[22]

The Great Trek no longer occupies the same place as it did in Afrikaner thinking a few decades ago, and studies on the Great Trek are no longer a central theme in Afrikaner historiography. But works on the Great Trek continue to appear. Some of the most recent research, so far from stimulating Afrikaner nationalism, tends to highlight the myths of Afrikaner historiography and to expose them. English-speaking historians have from time to time focused on myths in the Afrikaner's past, but Afrikaners themselves had not generally paid much attention to their work, which was often written in an attitude of hostility. It is thus a different matter when Afrikaner academics expose myths in Afrikaner historiography.

Following upon the publication in 1977 of his 1974 University of South Africa doctoral thesis, *Andries Pretorius in Natal*, which was undertaken under the promotership of C. F. J. Muller, B. J. Liebenberg became involved in a polemic concerning the oath supposed to have been taken some time before the battle of Blood River on 16 December 1838. Liebenberg had already been gently chided by other Afrikaans historians for not adopting as understanding an attitude as he might have done towards Pretorius's weaknesses and acts. What he presented was a portrayal of Pretorius that stripped him of the "hero" aura that Preller and others had conferred on him. This was a picture of Pretorius "warts and all" and the portrait was not altogether flattering. Liebenberg's further focusing on Blood River and its implications with regard to the Covenant came as an unpleasant blow to certain Afrikaners. If the controversy had been confined to the ivory towers of academic circles it may not have made much of a ripple at all. But it was brought to the notice of a wider public, a public that had been brought up to believe that God had intervened to give a small body of a few hundred Voortrekkers a great victory over an army of thousands of Zulus.

In an article in *Die Huisgenoot* of 16 December 1977 Liebenberg insisted that the Voortrekkers had won the battle because they had guns whereas the Zulus only had assegais, they had the protection of a fortified laager, a flat battlefield, without bushes, so that visibility was good, and a *sloot* and river preventing a massive attack by the Zulus from the south and east. A nice sunny day that kept the powder dry and the determination of the defenders were other factors. Predictably, Liebenberg was accused of having left out the most important element in the Boer victory, which was that God had given the Voortrekkers the victory. This was the parting of the ways between those who examined historical events as disinterestedly and dispassionately as possible and those who were happy to mix facts with mystical elements. Liebenberg expressed the professional historian's stand that although it was perfectly in order to maintain that God was working through human agency and in the course of history, it would be presumptuous of the historian to believe that he could discern God's plan. The historian had to rely on evidence, and there was no evidence of divine intervention – the Boer victory could be explained totally satisfactorily in terms of ordinary human evidence. Liebenberg further asked a number of awkward questions of those who maintained that it was God's intervention that had made the difference. If the historian ascribed success at Blood River to God, Liebenberg insisted, then he also had to explain why God had given the victory to the British in the Second Anglo-Boer War or allowed the Boers to be defeated by the Zulu at Italeni.[23]

The question of the Covenant was soon also brought into the limelight. According to the traditional version of events the Voortrekkers identified themselves with the Old Testament children of Israel, and in the divine services that they held for the members of Pretorius's commando in the days preceding the battle of the 16th December, those who ministered to the Boers emphasised the way in which God had given his children victory over their enemies. The parallels were clear. Some time before the encounter an oath was taken and a covenant entered into with God that should he give them victory over the Zulus, they would in turn build a church and commemorate the day each year. The annual celebration of the victory rests on the evidence of two contemporary documents by members of the commando, one the journal of Jan Bantjes and the other a letter by Andries Pretorius. There is a third document, composed by Sarel Cilliers, one of the ministers, and who has been credited with the actual making of the covenant. Cilliers's memories of what transpired in 1838 were some 33 years old when he gave his version of events on his deathbed in 1871. There are significant differences between the two contemporary documents and Cilliers's account. The documents make no mention of keeping the day as a sabbath, but they do mention the erection of a church. Cilliers, who maintains that they promised to always keep the day as a sabbath, said nothing about a church. G. B. A. Gerdener in his *Sarel Cilliers, die vader van Dingaansdag,* solved these discrepancies by bringing the three documents together and reconstructing an account that contained both the church that should be built and the keeping of the day as a sabbath. So what was later commemorated was the Cilliers tradition as manufactured by Gerdener in 1919.

The covenant was not observed in the Transvaal before 1864, and it was only in the wake of the encroaching British imperialism that it was "rediscovered". From 1886 it was observed throughout the Transvaal, and in the Free State from 1894. But it was not observed as a sabbath. In 1894 a commission of the volksraad of the South African Republic refused a request of 66 burgers for the day to be brought within the terms of the Sabbath Act. General Hertzog refused a similar request in 1925. Originally known as Dingaan's Day, it was renamed the Day of the Covenant in 1952 and it became a sabbath, which had to be observed by the whole population. Thus a promise to God to remember the day, and which was meant to apply only to those participating in the commando and their descendants, became a national day.

But the claim that the commemoration of the Day of the Covenant had no firm base in historical reality, did not endear historians to those who had imbibed these myths at school from their teachers and textbooks. It is ironic that the writer of probably the best-known of these school textbooks in the Transvaal, Professor F. A. van Jaarsveld, himself became a victim of their anger. Van Jaarsveld adapted, but those who had been brought up on his books to venerate the covenant and all that went with it, regarded him as a traitor.

Van Jaarsveld's attempts to demythologise the Day of the Covenant brought his name and picture into the homes of a great number of South Africans via the front pages of their morning newspapers. His address in the Senate Hall of the University of South Africa in March 1979, entitled "A historical mirror of Blood River", and which concentrated on the mythological elements in the events surrounding the battle of Blood River in 1838, and their enduring influence on Afrikaner national consciousness, was interrupted by Eugene Terre' Blanche and other members of the Afrikaner Weerstandsbeweging, who duly tarred and feathered van Jaarsveld, unfurled an enormous Vierkleur, and made a vague statement to the effect that they would not tolerate such anti-Afrikaner proceedings.[24]

P.J. van der Merwe[25]

Petrus Johannes van der Merwe was born on 2 December 1912 and his major historical works had all appeared by the time he was 35 years of age. Between 1945 and his death in 1979, he published only two works worthy of note and these could not really compare in their vision and scope with his earlier writing. Having completed his M.A. (*Die geskiedenis van die trekboer onder die Oos-Indiese Kompanje*) at Stellenbosch University in June 1933 under the tutelage of Willem Blommaert, in 1934 he departed for the Netherlands to do his doctorate, and remained there until graduating at the Rijksuniversiteit in Leiden in September 1937. His thesis was *Die noordwaartse beweging van die Boere voor die Groot Trek, 1770-1842*; his promoter was Johan Huizinga.

He returned to South Africa in 1937, and at the beginning of 1938 obtained a temporary lecturer's post at Stellenbosch University. He remained at Stellenbosch for the rest of his academic career, in due course replacing H. B. Thom as head of the department; he finally retired in 1977. The longest period he was away from Stellenbosch in that time was between 1951 and 1954 when, at the invitation of and at the expense of the Afrikaner community of Rhodesia, he undertook full-time research in that country with the aim of writing a book on the establishment of the Afrikaners north of the Limpopo.

Die noordwaartse beweging was published in The Hague in 1937. This was followed a year later by the publication in Cape Town of *Die trekboer in die geskiedenis van die Kaapkolonie (1657-1842)*; *Die Kafferoorlog van 1793* followed in 1940; in 1941 *Pioniers van die Dorsland* was published, and in 1945 *Trek: Studies oor die mobiliteit van die pioniersbevolking aan die Kaap*. Van der Merwe also published about 200 articles in newspapers and magazines, but not in academic journals. *Die noordwaartse beweging, Trekboer* and *Trek*, together, form a unit on the pioneering history of the Cape. In 1948 he won the prize of the Suid-Afrikaanse Akademie vir Wetenskap en Kuns for his pioneering history of the Afrikaner.

In 1962 he published *Nog verder noord, die Potgieterkommissie se besoek aan die gebied van die teenswoordige Suid-Rhodesië, 1836*. His last work published before his death was a short book on footnoting technique and the compiling of a bibliography, or source list, as he preferred to call it. *Bronnelys en voetnote* appeared in 1972 and there was also an English edition, *Source list and footnotes*. It was aimed at introducing uniformity into the technical aspects of historical writing, particularly with regard to the manuscripts submitted for consideration for publication in the Archives Yearbook for S.A. History. For some time after 1972 all manuscripts submitted to the Archives Commission had to be footnoted in accordance with the principles laid down by van der Merwe, and even in the mid-1980s, although those submitting work for publication were entitled to use other footnoting and reference systems, their attention was nevertheless drawn to the fact that the Archives Commission considered van der Merwe's system a good one.

Professor Muller could not be classified amongst those who wrote history from a specifically republican or nationalist standpoint, although the subject he chose was a favourite with the nationalists. Professor P. J. van der Merwe is an even less likely candidate for inclusion in that category. Not only did he heed Blommaert's advice to steer clear of political topics, he also chose a subject that was distinctly unfashionable at the time, and he approached it in a way that was somewhat unfamiliar to Afrikaner historians of the day. He focused attention on the pioneering history of the Afrikaner prior to the Great Trek, on the so-called *trekboers*, a term he applied to the half-nomadic frontier farmers who led the natural expansion of the colony to the interior. He demonstrated that historians like Gie, Thom and the English writers were wrong not to have made a distinction between the Voortrekkers and the *trekboers*.

He is seen today to have made one of the most significant contributions to South African historiography before 1945, but at the time there was a tendency to overlook his work as it deviated from the mainstream of Afrikaner preoccupation with the Great Trek. After all, the *trekboers* to whom van der Merwe devoted so much attention, were Afrikaners who did not go on the Great Trek, but who remained loyal to Britain. In other words they were not part of the republican Afrikaner movement – they were regarded as a lesser breed.

* * *

Moving away from the political and national preoccupations of the majority of Afrikaans historians, he concentrated on the emigration of the surplus population, the phenomena of bywoners, Boers without land, the desire for space, the trek spirit, economic adaptation and the process of expansion. He examined such aspects as changes of residence and the annual winter trek, water shortages and droughts, locusts and springbok and nomadism. And the questions he asked about the *trekboers* were also novel. What motivated them, how was the slow movement of the colonial border determined by natural circumstances? What did they believe in, how did they live, how did they adapt to their situation, how did they think, fight, work and suffer and still remain civilised? What were their relations with one another? How did they see life and the government?

These themes, and his approach, had more in common with social and economic history as studied in the 1970s than they did with the work of the majority of his contemporaries. This was partly due to the fact that his promoter, Johan Huizinga, was a noted cultural historian. Another influence on him was Frederick Jackson Turner, the American who had formulated a theory about the significance of the frontier on the development of American society. Like his contemporaries, van der Merwe based his work on a close study of archival sources, but he went beyond this, travelling some 24 000 kilometres in his car to speak to hundreds of people, documenting and adding this rich treasure of first-hand testimony to his other sources. Although W. M. Macmillan in his investigation into the lives of Poor Whites had undertaken field trips, van der Merwe's approach to rural regional history had not been undertaken by any other Afrikaner historian, and it was to be some time before any Afrikaner followed in his footsteps.

He was at pains not to judge either the *trekboers* or the San for their conduct on the frontiers, but to see their actions in terms of the situation existing at the time. Thus, the Boers, with their notions of private ownership of goods, could not be blamed for shooting San who stole their cattle any more than the San, who had no conceptions of private ownership, could be blamed for taking cattle and sheep when they were hungry. Such a view may be regarded in certain circles today as outmoded, when the focus is on various forms of primary resistance, and San thieving is seen as a form of indirect resistance to white penetration and loss of their land. But in the context of the late 1930s and early 1940s, van der Merwe was framing questions that Afrikaner historians as a whole were hardly beginning to ask in the 1970s. His broad approach and attempt to see both sides of the question, his probing of the social aspects of life among the Boers in the interior, was unique.

Van der Merwe also destroyed some of the myths that surrounded the Boers. In *Die Kafferoorlog* he examined Theal critically, and although he said that in the main he agreed with the Canadian-born historian, he revised the view then held that it had all been a matter of black thieving – conflicts over grazing and the activities of irresponsible whites were given a prominent place in his analysis. But if he implicitly rejected the one-sided and politically motivated accounts of many contemporary Afrikaners, he was equally critical of the "liberal" English-speaking historians like Walker and Macmillan, and he corrected statements they had made about the Boers.

It was the fact that he was a perfectionist that was largely responsible for his failure to produce any substantial work after 1945. He would not begin writing until he thought he had gathered every possible piece of information available. After the publication of *Trek* in 1945, the following year he began fieldwork for a book on the development of the "North West" between 1800 and 1900. He was at the same time gathering data on Griquatown and the Western Griqua between 1800 and 1946, and on missionary work in Kuruman in the nineteenth century. But he broke off his research in 1951 when approached by the Afrikaner Culture Union of Rhodesia (*Afrikanerkultuurunie van Rhodesië* [AKUR]) to write a complete history of the Afrikaners in Rhodesia, which it was hoped would be used in their schools. He agreed because this seemed to fit in well with his other task of dealing with Boer expansion north of the Cape. He left for Rhodesia at the end of March 1951. He spent three years mainly doing fieldwork, and one year based at the Salisbury archives. He returned to South Africa at the end of 1954, and took over Thom's position as head of the department.

By 1959 he had completed his research on Rhodesia, but he decided that before he could write the history of the Afrikaners north of the Limpopo he would need to undertake a number of preliminary studies. *Nog verder noord*, which appeared in 1962, was the first of these. In his major works, van der Merwe had paid great attention to detail, but it always remained subsidiary to the wider canvas. His care with lesser detail did not get in the way of the larger conception that informed his work. But in *Nog verder noord* one gets the feeling that the detail is all-important. In this book van der Merwe went out of his way to demonstrate the possibilities for interpretation inherent in a historical document. He took two texts of a single document comprising a few pages; his critical examination of them ended as a book of 166 pages.

He wrote a second preliminary work. Although he apparently completed this in 1966, it was not published until late in 1987 – some eight years after his death. In this work, *Die Matabeles en die Voortrekkers*, the detail is also very much in the forefront. In fact it could be argued that it is not so much a history as a detailed analysis of innumerable sources. This study of relations between the Boers and the Ndebele of Mzilikazi was only submitted to Tafelberg Publishers in 1975. It was agreed that since the manuscript was so long – a text of 724 pages on folio-size paper and a further 157 pages of references – it should be published in two volumes. Van der Merwe took it back to affect changes and presumably to cut it into two. That was the last the publishers saw of it. His wife found the manuscript in a drawer after his death, and on the recommendation of Professor J. J. Oberholster, the Archives Commission decided to publish it. Because there was much "polishing" to do, the book only appeared in 1987.[26]

The text of 428 pages, mostly on Ndebele-Boer attacks and counter-attacks, provides the reader with a fascinating insight into document analysis by one of the most thorough and painstakingly careful historians that South Africa has produced. Each document is weighed up and the value of its evidence set down in detail. The result provides us with an insight into all the sources that deal with the number of assegais found in the Boer laager after the battle of Vegkop, as well as all the information pertaining to the disappearance of two or three Boer children at the time of the Ndebele attacks.

Conclusions are cautiously arrived at only after the most exhaustive sifting of evidence has taken place in front of the reader. In the foreword to the book, the editors say that one of the main reasons for deciding to publish the book was that the brilliant research and source criticism would serve as a worthy example to South African historians, and postgraduate history students in particular. This may be so, but the work should also serve as a serious warning not to allow concern for detail to become an end in itself. The actual course of events is established in the most minute detail, but as with *Nog verder word*, the broader perspective that characterised his earlier work is missing.

This second preliminary study was as far as van der Merwe came to embarking on his Rhodesian history. It was a much bigger task than he had thought it would be; he also had a greater administrative burden than he had envisaged. The history so ardently desired by the Rhodesian Afrikaans community remained uncompleted, but at the same time the obligation placed on him to finish it, ruined his attempts to carry out his other projects. He completed none of them.

Although the Institute for Historical Research at the University of the Western Cape is continuing with van der Merwe's work on the history of the Afrikaners in Rhodesia, the need felt in the 1950s for a history to show that the Afrikaners had played a meaningful role in the development of the country, and to give them a sense of pride, a sense of belonging to the community, has passed with the arrival of black rule in Zimbabwe.

G. D. Scholtz[27]

An Afrikaner writer who, although he was not a professional historian, made a contribution to Afrikaner nationalist historiography, was G.D. Scholtz. What distinguishes him from others of his kind is that he attempted to enlarge the Afrikaners' breadth of vision by trying to convince them that the world outside really existed, and that it really did matter. Although he adopted a strongly nationalist approach and concentrated heavily on the dangers facing Afrikaner nationalism, he did not confine his examination to South Africa alone, but cast his net somewhat wider, looking at the situation in the context of the world at large.

Scholtz was a journalist, but he was no stranger to academic history; indeed, history was one of the majors in his B.A. degree which he completed at the University of South Africa in 1928. In 1929 he registered for the LL.B. degree at Unisa and completed this in 1932. He was not allowed to practise as an advocate, for having very strong Afrikaner nationalist principles – he refused to take the oath of allegiance to the British crown. In 1932 Scholtz changed direction, and registered for a M.A. in history at Unisa, using his knowledge of law to write *Die geskiedenis van die regspleging in die Oranje-Vrystaat 1854-1876*. He arrived in the Netherlands in December 1933. Enrolling for a doctoral degree in history at the Gemeentelike University in Amsterdam, he studied modern history under H. Brugmans. Scholtz graduated on 9 December 1936 with the thesis *Die konstitusie en staatsinstellings van die Oranje-Vrystaat 1854-1902*.

By January 1937 he was back in South Africa. After a short spell with *Die Volksblad* in Bloemfontein, he joined the newly-established *Die Transvaler*, of which Dr H. F. Verwoerd was the chief editor. Scholtz was foreign editor. In February 1960 Scholtz became chief editor of the paper. Shortly after joining the paper he began writing the rubric *Sake van die Dag*, and did so continuously until 1974, some four years after his retirement, a period of 37 years. In the last 18 months of his time at *Die Transvaler*, the directors of Voortrekkerpers relieved him of some of his editorial duties, including the writing of the daily leading article, so that he could devote time to a biography of Verwoerd.

Scholtz was a well-read man with wide interests and this is reflected in his work, which is not confined to history. Some of his writing was purely historical, some of it was predominantly historical but contained a strong didactic element; some of it could best be described as belonging to the history of ideas and some of it belonged more properly to the field of political science. Scholtz's first concern was the Afrikaner nation. Professor van Jaarsveld has referred to him as the historian of and for the Afrikaner.

The Anglo-Boer War occupies a prominent place in his purely historical work. The first book he wrote after completing his doctoral dissertation was *Europa en die Tweede Vryheidsoorlog* (1941). The appearance of his two-volume *Die oorsake van die Tweede Vryheidsoorlog 1899-1902* (1947) won him the Stals prize for historical writing from the Suid-Afrikaanse Akademie vir Wetenskap en Kuns.

He wrote as an Afrikaner nationalist, and his work is strongly nationalist. However, unlike so many of his fellow Afrikaner writers, he tried to place events in their broadest possible perspective. It was an article of faith with him that the past should be brought to bear on the present, it should be interpreted in terms of the present. He sought the causes of the war not only in Africa but in the world political situation generally. The war was brought about by a confrontation between an implacable Afrikaner nationalism and a Britain that was vitally concerned with her position in the world; British supremacy in South Africa and her prestige as a major power were at stake. A closer look at the South African situation drew Scholtz to the conclusion that the causes of the war really went as far back as the Great Trek and British imperialism at that time. Although ultimate responsibility for the war lay with the British, Scholtz does not absolve Kruger. He is critical of Kruger's handling of the Uitlander question and of Reitz's diplomacy. Scholtz was in fact no admirer of Paul Kruger. The president had considered surrendering in the war and he could not be compared, therefore, with President M. T. Steyn of the Orange Free State.

Scholtz also turned his hand to biography. His book on *Generaal Christiaan Frederik Beyers, 1869-1914* (1941) stemmed from his work and interest in the Anglo-Boer War. It had a patriotic intent. From this flowed *Die Rebellie 1914-1915* (1942). In his biography of *Dr. Nicolaas Johannes van der Merwe, 1888-1940* (1944), he entered the era of contemporary history and described a new kind of Afrikaner leader, not the military leader but the intellectual, the party leader. In a divided Afrikanerdom it had a mixed reception. His biography of Verwoerd (*Dr Hendrik Frensch Verwoerd, 1901-1966*), which is more than 600 pages long, was completed in September 1971. Written totally from Verwoerd's standpoint, one learns very little about the views of Verwoerd's opponents. This lack of perspective makes it a disappointing book.

The first of what Scholtz intended to be a ten-volume series on the development of the political thinking and philosophy of the Afrikaner, and which aimed at making the Afrikaner conscious of his calling, appeared in 1967. In the first volume of *Die politieke denke van die Afrikaner*, which deals with the period of rule of the Dutch East India Company at the Cape, Scholtz returns to a theme that he had dealt with before, blaming the Company for the fact that the Afrikaners were not a larger population group, that the economy was based on black labour and that the Afrikaner did not have a greater share in it. These were the basic sins of the Company, the wages of which were being paid in the present. It was a theme he had developed in *Het die Afrikaanse volk 'n toekoms?* which appeared in 1954. Three mistakes had been made during the period of the Dutch East India Company. Firstly, immigration was halted in 1706. Secondly, the Company's closing of all professions to the Afrikaner except that of a farmer, relegated the Afrikaner to the status of a rural being rather than that of a trader or merchant and thus was responsible for his economic backlog in the twentieth century. Thirdly, the use of non-white labour in the seventeenth century and later made urban whites dependent upon black labour and drew the Africans to the cities.

Scholtz was of the old school of Afrikaner historians, repeating the well-worn charges against H. C. D. Maynier and Andries Stockenström, resurrecting the familiar folk heroes without bothering overmuch to clothe them in modern garb. He saw the republican ideal that was realised in 1961 as stretching back to the republican expressions in the Cape in the eighteenth century, an attitude that Afrikaners like Giliomee and du Toit were later to challenge.

In volume 2 of *Politieke denke* the importance of the establishment of Boer republics in the interior in isolation is stressed – without this isolation which allowed the Afrikaner to develop free from outside interference, and the republican ideal, it would not have been possible to establish the republic in 1961. The Great Trek had brought about some temporary negative results such as the unnatural division of the Afrikaners, but they had soon become united again.

He completed eight of the ten volumes before he died. Volume 8 (published in 1984), dealt with events between 1939 and 1948. Volumes 5-8 covered the period after 1899. The series was not based on solid archival work, but on a number of selected works, and the contribution it made to Afrikaner history lay in the breadth of his perspective rather than in the uncovering and opening up of new sources.[28]

Scholtz had great respect for Strijdom and Verwoerd, but not for Smuts or Botha, nor really for Malan as he did not regard him as a convinced republican; apart from this, Scholtz did not trust Malan as he had given preference to the south above the north. *Generaals Hertzog en Smuts en die Britse Ryk* appeared in 1974, in which Scholtz's great liking for international politics is demonstrated. He saw Hertzog and Smuts in terms of a nationalist against a holist. He rejected Smuts, the holistic imperialist, and saw Hertzog as one of the most important creators of Afrikaner nationalism.

Scholtz also wrote a number of works that deal with South Africa as part of the larger world political scene. In his *Hoe die wêreldpolitiek gevoer word* (1952) and *Suid-Afrika en die wêreldpolitiek 1652-1954* he emphasised that the world had changed and that South Africa could no longer develop in isolation; the fate of South Africa was inextricably linked with what was happening in the rest of the world. In *Die stryd om die wêreld* he dealt with this theme again, with variations.

Die gevaar uit die Ooste, published in 1957, was an attempt to shake the Afrikaner out of his complacency and tell him about the sort of world his children would inherit; in 1964 he published '*n Swart Suid-Afrika?* He once again reiterated that the dependence upon black labour had been the curse of the past. Economic integration and political separation could not go together. *Die bedreiging van die liberalisme* followed in 1965 and aimed at awakening the Afrikaner to the dangers of liberalism, for in common with most South African nationalists, he saw liberalism as the means by which communism advanced.

F. A. van Jaarsveld

In the course of this chapter a number of references have been made to Professor F. A. van Jaarsveld, and in the footnotes to all the chapters his writings feature prominently. There is nothing surprising in this – he is by far and away the most prolific writer on South African history, and he has been at it for a good many years. He is also the most controversial one. This is because he believes the historian must be involved, must serve the community. He has never been afraid to air his views and has done so in innumerable articles in journals and newspapers, in radio talks, interviews and addresses. His comments have found their way onto the front pages of national newspapers.

In 1946 van Jaarsveld completed his M.A. at the University of Pretoria with *Die veldkornet en sy aandeel in die opbou van die Suid-Afrikaanse Republiek tot 1870*. His next work was *Die eenheidstrewe van die Republiekeinse Afrikaners (Deel I, Pioniershartstogte (1836-1864)* (1951), in which he dealt with the striving of various groups of Afrikaners in the Orange Free State and the Transvaal to form a united front in the mid-nineteenth century. He developed the idea of the unity of the two republics – the republican north, as opposed to the Cape and Natal – the colonial south – a division that numerous historians have found useful and adopted in their portrayal of the South African past.

In 1957 *Die ontwaking van die Afrikaanse nasionale bewussyn, 1868-1881*, was published, in which van Jaarsveld distinguished a number of phases in the development of Afrikaner nationalism. In the early 1970s he returned to the theme of the Afrikaners in the north, with a history of the disputes surrounding the Vaal River as a border. *Vaalrivier omstrede grenslyn* (completed in 1970 but only published in 1974) cleared up many problems, but it was not as thought provoking and stimulating as his earlier work. This was undoubtedly due as much to the nature of the subject as any other single factor. Dealing as it does with complicated border issues, it does not make for stimulating reading.

In the 1960s and early 1970s van Jaarsveld increasingly identified himself with the struggles and fears of the Afrikaners as they contemplated the future, and this reached a highpoint in 1971 with a series of radio talks which have been described as bordering on chauvinism.[29] Professor F. A. van Jaarsveld's *Van van Riebeeck tot Verwoerd* (1971) – later editions have the titles *Van van Riebeeck tot Vorster* and *Van van Riebeeck tot P.W. Botha* – is also very much in line with Afrikaner nationalist political thinking in its emphasis on the development of various "groups" in the past as an explanation of South Africa's later "multinational" development. In his preface, he made his aim clear: he was not striving towards completeness, but at indicating the significance of events, and their inter-connectedness. This was very much in line with his frequent criticism of the work of his predecessors and certain of his contemporaries, that they were simply stringing events together, compiling chronologies, rather than examining the *significance* of events. In general it was well received. He did not only concentrate on political history, but also on economic and social factors. Although the focus is on Afrikaners, his is the first Afrikaans history to give considerable space to blacks. The work has however been criticised as positing too much of a black-white divide – the "white Christian, pioneer, civilising" forces opposed to the "wild, untamed, barbaric", indigenous peoples.

His work has been characterised by his changing view of the Afrikaner and the situation in South Africa. The speed with which his perceptions sometimes altered makes it all the more difficult to characterise van Jaarsveld. He has gone through various stages. In his early work he tried above all to lay bare the mainsprings of what makes the Afrikaner tick, placing his history in a broad perspective. In the 1960s his own sentiments come through more clearly in his work and on occasion he acts as an Afrikaner apologist. In his more recent work he adopts a more critical approach to the Afrikaner's vision of his past and, as has been noted in connection with the Blood River covenant, has gone so far as to demythologise the Afrikaner's history, for which he suffered the ignominy of being tarred and feathered. His conclusion that an incorrect interpretation of the vow made by the Voortrekkers in 1838 had led to the observance of the Day of the Covenant as a sabbath, did not endear him to hardline Afrikaner nationalists.

He was accused of treachery to the cause of the Afrikaner. But what people have failed to see, as Johannes du Bruyn so perceptively indicated, is that his views derived from his involvement with Afrikaner history – his attempt to demythologise Blood River was in line with his concern for the Afrikaner – his concern that a narrow and sterile historical image would prevent the Afrikaner from being able to meet the future with confidence.[30]

* * *

Van Jaarsveld's major contribution to the study of South African history arguably has been his work on South African historiography. His theoretical studies represent one of his major contributions to Afrikaans historiography. It is pioneering work that demonstrates his originality, insight and imagination. It demonstrates a willingness to ask new questions, albeit within a narrow framework. Besides making available in Afrikaans a wide variety of studies on aspects of the South African past, his study in 1964, *The Afrikaner's interpretation of South African history*, which although it concentrated on the Afrikaner, did not do so exclusively, made available to English-speaking historians, both in South Africa and abroad, a balanced and incisive analysis of the main trends of South African historiography. His division of South African historical writing into Afrikaner republican, settler, imperialist and liberal schools, found wide acceptance. It is easier to use van Jaarsveld's earlier works on historiography as a guide to the various schools than it is to do so with his later writing, where he has become far more emotionally involved than was the case with his historiographical work in the 1960s.[31]

From his latest work it seems as if he is willing to ask new questions and encourage research into fresh directions, only on his own terms. He thus condemned rather than welcomed the attempt made by the *Oxford History* to see history in a fresh light. His reaction to *The shaping of South African Society 1652-1829*, which appeared in 1979, likewise showed little positive appreciation of the innovative nature of the work.[32]

Some other themes

Much attention has been devoted in this chapter to the Great Trek. The Second Anglo-Boer War was the other major theme of Afrikaner nationalist historiography. This, like the Great Trek, was by no means the preserve of

Afrikaner historians, and in more recent years the major contribution to the study of the Second Anglo-Boer War has been in English.[33]

In the course of this chapter some works dealing with the Second Anglo-Boer War have been mentioned, such as those of G. D. Scholtz. The Second Anglo-Boer War was a major rallying point for young Afrikaner nationalism, with the concentration camps in the forefront as a major grievance against the English – the camps had replaced Slagtersnek as a rallying cry.[34] As recently as the 1960s the State Historian of the four-volume history of the Second Anglo-Boer War,[35] portrayed Afrikaner history as a struggle against "foreign domination", a fight between nationalism and imperialism, and one which the Afrikaner should not forget. As he saw it the Anglo-Boer War was an attempt to exterminate the Afrikaner. Such views of the war did not differ all that much from those of Leyds 60 years earlier.

But these were not the only views, and certain Afrikaner historians were prepared to subject aspects of the war to rigorous scrutiny. Albert Grundlingh, in his M.A. dissertation, published as Die "Hendsoppers" en "Joiners"[36] broached the question of Boer traitors, a topic of some sensitivity to Afrikaner nationalists who liked to portray Afrikaner attitudes as monolithic and were reluctant to admit that there were a significant number of Afrikaners who had been less than enthusiastic in the fight against British imperialism.

The Second Anglo-Boer War remained a popular theme among historians. The military side of the war was highlighted in works dealing with individual campaigns or battles, such as Louis Botha and the Natal war front, the situation on the lower Tugela in February 1900, the battle of Spioenkop. Other works include the position of the Afrikaners in the Cape during the war and the trials of rebels; numerous publications deal with the reminiscences and memoirs of Boer leaders.[37] D. W. Krüger in his Die ander oorlog[38] handled the subject of public opinion in England with regard to the war.

There were, of course, many other topics that became the subject of historical inquiry. Some of them were obvious attempts at making history serve current political ends. One who, like Preller, came strongly under the influence of National Socialism, was J. Albert Coetzee, whose Potchefstroom doctoral thesis, Politieke groepering in die wording van die Afrikanernasie was published in 1941. Coetzee saw the history of South Africa as the history of the coming into being of a new nation – the Afrikaners. He put forward the view that the primary units of the human species were nations, each of which had a specific destiny. The Afrikaner's destiny was to bring Christian civilisation to South Africa and to control the country. This destiny would only be fulfilled when the Afrikaner had created an independent republic in South Africa, free from ties with Britain.

P. van Biljon's Grensbakens tussen Blank en Swart, was a 1937 University of Stellenbosch doctoral thesis published in 1947. White and black each had its own destiny, and their respective destinies could only be fulfilled if they were separated from each other geographically, in their own territories. But the main obstacle to this was the collusion of philanthropic missionaries and British commercial imperialism, which wanted to exploit the valuable South African market and which propagated the idea that black and white could be brought together into a single unity. It was the conflict between these two principles that had led to the Great Trek – the Afrikaner government of South Africa had a duty to restore the principle of segregated territories that had been wrongly channelled in another direction by these alien forces. Thus did van Biljon make history serve the needs of a developing Afrikaner ideology.

Constitutional and other political developments in the ranks of Afrikaners in the republics have been a prominent theme. Administrative systems and political institutions came under the microscope; the church, missionary societies and education were not neglected either. So far, only biographies of Voortrekker leaders have been mentioned, but there were also studies of other historical personalities; the history of language and literature was also examined. Although not covered very extensively, matters such as railway development and farming were also subjects of research.[39]

Afrikaans works on South African history gave very little attention to blacks. When blacks came into these histories, they did so only when their activities impinged on white consciousness, when they thwarted white aspirations for an abundant supply of cheap labour, or hampered the progress of "civilisation". Blacks were treated in early historiography mainly as a military threat, cattle thieves, vagrants, or more positively, as potential converts. They were two dimensional figures as they moved across the pages of historical works written by whites. There are some studies that deal with relations between various groups of blacks and various groups of whites, or with aspects of policy towards the blacks, or the Indian "question", but virtually nothing that deals with black societies in their own right, or as part of a common society.[40]

Old-style histories that pretend that blacks were only marginal to the history of South Africa continue to be published. *Five Hundred Years: A history of South Africa*, edited by Professor C. F. J. Muller, and published in both Afrikaans and English editions in 1967 and 1969 respectively, relegated the African side of the story to an Appendix. In a later edition in the early 1980s even this concession to the majority of the population of the country was absent in what was an unashamedly white history, written with the specific aim of recounting "the activities and experiences . . . of the white man in South Africa". So even in the early 1980s a white history could still be passed off as a history of South Africa, with the first chapter being devoted to "Explorers and circumnavigators of the Cape", as if nothing of any consequence in the "history of South Africa" had occurred before then.

With a few exceptions, the topics researched were taken from the nineteenth century and were specifically *Afrikaans*. The establishment of Union in 1910 did not really become a popular subject among Afrikaners, and such works as have been done focus almost exclusively on political relationships between whites. A few biographies of relevance to the period after 1910 have been undertaken, and deal with Afrikaans leaders such as Hertzog, Malan, Strijdom and Verwoerd. D. W. Krüger's *The age of the generals* discusses South African history during the period it was dominated by Louis Botha, Jan Smuts and Barry Hertzog. A more recent work is J. P. Brits's authoritative study of Tielman Roos.[41] The mineworkers strike of 1922 has recently been the subject of historical inquiry.[42] The heavy concentration among Afrikaner historians on political history and the lives of political and military leaders has meant that social and economic history has been very neglected. A recent attempt to fill the gap is a study of the Afrikaners in Johannesburg.[43]

Many of these Afrikaans works were so loaded down with detail and so closely focused on local archives that they lost sight of the wider picture, so that often one could not see the wood for the trees. As an example of this one may take S. L. Barnard's and A. H. Marais's *Die Verenigde Party: Die groot eksperiment* (1982), a useful work if one wants to know where any particular United Party leader was on a specific day, which meeting he was addressing, but is otherwise largely devoid of insights, particularly with regard to the period in which the United Party formed the government of the country. Far more detailed, exhaustingly so, and in line with the Afrikaner's vision of his past, is *Die Nasionale Party*, a research project of the University of the Orange Free State's Institute of Contemporary History, and edited by J. H. le Roux and P. W. Coetzer. By 1987 four volumes had appeared, dealing with events up to 1940. A further two volumes are planned, which will take the narrative up to 1961.

It is worth noting that although Afrikaners have written about non-Afrikaners, such as J. S. Bergh's work on Charles Brownlee and P. H. Kapp's contributions on Dr John Philip,[44] while the work by Barnard and Marais on the United Party cited above includes both Afrikaners and English, in general there are remarkably few Afrikaans works that deal with any broader issues outside the Afrikaner fold. Thus there are no equivalents in Afrikaans of M. Roberts and A. E. G. Trollip's *The South African opposition, 1939-1945: An essay in contemporary history* (London, 1947), T. R. H. Davenport's *The Afrikaner Bond: The history of a South African political party, 1880-1911* (Cape Town, 1966), or C. T. Gordon's *The growth of Boer opposition to Kruger, 1890-1895* (Cape Town, 1970). Two more recent works that have made contributions to the history of the Afrikaner are T. Dunbar Moodie's *The rise of Afrikanerdom: Power, apartheid, and the Afrikaner civil religion* (Berkeley 1975), which deals with the civil religion of the Afrikaners in the 1930s, and Irving Hexham's *The irony of apartheid: The struggle for national independence of Afrikaner Calvinism against British imperialism* (New York, 1981), which traces the origins of Christian Nationalism in the early part of the 20th century.

* * *

There were attempts at seeing South Africa within a broader context. A notable attempt in this direction was made in 1951 when 25 contributors produced *Geskiedenis van Suid-Afrika* in two volumes under the editorship of A. J. H. van der Walt, J. A. Wiid and A. L. Geyer, but the result was not a meaningful integrated image of the past that gave due weight to a wide variety of factors. The quality of the contributions and the basic assumptions of the authors, although all of them saw their subjects broadly speaking through Afrikaner nationalist eyes, were too different to give any unity to the work as a whole. The way the South African past was divided, chronologically in the first volume, and thematically in the second, only added to the fractured picture that emerged. To coincide with the 1952 Van Riebeeck Festival, the five-volume *Drie eeue: Die verhaal van ons vaderland* appeared, the main contributors being A. J. Böeseken, D. W. Krüger and A. Kieser. It was a "popular" history. The three-volume *Kultuurgeskiedenis van die Afrikaner* was published in 1950 under the editorship of C. M. van den Heever and P. de v. Pienaar.

This Afrikaner-centric history became very local, almost parochial, and little was done to take cognisance of the wider background to South African history. In 1924, however, S. F. N. Gie in his *Geskiedenis vir Suid-Afrika* tried to fit South African history into the framework of European history, though he did not succeed in integrating South African history into the European past; what he really did was to present a parallel picture of what was happening in South Africa and Europe at the same time. The vital element of the interaction of Europe and South Africa was missing. An attempt to consider the wider picture was the 1957 *Portugese ontdekkers om die Kaap* of Dr W. J. de Kock.

The demythologising of part of the Great Trek saga has been mentioned. Another area in which an attempt has been made to penetrate beyond the myths is the work of two members of the Heese family. In 1973 J. A. Heese published *Slagtersnek en sy mense* and in 1984 his son, J. H. Heese, published *Groep sonder grense: Die rol en status van die gemengde bevolking aan die Kaap, 1652-1795.*

AFRIKANER HISTORY AT THE CROSSROADS

Professor F. A. van Jaarsveld's swift, often bewilderingly rapid changes, may be seen, in one sense at least, as symptomatic of the loss of direction of Afrikaner historians as a whole, and their search for something new to replace their old values, which are increasingly seen to be irrelevant in the present situation in South Africa. In articles and books since the 1970s, van Jaarsveld has been pleading for renewal, his message being that Afrikaans historical writing is in a crisis as a result of methodological "petrification" and the failure of historians to recognise the demands of a modern, industrialised South Africa.

The Afrikaners' use of the past was primarily a functional one and it served them well as they sought to maintain their identity in the face of British culture. But with the coming of a republic in 1961, which appeared to be the glorious triumph of a long term Afrikaner struggle to throw off foreign shackles, Afrikaner urbanisation and the emergence of a well-to-do class, nineteenth century rural republican values no longer had the same relevance or appeal for Afrikaners – in short, their view of history had outlived its usefulness. "The Afrikaner had won the constitutional struggle against the Briton", van Jaarsveld wrote in his analysis of the situation, "but at the very moment that he was about to reap the rewards of his victory in a new Republic, he stood confronted with the challenge of a non-white majority, which, in conjunction with the outside world, threatened to deprive him of his gains . . . A national myth has already become established – that South Africa is an innocent nation and the victim of attack in an evil world; and that attempts to solve the racial problem by territorial divisions or separate development are 'misunderstood'."[45]

Conservative Afrikaners attempted to restimulate Afrikaner nationalism by returning to the Afrikaners' past, but that past no longer had any appeal for the majority of Afrikaners. The urban Afrikaner could not associate himself with that past, or if he did, it did not seem to say anything to him. Afrikaner nationalism had needed the stimulation of a white English political opposition and British imperialism. But the white English opposition in South Africa itself has crumbled, British imperialism has disappeared from Africa. With the withdrawal of Europe from Africa, which began with the independence of the Gold Coast as Ghana in 1957, Africa was no longer seen as an appendage of Europe, but as an area of study in its own right. The struggle of the blacks in Africa towards independence was now a theme that historians in newly independent states began to tackle. The focus became black nationalism, and instead of themselves being seen as the victims of imperialism, the Afrikaners found themselves portrayed as imperialists and oppressors.

The situation in which South Africa found itself at the end of 1987, in the midst of a state of emergency that showed no signs of being lifted, rendered the Afrikaner's nationalist vision of his past increasingly irrelevant. As a guide to the present and the future, to see South African history in terms of the struggle of Afrikaner nationalism to fulfill its destiny, makes no sense at all. From the perspective of 1987 the Nationalist Party victory at the polls in 1948 and the advent of the republic in 1961 have lost much of the significance that they appeared to have in the 1960s.

The dilemma in which Afrikaner historiography found itself was complicated at the same time by the fact that while they were becoming aware that their own particular view of the past was a poor guide to the present or to the future, their methodology was also being challenged. The type of themes that were relevant for Afrikaners were the state, politics, diplomatic relations, the study of volk heroes. This was in line with the sort of themes being studied in Europe, with scientific methods grounded in Ranke. But the study of history in Europe underwent a change after the Second World War. The "political" and "national" themes were replaced by themes that seemed to have a particular relevance for an urbanised and industrial world, and attention was given to phenomena like class structures and anonymous historical processes. A Europe that was increasingly socialist placed more emphasis on socio-economic developments, on the lives of ordinary men and women, on their activities as farmers and labourers, on the way they made ends meet or did not make ends meet, on what occupied their thoughts, on their cultural activities. No longer were the comings and goings of the great the principal subject of research. To study these mass phenomena, historians in Europe borrowed the techniques of the social sciences, and history thus became an interdisciplinary study. Narrative history was eclipsed by the impersonal and collective, studied quantitatively rather than qualitatively. In the studies of English-speaking historians working on South African topics, the centre of the stage came to be held not merely by ordinary people instead of prime ministers and Voortrekker leaders, but by black people in particular.[46]

And just to add to the Afrikaner's problems of adjusting to a new historical scene, was the fact that much of these new preoccupations of historians were clothed in neo-Marxist language and class analysis. It was not enough that South Africa, as nationalist politicians and generals kept telling them, was facing a determined onslaught from the communist world, aimed at bringing South Africa to its knees; as historians, they had to face a similar onslaught, and it seemed to them as if the two were linked, that much of the new history emanating from the neo-Marxist camp had a revolutionary aim.

So the Afrikaner found his old vision of South African history, the history of the struggles of the Afrikaners to maintain their own identity and achieve victory for their republican ideals, outdated. But the new methods and emphasis on the lives of ordinary people caught up in urbanised and industrialised South Africa, likewise passed the Afrikaner by. His isolation from the European community of scholars seemed complete.

The question then was, where do we go from here? In his *Moderne geskiedskrywing* (1982) van Jaarsveld called for renewal, not only because of his conviction that Afrikaans historical writing had serious shortcomings, but also as a result of the recent constitutional changes in the country. It is this call that has aroused the misgivings of some of the younger Afrikaner historians about the possible direction in which Afrikaner historiography is moving. Although van Jaarsveld did not link his plea for change solely to the new political dispensation, his statement that there was a need to re-examine the past in the light of the new political developments, has made this aspect the one which commands most attention.[47]

Although there is much disagreement about the true nature of the new constitutional dispensation, with many people writing it off as "cosmetic" and others saying that the changes, in fact, entrench apartheid, the fact remains that to the large majority of Afrikaners the changes are seen as the beginning of a new era of power sharing, with Indians and Coloureds at any rate, and a new acceptance of the permanence of urban blacks and of the necessity for making some arrangement to accommodate their aspirations. In this new climate, where there is undoubtedly more contact across the colour line, prohibition on inter-racial mixing and marriages has been repealed and there is more freedom of association, the Afrikaner finds himself at the crossroads. The unrest in black townships that reached a highpoint in Soweto in 1976, and which, after simmering for a number of years flared up into the worst unrest ever in 1985, and the declaration of a countrywide state of emergency in 1986, also had a profound effect on Afrikaner thinking. The long-term future of the whites in South Africa, in isolation from other groups, could no longer be taken for granted. Afrikaner historiography, no less, finds itself at a major junction.

Some young Afrikaner historians believe that van Jaarsveld's plea for renewal carries within it the very reasons why Afrikaans historical writing finds itself in a dilemma, for he links his cry for renewal to government policy. Van Jaarsveld seems to suggest that historians can help to make it easier to carry out government policy, saying that knowledge about the mentality and modes of thought of various peoples can help to smooth relations and execute government policy.[48]

It has been argued that the effects of the debate preceding the introduction of a new South African constitution are already evident in that in the new climate the old "traitorous liberal" Afrikaner figures of the past are being brought in from the cold, and being given a new respectability. For example, men like landdrost Maynier of Graaff-Reinet, reviled in Afrikaans history books for standing against the "volkswil" and championing the rights of the Khoikhoi, and Andries Stockenström, another defender of black interests on the frontier, have been held up as examples of Afrikaner racial tolerance, as representatives of an honourable Afrikaner tradition.[49] Albert Grundlingh warns that if Afrikaans history is written to serve the ends of the recent political developments "one may find histories in which, for example, greater attention is paid to the 'Coloureds', but the history of their constant exploitation and intermittent resistance glossed over in favour of an approach which emphasises their 'positive' contribution to white South Africa in perhaps the economic and military fields – an interpretation which would be in keeping with their envisaged role as junior partners in government. Such a history, in which the 'Coloured' past would be distorted through extreme presentism . . . would also parallel recent trends in education for Blacks, where there has been a move towards the retribalization of the past, the establishment of a new ethnic idyll in which black heroic figures are invoked to legitimize separate development. Thus Shaka is divorced from his historical context, and he, instead of H. F. Verwoerd, is seen to be the original 'creator' of 'homelands'."[50]

Indeed, Grundlingh, who wrote the above early in 1984, was not far off the mark, and in a interview with a newspaper reporter in February 1985 van Jaarsveld said of the 1809 Caledon laws to prevent vagrancy among the Khoi-Khoi, that in essence the laws "were not a question of compelling the brown people of the Cape to work for whites. It was a question of labour. Instead of emphasising the pass laws to keep the brown people under control what can be emphasised is labour, especially after slavery [the slave trade] was abolished in 1807. One must emphasise that the Khoi-Khoi was a separate group living in South Africa which integrated into white society. One can present the history of the brown people in a very positive way, and tell the pupils how they contributed to the building of the farms in the Cape."[51]

Although individual Afrikaners have spanned the ideological gulf, there are no signs that as yet Afrikaans historians as a whole are prepared to confront the implications of the revisionist history of the past 15 or so years squarely. Since 1945, Afrikaner historians have become increasingly isolated from the international community, and instead of proceeding abroad for post-doctoral work as they had done before the war, this was conducted entirely in South Africa. This was one reason for the lack of contact with the wider international historical community, while increasing political alienation widened the gulf. The fact that historians outside South Africa could not read Afrikaans also hampered dialogue with historians elsewhere.

So the new ferment that began in historical circles between so-called "liberal" and "radical" historians from the early 1970s did not make its mark among Afrikaners, the majority of whom continued with their traditional research methods and themes. The quantitative methods and other methodological influences that gained favour as a result of closer contact between history and the other social sciences passed them by, as did the socio-economic themes to reflect a modern industrialising South Africa. Most of their research was concerned with the Afrikaner and the whites in general. Of course there had always been a certain amount of disagreement, at times fundamental, between the conservative and liberal viewpoints, but it was the emergence of the radical, revisionist point of view that caused such trauma for Afrikaans historians.

Many Afrikaans historians, allowing themselves to be led by Harrison Wright's arbitrary classification of South African historians, in the late 1970s and early 1980s in particular rejected the "new" history as "radical", "activistic" and "neo-Marxist" – these very labels were for many Afrikaner historians enough to bring the new works under suspicion and to cast doubt on their "scientific" nature. It was the linking of the new approach to Marxism that presented the biggest stumbling block for Afrikaners, for while some of them see the need for renewal in the historical work being done by Afrikaners, they remain distrustful in the extreme of Marxist influences. In his more recent works, and no doubt as a result of the obvious success enjoyed by radical history in some spheres, van Jaarsveld has become far more attuned to the new approach, although still abhorring anything smacking of Marxism. A close reading of van Jaarsveld suggests that his detestation of Marxist history is surpassed only by his rejection of liberal histories. The Marxists, one may infer, are to be preferred to the liberals, for in their interpretation of South African history they place the blame for the mistakes of the past on world capitalism and the representatives of capital in South Africa, whereas the liberals place the blame squarely on the Afrikaners.[52]

Van Jaarsveld's arguments are sometimes tortuous, and while criticising the approach of the historical materialists, he also calls for work to be undertaken on rural depopulation and urbanisation, poverty, the social history of the Voortrekkers and the Boer republics, and for attention to be given to rural agricultural history. He encourages Afrikaners to adapt their working methods and adopt an interdisciplinary approach. Afrikaners are exhorted to work structurally and to research historical phenomena that affect the people at large, thus to move away from "political" history. He concludes that as long as a structure is not made absolute, as in the case of Marx, it may be a valuable supplement for the historian and increase the potential for historical interpretation; for he admits that for too long collective phenomena that fall beyond the scope of individual decisions have been neglected. He also makes the point that the concept of class, a central feature of Marx's theory, may be used as an accepted reality without having to accept Marxism. In fact, van Jaarsveld has, on occasion, argued, although not very convincingly, that Afrikaners have indeed already tackled socio-economic themes, pointing to studies on the movement of Afrikaners away from rural areas to the urban centres, and the position of blacks on the Rand.[53]

But despite his pleas for renewal, van Jaarsveld has not been particularly sympathetic towards those Afrikaners who have struck out boldly in a new direction. Afrikaners like Hermann Giliomee have been prepared to face the challenge presented by Marxist writing, and to examine the evidence rather than engage in emotional outbursts or pretend that historical materialism has nothing to say to them. Giliomee has not so much rejected a class analysis of Cape history as given a new sophistication to the analysis of the racial origins of South African society. From the tone of his discussion of the 1979 publication, *The shaping of South African society, 1652-1920*, edited by Giliomee and the American historian, Richard Elphick, it is clear that van Jaarsveld does not approve of the fact that Giliomee sees white domination of blacks as a major theme of our history, or of his portrayal of the Cape as part of the world capitalist economy. In Giliomee's work, van Jaarsveld complains, no longer is the Cape regarded primarily as the fatherland of the white population group, but as a typical colonial society comprised of "white settlers" or colonisers on the one hand, and the indigenous colonised and slaves on the other. This society is then compared to other slave societies in America and elsewhere. The history of the white free burghers, including the Patriot movement of the late eighteenth century, is stripped of its heroic and democratic dimensions. The whites, and here is the nub, are seen as "white settlers" in someone else's land. Van Jaarsveld sees what he calls the "derived" views of Giliomee as springing from the fact that Giliomee was a "follower" of Leonard Thompson, whom van Jaarsveld describes as "a British immigrant who became professor of history at the University of Cape Town, and voluntarily left the country because of his frustration at the coming of a republic in 1961, establishing himself in America where he was seen as a 'refugee' of an unfree apartheid-land."[54]

Giliomee has indeed been in the vanguard of those who have broadened the study of South African history by viewing it in its widest possible context. The uniqueness of the South African situation, so often accepted as an article of faith rather than analysed, is put to the test by Giliomee. He has studied comparable elements in other societies to see what was common and what was different in their experiences, and in this way has come to some conclusions about the South African situation. A few examples from his inaugural address in mid-1986 will demonstrate the possibilities inherent in casting one's net beyond the shores of South Africa.[55]

Giliomee compares South Africa and Brazil as two colonial slave societies. He describes South Africa as having "a racial order of society in contrast to Brazil's class order". In South Africa it is *whites* who have power, wealth and status, and blacks who generally do not. In Brazil it is *rich* people who have status and power, and *poor* people who generally do not. He addresses himself to the question as to why the two societies should have developed so differently. He suggests that the essential difference was the growth in Brazil in the nineteenth century of a large coloured or mulatto population which filled intermediate positions between those occupied by either colonists or slaves. There were many such posts in the army, and numerous employment opportunities as slave overseers, hawkers or artisans. A large number of such jobs, taken together with a dearth of white women, explains the growth of a large coloured group, the existence of which "made it impossible to apply racial discrimination consistently."

In the Cape however, there were few such intermediate positions. The Dutch East India Company did little to encourage diversification. Few slaves were manumitted, while by the eighteenth century the shortfall of white women had been eliminated. Thus, whereas in 1690 there were 100 women to 260 men, by 1770 there were 100 women to every 140 men. Women were sufficiently numerous to act as a serious brake on the conclusion of mixed marriages. Giliomee points out that a distinction should be made between women of northern European extraction who found their way to North

America, Australia and South Africa, and those of Southern European descent who went to Brazil and elsewhere in South America. Giliomee writes that "The former had a relatively stronger social position and status in family and public life and were much more able to prevent their sons from marrying non-whites or their husbands from legitimising the offspring of their extramarital affairs." It has been observed that women "generally tend to refrain from matrimonial and social relations with men of a social and cultural stratum lower than their own . . . Undoubtedly this attitude would also have expressed itself in severe pressure exerted by women on their children to marry within the white group."[56]

It is not only with Brazil that parallels are sought. The position of the whites in the Cape is compared to that of the whites in Virginia, and he comes to the conclusion that in both societies there was "no need to curtail white liberties. Politically the class divisions among whites in these colonies steadily lost political significance from the early eighteenth century onwards and a spirit of white egalitarianism was born". But this could only apply while there was still land to be had for the taking. If there had been no more land available after 1700 the lower class whites would have had to find employment working for others, and South Africa would have had a very different history. But the availability of land on the frontier gave "middle-ranking" farmers the opportunity of becoming independent farmers. Egalitarianism on the frontier was confined to whites as the frontier was too poor to produce equality and freedom for everyone. In this respect, Giliomee feels that it should be compared with the American South rather than the West.

In South Africa the need for a large intermediate group like that in Brazil only emerged with the rapid economic growth of the 1960s. Blacks came to fill the vacuum, but the growth was not maintained in the 1970s, and the number of jobs did not increase. Giliomee sees the sudden halting of this process as being partly responsible for South Africa's turmoil in the mid-1980s.

He writes that in South Africa in the early 1960s "there was the almost universal expectation that education would create a responsible [black] middle class with a stake in the system and a vested interest in capitalist development and political stability. However, in the past two decades, evidence from the Third World has demonstrated overwhelmingly that education has a stabilizing function only when there is a rapid increase in job opportunities and an efficient labour market. When these conditions are not met education can be a major obstacle to development and stability". He then illustrates this with reference to Lebanon.

If Afrikaner nationalists were unhappy with the view of South Africa as a typical colonial and slave society, they were even more so with the direct attacks on the nationalist version of Afrikaner history. The appearance in 1983 of *Afrikaner political thought: Analysis and documents,* vol. 1, *1780-1850,* by Hermann Giliomee and his Stellenbosch colleague, André du Toit, was a direct challenge to those Afrikaner historians like Scholtz who had projected the Afrikaner republican ideal backwards into the eighteenth century. Although Afrikaner nationalism only had its origins in the late nineteenth century it soon appropriated the entire history of the Afrikaner, reforming it in its own nationalist image. This, the authors declared, "leads to a double distortion of Afrikaner history. On the one hand, everything that does not fit the nationalist paradigm is excised from Afrikaner history as such. Since Afrikaner history is defined in nationalist terms, that which does not fit the latter does not belong to the former."[57]

If van Jaarsveld was critical of the University of Stellenbosch historian, he was even more so of du Toit, a political philosopher who, van Jaarsveld informs us, had "ventured into the field of history without having received training in the subject". Du Toit, in van Jaarsveld's view, was an outspoken propagator of Thompson's ideas, on Thompson's advice having taken up the subject of the demythologising of Afrikaner history. Du Toit's attacks on the traditional portrayal of Afrikaner history, says van Jaarsveld, should be seen in the light of the fact that du Toit was regarded in Stellenbosch as a "far left opponent of the National Party . . . with a grudge against Afrikanerdom".[58]

Du Toit has spelled out his attacks on Afrikaner nationalist history in some detail, demythologising Afrikaner history and encouraging Afrikaners to view their past afresh. He attacks what he calls the myth of the " 'Calvinist' origins of Afrikaner nationalism". In terms of this myth, in the isolated conditions in the interior the cultural traits which the Afrikaners brought over with them from Europe became "fixated . . . as a kind of 'primitive Calvinism' which eventually gave rise to a Chosen People ideology among early Afrikaners. It is held that Afrikaner ideas on their calling and mission served both as a central motivation for the Great Trek and as legitimations for the conquest and subordination of indigenous peoples, thus providing the root sources for modern Afrikaner nationalism and the ideology of apartheid."[59]

Du Toit argues that "in actual fact there is very little, if any, contemporary evidence that might count unambiguously in support of the presence among early Afrikaners of a set of popular beliefs that could be recognised as 'primitive Calvinism' nor of any social ideology of a Chosen People with a national mission." It was the English missionary David Livingstone who in the middle of the nineteenth century put forward the view that the Afrikaners considered themselves as a Chosen People. Theal took this over in his history, further popularising it. Du Toit says that the Afrikaners themselves only began expressing this view towards the end of the nineteenth century, with the emergence of Afrikaner nationalism. Although Afrikaner nationalism only developed after 1880, Afrikaner nationalists projected this nationalism backwards in time to incorporate the entire history of the Afrikaner. They reinterpreted the whole history of the Afrikaners in the nationalist idiom. When these nationalists "claimed the existence of, inter alia, an authentic core tradition of Afrikaner Calvinism and the prevalence of Chosen People notions among early Afrikaners this served the purpose of providing a myth of origin for latterday Afrikaner nationalism."[60]

Du Toit sees very great danger in the appropriation by the nationalists of the whole history of the Afrikaner, and the insistence by the nationalists that "Afrikaner survival cannot be separated from continued Afrikaner nationalist power". He describes "the identification of all Afrikaners and of Afrikaner culture generally with Afrikaner nationalism" as "highly problematic". "The very politics of ethnic mobilization which in the past had served the Afrikaner cause so well for so long must now appear to involve very high risks. At a general and somewhat abstract level the risk is that if Afrikaner culture is tied too closely with the power structure of the apartheid state then a possible failure of Afrikaner nationalist power must involve more than a political defeat only. A Black 'liberation movement' coming to power and sweeping away what it regards as the oppressive structures and symbols of apartheid can hardly be expected not to regard the cultural institutions, social values and ethnic symbols of Afrikaners as very much part and parcel of that same oppressive system. After all, they would only be taking Afrikaner nationalism at its own word." Du Toit questions whether this "Nationalist strategy of harnessing all possible Afrikaner cultural and ethnic resources to bolster Nationalist power" is really necessary. He asks whether it would "not better serve the cause of long term Afrikaner survival to sever this close identification of Afrikaner cultural concerns and the policies and racial ideologies espoused by the National Party, if that could be done?"[61]

Giliomee and du Toit, both now at the University of Cape Town, for the most part do not publish their work in Afrikaans. They have become active participants in the debate, seeking the widest possible audience for their views, increasingly addressing their conclusions to the more receptive ears of their English-speaking colleagues in South Africa and abroad.[62]

NOTES

1 F. A. van Jaarsveld, *The Afrikaner's interpretation of South African history*, Cape Town, 1964, p. 55.

2 Ibid., p. 35.

3 S. J. du Toit, *Di geskiedenis van ons land in di taal van ons volk*, pp. 84, 89-90. The translations are taken from L. M. Thompson, "Afrikaner nationalist historiography and the policy of apartheid", *Journal of African History*, 3(1), 1962, p. 128, and van Jaarsveld, *The Afrikaner's interpretation*, pp. 39–40.

4 Translated and quoted in van Jaarsveld, *The Afrikaner's interpretation*, p. 42.

5 F. J. le Roux and D. J. van Zyl (eds), *'n Eeu van onreg*, Cape Town and Pretoria, 1985. In the introduction Professor van Zyl discusses the question of authorship. The information on Roos's expertise in numismatics and the positions he held later in government do not come from van Zyl's introduction but from a review of the book by A. H. Duminy in the *South African Historical Journal*, 18, 1986, pp. 252-253. See also W. J. de Kock, *Jacob de Villiers Roos 1869–1940: Lewenskets van 'n veelsydige Afrikaner*, Cape Town, 1958.

6 Reitz, F. W. (issued by), *A century of wrong*, London, 1900. The quotes come from pp. 6, 26, 43 and 98.

7 Van Jaarsveld, *The Afrikaner's interpretation*, pp. 43-44.

8 Ibid., pp. 94–104.

9 F. A. van Jaarsveld, "Afrikaner historiography" in D. I. Ray, P. Shinnie and D. Williams (eds), *Into the 80s: The proceedings of the Eleventh Annual Conference of the Canadian Association of African Studies*, vol. 1, Vancouver, 1981, p. 237.

10 Van Jaarsveld, *The Afrikaner's interpretation*, pp. 7, 57, 125.

11 See pp. 112–115.

12 This discussion on Preller is based on the following sources: B. J. Liebenberg, "Gustav Preller as historikus", *Tydskrif vir Geesteswetenskappe*, 15(4), December 1975, pp. 243–250; J. J. Oberholster, "Die neerslag van die Romantiek op ons geskiedskryw ng: Gustav S. Preller", *Tydskrif vir Geesteswetenskappe*, December 1966, pp. 312–321; D. W. Krüger, "G. S. Preller as geskiedskrywer", *Koers*, 11(6), 1944, pp. 195–198. The above sources are all reprinted in B. J. Liebenberg (comp.), *Trends in the South African historiography*, Unisa, Pretoria, 1986. See also van Jaarsveld, *The Afrikaner's interpretation*, pp. 78–80.

13 Van Jaarsveld, *The Afrikaner's interpretation*, p. 85.

14 C. F. J. Muller, "Die Groot Trek", *Die hervertolking van ons geskiedenis*, Communications of the University of South Africa, B. 19, Pretoria, 1963, reprinted in Liebenberg, *Trends*, pp. 58–91.

15 See also van Jaarsveld, *The Afrikaner's interpretation*, pp. 81–82.

16 Ibid., pp. 89–90.

17 Ibid., Quoted by van Jaarsveld, pp. 87–89.

18 B. J. Liebenberg, "Professor C. F. J. Muller en die Groot Trek", *Kleio*, 12(1 & 2), 1980, p. 8. This is reprinted in Liebenberg, *Trends* pp. 92–98.

19 C. F. J. Muller, *Leiers na die noorde*, Cape Town, 1976, p. 16.

20 G. D. Scholtz, *Die oorsake van die Tweede Vryheidsoorlog 1899–1902*, vol. 1, Johannesburg, 1947, p. 23.

21 J. A. Wiid, "Die betekenis van die Groot Trek", *Die Huisgenoot*, December 1938 – Groot Trek-gedenkuitgawe, pp. 19–21.

22 A. J. H. van der Walt, J. A. Wiid and A. L. Geyer (eds), *Geskiedenis van Suid-Afrika*, vol. 1, Cape Town, 1951, p. 264.

23 *Die Huisgenoot*, 16 December 1977 (pp. 52–55), 27 January (p.4), 17 February (p.4), 10 March 1978 (pp. 4,6).

24 Van Jaarsveld's address "A historical mirror of Blood River", was later published in A. König and H. Keane (eds), *The meaning of history*, Unisa, Pretoria, 1980, pp. 8–59. An Afrikaans version, "Historiese spiëel van Bloedrivier", was published in *Die evolusie van apartheid*, Cape Town, 1979, pp. 46–89.

25 F. A. van Jaarsveld, "P. J. Merwe: Ondersoeker van die Afrikaner se landelike pioniersgeskiedenis" in *Wie en wat is die Afrikaner?*, Cape Town, 1981, pp. 129–175. This was based on a tribute to van der Merwe delivered at the University of Stellenbosch on 14 October 1979.

26 Foreword to P. J. van der Merwe, *Die Matabeles en die Voortrekkers*, Archives Year Book for S.A. History, 1986, vol. 2.

27 F. A. van Jaarsveld, "G. D. Scholtz: Historikus van en vir die Afrikaner" in *Die evolusie van apartheid*, pp. 90–121. Taken from a paper delivered at the Randse Afrikaanse Universiteit in August 1975 on the occasion of Scholtz's 70th birthday.

28 See J. P. Brits's review of volume 8 of *Politieke denke* in *Kleio*, 17,1985, pp. 124–127.

29 Johannes du Bruyn, "F. A. van Jaarsveld: Afrikaner historikus en vernuwer", *Historia*, 27(1), 1982, p. 59. Du Bruyn is here referring to van Jaarsveld's *Afrikaner quo vadis?*, Johannesburg, 1971.

30 Du Bruyn, "F. A. van Jaarsveld", p. 61.

31 Some of van Jaarsveld's more recent works that may be classified as having a largely theoretical or historiographical content include: *Geskiedkundige verkenninge*, Pretoria, 1974; *Die evolusie van apartheid*, Cape Town, 1979; *Wie en wat is die Afrikaner?*, Cape Town, 1981.

These books consist of articles previously published in journals, and addresses delivered on various occasions. His two most recent full-length books are *Moderne geskiedskrywing: Opstelle oor 'n nuwe benadering tot geskiedenis*, Durban and Pretoria, 1982 and *Omstrede Suid-Afrikaanse verlede: Geskiedenisideologie en die historiese skuldvraagstuk*, Johannesburg and Cape Town, 1984.

32 Van Jaarsveld, *Geskiedkundige verkenninge*, pp. 166-186 and *Omstrede verlede*. See also B. J. Liebenberg, " 'Omstrede Suid-Afrikaanse verlede' – 'n omstrede boek deur 'n omstrede skrywer", *Kleio*, 17, 1985, pp. 104–114.

33 S. B. Spies, *Methods of barbarism? Roberts and Kitchener and civilians in the Boer republics, January 1900 to May 1902*, Cape Town, 1977; T. Pakenham, *The Boer War*, Johannesburg, 1979; P. Warwick and S. B. Spies (eds), *The South African War, 1899-1902*, London, 1980; P. Warwick, *Black people and the South African War, 1899–1902*, Cambridge, 1983.

34 In bitter vein is J. C. Otto's, *Die konsentrasiekampe*, Cape Town, 1954. An academic study is J. L. Hattingh's *Die Irenekonsentrasiekamp*, Archives Year Book for S. A. History, 1967,1.

35 J. H. Breytenbach, *Die geskiedenis van die Tweede Vryheidsoorlog in Suid-Afrika*, 4 vols, Pretoria, 1969–1977.

36 A. M. Grundlingh, *Die 'Hendsoppers' en 'Joiners': Die rasionaal en verskynsel van verraad*, Cape Town, 1979.

37 A. G. Oberholster (ed.) *Dagboek van H. C. Bredell, 1900-1904*, Pretoria, 1972; M. C. E. van Schoor (ed.), *Dagboek van Hugo H. van Niekerk*, Christiaan de Wet-Annale, vol. 1, 1972; T. van Rensburg, *Oorlogsjoernaal van S. J. Burger 1899–1902*, Pretoria, 1977; O. J. O. Ferreira (ed.), *Krijgsgevangenskap van L. C. Ruijssenaers, 1899–1902*, Pretoria, 1977; A. G. Oberholster (ed.), *Oorlogsdagboek van Jan F. E. Celliers 1899–1902*, Pretoria, 1978. The above works listed as published in Pretoria form part of a Source Publications series of the Human Sciences Research Council. Not all these diaries and memoirs are published in Afrikaans. See for example, J. P. Brits (ed.), *Diary of a National Scout: P. J. du Toit 1900–1902*, Pretoria, 1974 and O. J. O. Ferreira (ed.), *Memoirs of General Ben Bouwer*, Pretoria, 1980. A number of studies on the military aspects of the war have appeared in various volumes of the Archives Year Book for S. A. History. They include: C. M. Bakkes, *Die militêre situasie aan die benede-Tugela op die vooraand van die Britse deurbraak by Pietershoogte (26 Februarie 1900)*, 1967, vol. 1; J. H. Cilliers, *Die slag van Spioenkop (24 Jan. 1900)*, 1960, vol. 2; J. H. Snyman, *Rebelle-verhoor in Kaapland gedurende die Tweede-Vryheidsoorlog met spesiale verwysing na die militêre howe (1899–1902)*, 1962; J. H. Snyman, *Die Afrikaner in Kaapland, 1899-1902*, 1979, vol. 2. Other works dealing with the conduct of the war are C. J. Barnard, *Generaal Louis Botha op die Natalse front, 1899-1900*, Cape Town, 1970; C. J. Scheepers Strydom, *Kaapland en die Tweede Vryheidsoorlog*, Cape Town, 1947. A number of unpublished theses on the war have also been undertaken: J. P. Botha, *Die beleg van Mafeking tydens die Anglo-Boereoorlog*, D. Litt. et Phil., Unisa, 1967; J. L. Basson, *Die slag van Paardeberg*, M. A., U. P., 1971; M. H. Buys, *Militêre regering in Transvaal, 1900–1902*, D. Phil; U. P., 1972; H. A. Mocke, *Die slag van Colenso, 15 Desember 1899*, M. A., U. P., 1966; C. W. Zollner, *Duitsland en die Tweede Vryheidsoorlog*, M. A., U. O. V. S., 1968.

38 D. W. Krüger, *Die ander oorlog: Die stryd om die openbare mening in Engeland gedurende die Tweede Vryheidsoorlog*, Cape Town, 1974.

39 For a list of works in these spheres consult the relevant sections in C. F. J. Muller, F. A. van Jaarsveld, Theo van Wijk and M. Boucher (eds), *South African history and historians – a bibliography*, Pretoria, 1979, which includes works published up to March 1979.

40 See C. C. Eloff, *Die verhouding tussen die Oranje-Vrystaat en Basoetoland, 1878-1884*, Archives Year Book for S.A. History, 1980, vol. 2 and also *Oranje-Vrystaat en Basoetoland, 1884-1902: 'n Verhoudingstudie*, Pretoria, 1984. Other Archives Year Book contributions include C. J. Beyers, *Die Indiërvraagstuk in Natal, 1870–1910"*, 1971, vol. 2; J. J. Fourie, *Die koms van die Bantoe na die Rand en hulle posisie aldaar, 1886–1899*, 1979, vol. 1; O. Geyser, *Die Bantoebeleid van Theophilus Shepstone, 1865-1875*, 1968, vol. 1; F. J. Nöthling, *Die vestiging van gekleurdes*

in en om Petoria, 1900–1914, 1982, vol. 1; H. J. van Aswegen, *Die verhoudinge tussen Blank en Nie-Blank in die Oranje-Vrystaat, 1854–1902,* 1971, vol. 1; A. J. van Wyk, *Dinuzulu en die Usutu-opstand van 1888.* 1979, vol. 1. See also A. J. Potgieter, *Die swartes aan die Witwatersrand, 1900–1933,* D. Phil., R.A.U., 1978; J. P. F. Moolman, *Die Boer se siening van en houding teenoor die Bantoe in Transvaal tot 1860,* M. A., U.P., 1975.

41 D. J. Kriek, *Generaal J. B. M. Hertzog se opvattings oor die verhoudinge tussen die Afrikaans-en Engelssprekendes na uniewording,* D. Phil, U. P., 1971; J. D. Naude, *Generaal J. B. M. Hertzog en die ontstaan van die Nasionale Party, 1913-1914,* Johannesburg, 1970; D. W. Krüger, *The age of the generals: A short political history of the Union of South Africa, 1910-1948,* Johannesburg, 1961; J. P. Brits, *Tielman Roos: Sy rol in die Suid-Afrikaanse politiek, 1907-1935,* Pretoria, 1979. (A revised version of this book has recently been translated into English. *Tielman Roos: Political prophet or opportunist?,* Pretoria, 1987.)

42 A. G. Oberholster, *Die mynwerkersstaking Witwatersrand, 1922,* Pretoria, 1982.

43 E. L. P. Stals (ed.), *Afrikaners in die Goudstad,* vol. 1, *1886-1924,* Cape Town and Pretoria, 1978.

44 J. S. Bergh, *Die lewe van Charles Pacalt Brownlee tot 1857,* Archives Year Book for S. A. History, 1981; P. H. Kapp, *Dr. John Philip: Die grondlegger van liberalisme in Suid Afrika,* Archives Year Book for S. A. History, 1985, vol. 2. Kapp's unpublished M. A. (Stellenbosch University 1966) and D. Phil. thesis (Stellenbosch, 1974) also dealt with Philip.

45 Van Jaarsveld, *The Afrikaner's interpretation,* pp. 148–149.

46 See *inter alia, Moderne geskiedskrywing,* pp. 141–142 and *Omstrede verlede,* pp. 26–32.

47 Johannes du Bruyn, "F. A. van Jaarsveld – en 'n nuwe Afrikaanse geskiedskrywing?", *Kleio,* 16, 1984, pp. 64–72.

48 Ibid.

49 Bloomberg made these claims in *The Cape Times,* 3 January 1984; the report was taken over by the *Rand Daily Mail* of 20 January 1984. Albert Grundlingh, "George Orwell's 'Nineteen Eighty-Four': Some reflections on its relevance to the study of history in South Africa", *Kleio,* 16, 1984, pp. 20-33, believes that Bloomberg "overstates his case and is clearly only partially informed." (p. 27) Grundlingh writes that if Bloomberg was referring specifically to the work of A. du Toit and H. Giliomee, *Afrikaner political thought: Analysis and documents,* vol. I, *1780-1850,* Cape Town, 1983, "to claim that they are writing a history to specifically demonstrate the non-racial aspect of the Afrikaner past which would be acceptable to all shades of 'verligte' Afrikaners, with the further suggestion that their history is in line with government thinking, is not merely simplistic but untrue." Grundlingh goes on to write that: "The innovative work of Du Toit and Giliomee has moved far beyond any variation of 'verligte' Afrikaner thinking." (p. 27)

50 Grundlingh, "George Orwell's 'Nineteen Eighty-Four' ", p. 28.

51 *Sunday Express,* 3 February 1985.

52 See van Jaarsveld, *Omstrede verlede,* pp. 72–88, 107–108 for positive remarks about the radicals, and pp. 57–66 for his opinion of the liberals. See also Liebenberg, " 'n Omstrede boek", pp. 108–109.

53 See *Moderne geskiedskrywing,* p. 129 and *Die indiwidualiserende of strukturele benadering tot die geskiedskrywing en onderrig in Suid-Afrika?,* Ninth Biennial National Conference of the South African Historical Society, 17–19 January 1983, RAU, Conference Papers, part 1, p. 49. Some of the works cited by van Jaarsveld to back up his assertion are Nöthling, Moolman, Potgieter and Fourie cited above in fn 40. Whatever the merits of these works, however, they can hardly be classified as studying mass phenomena or structural history in a way that has been informed by urbanisation studies as reflected in Europe or by the radicals in South Africa.

54 Van Jaarsveld, *Omstrede verlede,* pp. 66–67.

55 "The history in our politics", Inaugural lecture, University of Cape Town, 11 June 1986, New Series, no. 126.

56 The above statistics and observations about women do not come from Giliomee's inaugural lecture but from his article "Eighteenth century Cape society and its historiography: Culture, race, and class", *Social Dynamics*, 9(1), 1983, pp. 25–26.

57 Du Toit and Giliomee, *Afrikaner political thought*, p. xv.

58 Van Jaarsveld, *Omstrede verlede*, pp. 67–71. The basis for van Jaarsveld's anger was that a lecture he had delivered in 1961 and which appeared in translation in 1964 as "The ideas of the Afrikaner on his calling and mission" (*The Afrikaner's interpretation*, pp. 1–32), should have been subjected to such rigorous scrutiny twenty years later by du Toit when he was a Fellow of the Southern African Research Program at Yale University. See André du Toit, "Captive to the Nationalist paradigm: Prof. F. A. van Jaarsveld and the historical evidence for the Afrikaner's ideas on his Calling and Mission", *South African Historical Journal*, 16, 1984, pp. 49–80, and F. A. van Jaarsveld, "André du Toit: Much Ado about Nothing", p. 81.

59 Du Toit, "Captive to the Nationalist paradigm", p. 49.

60 Ibid. pp. 50–51; See also du Toit, "No Chosen People: The myth of the Calvinist origins of Afrikaner nationalism and racial ideology", *American Historical Review*,88(4), 1983, pp. 920–952.

61 "Facing up to the future: Some personal reflections on the predicament of Afrikaner intellectuals in the legitimation crisis of Afrikaner nationalism and the apartheid state", *Social Dynamics*, 7(2), 1981, p. 10.

62 For more details about Giliomee's views on the nature of Cape society, see fn 49 above and also The pre-industrial Cape in Chapter 5.

4 The liberal trend in South African historiography up to the end of the 1960s

All the schools of historical writing discussed thus far shared a common anti-black tendency. The histories they produced were written from a white viewpoint. South Africa was not unique in this respect, and it was only after the First World War that this attitude began to be challenged in the world at large.

In South Africa the impetus to take a fresh look at the role of blacks in history was provided by rapid industrialisation and the social and economic problems that attended it. The gradual political awakening of the blacks and the new situation of black poverty alongside and in competition with white poverty in the economically integrated urban communities, whence both white and black had been drawn from the rural districts, became a major focus of attention among certain liberals concerned about black welfare. And it was this that gave rise to another strain in South African historiography which emerged in the 1920s and which has come down to us as the liberal school. It was, therefore, a contemporary issue that directed the attention of liberals to the past. The liberal historians were part of the wider community of liberal economists, anthropologists, sociologists and political scientists that came into being between the two world wars, the intellectual foundations for which were classical liberalism.

Unlike the other strains of South African historical writing, the liberal historical school had very few practitioners. Foremost among them were

W. M. Macmillan and his pupil, C. W. de Kiewiet. They wrote at a time when many thinking people were concerned about the effects of urbanisation and industrialisation in South Africa. Macmillan wrote in the 1920s, in an age of depression, focusing attention on the emergence of the Poor White and the resurgence of Afrikaner nationalism after the Second Anglo-Boer War. De Kiewiet wrote a few years later, and his preoccupations were a little different. He was also writing for a different audience, and while Macmillan's work was aimed at a South African audience, and white policymakers in particular, de Kiewiet in his principal work was looking at South Africa in the context of the British Empire when the threat of Hitler to that empire loomed large.

What made their work so different from other writing on South African history was that it dealt with social and economic issues and gave greater prominence to the role of blacks in South African history. What was new in their vision was their rejection of a "segregated" history and the placing of people of colour in an integrated past as a factor of equal importance with whites. These liberal historians rejected racial discrimination and evinced a great concern for black welfare, but they did not actually study black society itself. The distinction other historians had made between "savagery" and "civilisation" was retained; they still thought in racial categories, and saw indigenous black culture as inferior. For the most part they did not see black society as something that should be retained – they envisaged an ideal future in which the blacks would be "civilised" and integrated into white society. They did not regret the break-up of indigenous African society. Thus, Macmillan saw the frontier wars of the nineteenth century as "mere stages in the triumph of the robust colonial community over the forces of barbarism which hemmed it in".[1] Eric Walker, another liberal historian, in a lecture in 1930 noted, without concern, that a "tribal system . . . always crumbles sooner or later in contact with Western civilization, even when it is not forcibly broken up".[2] In many ways their attitude was paternalistic, but they at least dispelled the notion that South African history could be studied without making blacks an integral part of it; there was interaction between whites and blacks. Interaction was to become a major theme in liberal history, not only at the time but into the 1970s.

W. M. MACMILLAN

The Rev. John Macmillan, having graduated from King's College, Aberdeen, and taken a four-year training course for the ministry of the Free Kirk, was ordained in 1864, and almost immediately sent off to Madras in India where he spent 14 years as a teacher at the Free Kirk mission. When he returned to Scotland in 1878 he had a wife and six children. William Miller, the seventh child, was the youngest by seven years, and was born in Aberdeen in 1885. Back in Scotland, John taught, even venturing to open his own private school.

When he was forced to close it, he decided to come to South Africa, eventually taking charge of the Eikenhof residence at Victoria College in Stellenbosch; he supplemented his salary by teaching.[3]

The red-headed, six-year-old William Macmillan initially settled in well in his new home, but after the Jameson Raid which divided the community politically, he found himself "one of a small minority at loggerheads with the great majority of my schoolfellows". His brother Bertie, who enrolled with the Volunteers at Somerset East to fight on the British side in the Anglo-Boer war, was killed in action in September 1900.[4] The feeling of cultural alienation as a member of a small Scots community in an overwhelmingly Afrikaner nationalist town, helped to give form to Macmillan's views, as did the history he learnt in Stellenbosch. Clearly he did not enjoy his lessons on the Black Circuit and Slagtersnek where "the obvious culprit was meant to be the British Government", nor the story of Retief's murder, where "this time the villain was the African", nor the assurances by his teachers "in one and the same breath that the Trekkers had no slaves, but that they deeply resented the way in which compensation for slaves had been paid out by the British government". "I chafed as I have done ever since," he wrote, "at the favourite national stories of what very unfairly was then called Cape history."[5]

While he was still a student at Victoria College, it was decided by the family that William would go to Aberdeen and read for the four-year M.A. course. However, before these plans could be put into effect, he was awarded a Rhodes scholarship after Tobie Muller, father of Professor C. F. J. Muller, had turned it down as he was opposed to everything for which Rhodes had stood. Macmillan went to Merton College, Oxford, in 1903, where he was persuaded to read History rather than the Classics he had originally decided upon.[6]

Macmillan absorbed the political and intellectual climate of Britain and this was to have a decisive influence on his views. English working class consciousness had lost its earlier revolutionary flavour, and there was great support for reformist and evolutionary change. In common with this trend, Macmillan developed a strong distaste for revolutionary method and practice. The way to change things was gradually, through modifying existing institutions. This fitted in well with the favour enjoyed by Fabianism at this time, another major influence on Macmillan. The Fabians, and Macmillan with them, believed that all that was required to effect change was to demonstrate your case with convincing evidence, that this would persuade others of the proper course to follow. Much attention was being given at the time to studies in poverty in London and York; this was the time of the east London settlement of Toynbee Hall where in the words of Jeremy Krikler, "people from the universities could live with the poor, study their conditions and attempt to improve the latter's lives and education. The political boundaries of this milieu were clearly demarcated: a belief in the necessity for social change was to be inculcated in the powers that were through the collection and presentation of data which revealed the extent of poverty and the gains in 'efficiency' that would be achieved through the expansion of the state's powers: the existing institutions of society – and the modified versions of them produced by their subsequent evolution – were to be the agents of such change; and, finally, such change as was effected was to be incremental, and gradual in nature – i.e. evolutionary rather than revolutionary."[7]

Macmillan became very involved with the question of poverty. Besides the above influences, he also had direct experience of poverty. His own immediate family struggled financially. His father could not make ends meet after the closing down of the Eikenhof residence, and was unable to find adequate work in the hostile postwar atmosphere of Stellenbosch.[8] William was also deeply moved by a visit to his uncle's family in the Scottish Highlands where they were crofters. He was made painfully aware of the plight of tenant farmers in general.[9]

Macmillan took up divinity studies in Aberdeen in 1906. In 1910 he had a short but very important stay at the König Wilhelm University in Berlin, where he immersed himself in studies on poor-relief. He decided to complete his divinity studies at Glasgow, but he had been there only a few months when he heard that an application he had sent to Rhodes University College in Grahamstown had been successful.[10]

By February 1911 he was back in South Africa, in charge of the newly created Department of History and Economics at Rhodes University College. Macmillan by this time had very firm ideas. He had a great "belief in the power of ideas buttressed by convincing evidence, in the need to achieve change through the reforming of existing institutions and policies, a distrust of revolutionary theory and method, a firm adherence to a socially-concerned Christianity."[11]

His concern for the poor soon found expression in the publication in 1915 of *Sanitary reform for Grahamstown* and *A study of economic conditions in a non-industrial South African town*. The latter of these two publications was in many ways a classically Fabian tract in that the data were presented with a view to persuading the authorities to take social action, reforms were suggested in which local government featured prominently, and which, it was envisaged, could take place within the existing structure of society. In this essay, Macmillan was concerned above all with the white poor, and he argued that it was competition in the market place from cheap, unskilled black labour that tended "to degrade whites down to and below their level". The answer was for white working men and the white public to organise themselves to prevent this.[12] He was soon to be arguing on very different lines.

In 1917 he left Grahamstown for Johannesburg, taking up the Chair of History at the School of Mines, which in 1922 was to become the University of the Witwatersrand. Between 1919 and his departure from South Africa in 1932, he published a number of studies, four of which in particular were very well received in English-speaking intellectual circles. Although he only died in 1974, after he left South Africa he published nothing of significance on South Africa, and his career abroad was something of an anticlimax as far as the study of South African history is concerned. He taught for some seven years at St. Andrews University in Fife (1947-1954) and had a short spell after that at the University of the West Indies in Jamaica. He was awarded honorary doctorates by the universities of Oxford in 1957, Natal in 1962 and Edinburgh in 1973.[13]

The slums of Johannesburg with their large number of poor Afrikaners who had moved there from the rural areas of the country drew his attention. In particular, the situation "invited research into the conditions in the backveld from which they came."[14] Making good use of sociology and economics in particular, Macmillan undertook an interdisciplinary study of South African social history, widening the traditional vision of "sources" to include field trips to the areas about which he was writing. He gained intimate firsthand knowledge of the conditions of the Afrikaner rural poor. The results of his research were given in a series of five public lectures and were published in what Macmillan refers to as "a large [104-page] pamphlet".[15] In this work, *The South African agrarian problem and its historical development* (Johannesburg, 1919), Macmillan traced the question of poverty from the days of the Dutch East India Company through to twentieth century urbanisation.

This was a very important work for the development of rural historical studies, and is recognised as such in the tribute paid to it by William Beinart and Peter Delius in the mid 1980s.[16] Although he did not give any real attention to the class struggle, in other ways he did raise issues that later researchers, right up to the 1980s, were to take up and explore further in different ways. He pointed to the connection between the injection of capital and the commercialisation of agriculture on the one hand, and the increasing landlessness and poverty of many rural Afrikaners on the other. He emphasised the effects of the discovery of minerals on the sudden emergence of industrial centres with the creation of new markets, which could not be satisfied by the predominantly subsistence type agriculture practised by most Boers. Agriculture had to be capitalised and commercialised. This issue was to become a major theme of historical studies in the 1970s and 1980s.[17] The roots of the "agrarian problem" were the problems faced by Afrikaners in adjusting to the new situation. Because of the legacy of attitudes formed on the frontier, they were ill-equipped to make the adjustment. Used to regarding large farms as a birthright, isolated from markets, dependent upon slave or cheap Khoi labour, which gave them an aversion to heavy manual labour, at least in the service of someone else, the Afrikaners experienced great difficulty in making their way in the mining towns of an industrialising South Africa. The transition to capitalism brought with it a crisis for many of the rural poor.[18]

At first Macmillan concentrated on the Poor Whites, but because of the integrated nature of the economy he soon became convinced that it was not possible to separate the study of the Poor White from that of the Poor Black. *The South African agrarian problem*, he wrote, "marked a turning point in my life and work, a diversion from poor-whites to poor-blacks". His personal ventures into the field made him realise that he had thus far "dealt with only the tip of the iceberg".[19] He now stressed that the welfare of the coloured races was irrevocably tied up with the welfare of the whites as well, that they could not be separated. The history of South Africa was the history of its total population, he asserted. He was the first historian working on South African history to see this. He was also the first historian to move away from the political history that dominated historical studies. "The South African history," he wrote, "which is really significant is that which tells us about the everyday life of the people, how they lived, what they thought, and what they worked at ... what they produced and what and where they marketed, and the whole of their social organisation."[20] This has a very modern ring to it, and anticipates the way historians in the 1970s and 1980s were to define social history. Macmillan believed that the key to the racial question was to be found in the spheres of land and labour.

Although *Complex South Africa: An economic footnote to history* (London, 1930), was not his next work, it is convenient to discuss it here as it was an analysis along the same lines as the *Agrarian problem*, except that it focused on the black poor. He emphasised the socio-economic base of history, paying particular attention to race contact in the towns and the rural areas. As in the case of the rural white population, dispossession was at the root of the plight of rural blacks. But the situation had been far more traumatic for the blacks: "They have been called upon, in the space of three generations or less, to adapt themselves, somehow or other, to live on what may be put at a rough estimate at about one-fifth of the land they lately held."[21]

Macmillan had come a long way since his Grahamstown publications, where he had implied that the Poor White problem was caused by competition from blacks and that the remedy was somehow to prevent this. In *Complex South Africa* he argued that "the Poor Whites are little more than the 'reservoir' of unemployed to be found wherever Western industrialism has dislocated an old agrarian system." This was the basic problem, and the solution lay in agrarian reform. But if in fact competition from cheap and unskilled black labour was a factor in the making of the Poor White, the answer was to improve the lot of the blacks, rather than to cry for the institution of industrial colour bars, "which can only, and do all too effectively, make the natives poorer still, and to that extent an ever more real 'menace' ".[22]

Macmillan became very involved in workers' movements, lecturing on labour relations. In the early 1920s he became president of the Workers' Educational Association, later also extending his activities to black workers, particularly those unionised by the Industrial and Commercial Workers' Union.[23] On occasion he had interviews with both Smuts and Hertzog. In a meeting with Hertzog, Macmillan referred to the terrible conditions he had found in the reserves, "suggesting that if they [the government] thought I had misread the conditions in the Reserves I should be happy to pursue my investigations in any other district of their own choosing". This had a sequel when in 1925 the government took Macmillan up on his offer and told him he could make a study of the Herschel district, an isolated part of the north-eastern Cape, with the Free State on one side of it, and the mountains of Lesotho on the other. Macmillan undertook the survey, but hearing nothing at all from the government on the matter, he published his findings on the Herschel district in *Complex South Africa*.[24] Macmillan's study of conditions there was largely responsible for Colin Bundy in the 1970s taking the Herschel peasantry as a case study in his work on the South African peasantry.[25]

In the mid-1980s *Complex South Africa* is recognised as the first study to have examined the nature of white accumulation in the countryside and also the changing nature of exploitation and relationships on farms. Even in the 1980s Macmillan's work embodies insights that "remain striking". Although historians who followed Macmillan took up his lead, incorporating strands of his synthesis into their work, "few drew on the full range of his ideas".[26]

* * *

Macmillan said of the South African historical scene that "what passed for South African history when I started my teaching career was the tale of the conquest of a new country by lonely and scattered white men, with no regard whatever for the interests or the fate of Bushmen, Hottentots, the mixed races or the African tribes. History was the triumph of white power in crushing all these peoples. In this strictly 'authorised version' of the story there was one white man, a missionary leader, who remembered the weaker peoples and incurred terrible ill-will in his attempts to help them: as a result of his efforts this man, the famous Dr. John Philip, had become the personal devil of the drama, blamed for everything that went wrong."[27]

It was this version of South African history that Macmillan was intent on revising. The papers of the early nineteenth century missionary Dr John Philip were made available to Macmillan in 1920, and his study of these gave a new direction to his research; he worked on these papers until the middle of 1923, using this hitherto untapped source in the writing of *The Cape Colour Question* (London, 1927). Macmillan believed that "the generally received view of Philip's work sorely needs restatement, for it is still that of his colonial contemporaries and opponents. Even historians have accepted, endorsed, and enlarged the categorical charge of his opponents, that Philip was 'more a *politician* than a missionary'."[28] But Macmillan was not so much concerned with Philip himself as with Philip's policies. His defence of the missionary against the charges that had been levelled by the likes of Theal and Cory was secondary to his principal aim of persuading the powers that be to apply to the Africans "the enlightened principles which underlie the advance towards political and social freedom in the Cape Colony before 1853".[29] He was thus addressing himself to the policymakers in the government.

The book was the fruit of the conviction that an understanding of the "Colour Question" insofar as it related to the indigenous Khoikhoi was "an indispensable preliminary to any hopeful approach to the complex problems that remain".[30] *The Cape Colour Question* is more a study of the political and legal status of the Khoikhoi than it is of the Khoikhoi themselves. He saw the legislation of 1809 and Ordinance 50 of 1828 as representing the conflicting principles of oppression and freedom. In the 1920s it seemed to Macmillan that South Africa was taking the road of the 1809 Khoikhoi codes rather than what he saw as the enlightened road of Ordinance 50. He had a touching faith in the ability of legislation to put matters right. All it required were the necessary laws to secure people's rights. Until recently Ordinance 50 was seen as a great triumph of philanthropism, engineered by Philip, in freeing persons of colour from the restrictions imposed on them and in granting them equality with whites before the law.[31] He advocated the application of Ordinance 50 as a solution to South Africa's problems. The message of *The Cape Colour Question* is that the position of the Coloureds had been satisfactorily secured by granting them legal equality – this was also the way to solve the colour question as it concerned the Africans. It was the freedom that had been granted to the Khoikhoi that, despite their "generations of slum life", was allowing "civilisation" to triumph among their descendants. He warned that as far as seeking an acceptable solution to the complex situation posed by the Africans, whites should realise that "civilisation" lay in granting freedom, not in imposing the sort of restrictions that had been attempted in the case of the Khoikhoi and which had failed. "To-day it is the far more numerous 'Bantu' who are being uprooted from the land and driven into the slums", he wrote. "Even while the descendants of the "Hottentots' [Khoikhoi] are being legally recognized as a 'civilized' people, the old restrictions, and new, are being urged, in much the same terms, as a cure for the 'lazy thieving vagabondage' of the Natives; as if similar measures had not been tried, and failed, in the eighteen-thirties. There is the old pathetic faith in the efficacy of a Pass Law, and in new and more oppressive restrictions like a 'Colour Bar'." As far as Macmillan was concerned: "If by general agreement the 'Eurafricans', with all their manifest weaknesses, rank to-day as a civilized people, this is the result not of the policy of restrictions, but of the measure of freedom allowed them."[32]

Bantu, Boer, and Briton: The making of the South African Native problem (London, 1929), was likewise based on the voluminous Philip papers. Macmillan analysed Philip's views and applied them to modern South Africa, studying them in the light of the new cultural climate brought about by urbanisation and the resurgence of Afrikanerdom. Macmillan examined white conquest of the blacks, the way they were dispossessed, their resistance on the moving frontier to white penetration, the way the blacks lost their land and were transformed into farm labourers or poor peasants living in reserves that were unviable, and their consequent migration as wage earners to the cities where they came into competition with poverty-stricken rural whites. Macmillan saw in the application of the principles of freedom and equality that had guided Philip the solution to the problems of South Africa. He was a pragmatist, who found in the past lessons that could be applied in the present. For him, history was a social science with practical applicability; he was thus an activist, trying to persuade the government to abandon segregation, and he did not hesitate to make the transition from historical conclusion to current political comment. In *Bantu, Boer, and Briton* he thus advocated the extension of the franchise to certain Africans: "The Natives ready to qualify for the jealously guarded privilege of the franchise are a mere handful," he argued, "and their number increases all too slowly. Wisdom demands that White South Africa bind this handful to itself, and secure their co-operation in devising a policy for leading up to civilization the great backward masses who must, for many years, remain incapable of independent political thought and action."[33]

Bantu, Boer, and Briton was the last book to be based on Philip's papers, for in 1931, two years after its publication, this valuable collection was lost in a fire that destroyed part of the library of the University of the Witwatersrand.[34]

Macmillan claimed that his study was "a radically new interpretation of known and generally undisputed facts", in that "the predicament of the natives, involved perforce in a struggle with encroaching European colonists, has never been taken into account".[35] He saw the frontier not as the meeting place between civilised and uncivilised, Christian and heathen, but as a clash of pastoralists over land and cattle. He gave attention to the blacks, but not in their own right. Jeff Peires was thinking of Macmillan in particular when he wrote of the liberal attitude towards the Xhosa that: "The mighty edifices of Theal and Cory have fixed the predatory barbarian image of the Xhosa in the school-books up till now. The liberal historians of the twentieth century, although sympathetic to the Xhosa, still concentrated on the Colonists. Instead of rapacious Xhosa depriving peace-loving Colonists of their cattle, they tended to depict rapacious Colonists depriving peace-loving Xhosa of their land."[36]

He took sides with the blacks in their actions on the frontier. He admitted that they stole cattle. However, "it was not a lust for colonial cattle, but a passion to defend their own land which kept chiefs like Maqoma, the most 'turbulent' of the Xhosa leaders, in chronic unrest".[37] Blacks are seen as victims, suffering injustice, pawns in the hands of the whites. He had a rather idealistic and romanticised image of Africans. Africans "as a people are long-suffering and law-abiding . . . singularly amenable to just government. They have never known slavery. Even in defeat which left them powerless and without status their leaders put their case not only with eloquence and logic but with amazing good humour and tact. They are kindly and cheerful and, as in the famous story of the last days of Dr. Livingstone, faithful – a people most suitably summed up in the untranslatable German word, *gemüthlich*."[38]

What was also new in his history was that he gave a prominent place to interaction between white and black on the frontier – Theal and Cory's accounts had been dominated by the frontier wars. Macmillan showed that this was only one side of the coin, that there was also much peaceful co-existence – strong economic bonds, and white dependence upon black labour betokened peaceful relations. Macmillan also maintained that Theal and Cory had overemphasised the racial aspect of conflict; but as he saw it, it was not race but land that had been at the heart of the conflict.

With typical Fabian naivety, he believed that all that was necessary to set things right was to show the authorities what was wrong, to back it up with convincing evidence. He was thus addressing the powers that be, his message was not directed at rallying the oppressed. He was naive however in this hope that convincing arguments would accomplish what he wanted. In his autobiography written many years later, he seemed to appreciate this. "In my innocence, however," he wrote, "I overlooked the fact that the ruling classes in South Africa have a genius for merely ignoring inconvenient facts, however accurate, and in all these years I never succeeded in making the facts bite. It might have been better had I thrown caution to the winds, and worked for a straight fight."[39]

The Afrikaner community ignored his work and labelled him a liberal and negrophile, an advocate of blood mixing, all of which was more than enough to damn him in their eyes.[40] The views put forward in his books did not find their way into school history textbooks, and those who controlled the syllabi and choice of textbooks determined to keep Macmillan's "heresies" far away from the eyes and minds of the youth. But if one looks in the mid-1980s at the importance accorded to rural studies and to the relationship between "town and countryside",[41] then one can make another evaluation of Macmillan: he pointed the way. More than anyone else, he identified and defined "the agrarian problem". In the 1970s the development of historical materialism and class analysis enabled historians to take his ideas further, to develop and clothe them in a more sophisticated analysis. Macmillan was also the first historian to put the "other side" of the frontier tale, to give another portrayal of the role of missionaries to counter the picture that Theal and Cory had painted. Above all, he was the first historian to treat the history of South Africa as the history of all its people, not just the history of the whites.

C. W. DE KIEWIET

The most extravagant praise for a historian of the liberal school has been reserved for Macmillan's pupil, C. W. de Kiewiet. In 1964 van Jaarsveld described him as "perhaps the brightest star to glow in the firmament of South African historiography", [42] while Christopher Saunders in the mid-1980s wrote of de Kiewiet's *A history of South Africa: Social and economic*, published in 1941, that it "remains one of the most-used general histories" of South Africa. "No other single work by a professional historian on South Africa", he declared, "has been so influential, so often cited and quoted." He believes it is the "single greatest work ever written on South African history."[43]

This claim will not be universally accepted, but it has a certain validity. The book covered the whole of South African history. Although he owed much to Macmillan's pioneering work, and in many respects simply followed his lead, Macmillan's findings were spread over a number of works that covered specific areas of South African history and he did not produce a history of South Africa. Walker's *A history of South Africa*, because of its detail and comprehensiveness, was probably used more by university students and teachers than was de Kiewiet's work, but it did not contain any serious analysis of processes, of what South African history "was all about".

De Kiewiet was born in Rotterdam in the Netherlands in 1902, and came to South Africa with his parents in 1903. His M.A. thesis was burnt in the fire in the library of the University of the Witwatersrand in 1931, and no copies of it apparently survive. Its title was possibly *Government, emigrants, missionaries and natives on the northern frontier, 1832-1846*, which is what appears on the degree certificate, or *Government, colonists, missionaries and natives on the north-eastern frontier and beyond, 1832-1846*.[44] It was supervised by Macmillan. In 1925 de Kiewiet proceeded to the University of London, where he completed his doctorate in 1927 under the tutelage of the well-known Professor A. P. Newton. A slightly revised version of the thesis was published in 1929 as *British colonial policy and the South African republics, 1848-1872*. He demonstrated that South African history could not be studied in isolation, that it could not be divorced from what was happening in Britain itself or in other British colonies. Thus the British withdrawal from the South African interior signalled by the Conventions policy of 1852-1854 was not simply the result of a desire to avoid expense and limit responsibilities. If the Voortrekkers were to be followed, Britain would have to accept responsibility for their actions up to the Equator and beyond. The decision not to assume this responsibility had to be seen in the light of other imperial commitments. In South Africa itself, Sir Harry Smith's eastern frontier policy at the Cape had collapsed, while further abroad the position in New Zealand was precarious, and Britain had also to take into account the effects of the Crimean War and the Indian Mutiny. Nor could the South African situation be reduced to a clash of interests between the British government and the Afrikaners, for the existence of blacks played the decisive role in developments.[45]

In the same year as the above publication de Kiewiet obtained a post in the Department of History of the State University of Iowa. He spent the remainder of his life, with the exception of a number of visits abroad, in the United States. On occasions, however, he contemplated a return to South Africa, in 1934 going as far as to apply for the chair at the University of the Witwatersrand vacated by Macmillan. General Smuts, however, intervened to secure the post for Leo Fouché, the University of Pretoria historian – whose politics were more in keeping with his own than those of the liberal de Kiewiet. When the Wits chair again fell vacant in 1944 he considered putting in an application but was dissuaded from doing so by his wife's reluctance to leave America. By this time de Kiewiet had already been at Cornell University for some three years. He became President of the University of Rochester in 1951, remaining there until 1961.

In the 1930s he returned to London for a spell to continue the research on British colonial policy that he had started with his doctorate. *The imperial factor in South Africa: A study in politics and economics* was the result of these labours and was published in 1937. In this he followed the convolutions of imperial policy up to the 1880s. Further than this he could not go, as the Public Record Office documents beyond the mid-1880s were closed to researchers.

In this book de Kiewiet was at pains to show that Theal had been unfair in his judgement about the ignorant meddling of Britain in South African affairs. He stressed the difficulties facing British officials; although British policy had evinced many shortcomings and they had many failures, the British had acted with "high motives and worthy ends".[46] There was more than blatant imperialism to Lord Carnarvon's federation scheme in the 1870s. The Great Trek and the opening up of the diamond fields had created a demand for land and labour that had resulted in the Africans being crowded into smaller spaces. The frontier wars that seemed to erupt in every direction were the physical evidence of these pressures on the blacks. Only a central authority over the whole country could find a remedy, and Carnarvon's scheme had this in mind. The earlier withdrawal of the British in the 1850s had been a mistake because it had left no central authority that could fill the vacuum caused by the departure of the imperial factor. Federation, de Kiewiet showed, was aimed not at expanding the empire, ut envisaged a possible British withdrawal, once the various communities in the country had come together to act in concert. To the extent that he was saying that the British could consider a withdrawal once they had created the sort of society that would serve their interests, he was anticipating a principal argument of Shula Marks and Anthony Atmore in the early 1970s, and which itself gave impetus to research in a new direction.[47]

Although imperial policy was the central point of focus, and the internal structure of African societies was not studied at the same level and depth as white society, de Kiewiet, like Macmillan, made it clear that black-white relations were important in the study of South African history. Like Macmillan, he believed that Theal and Cory had gone overboard in giving such prominence to the many frontier wars – this had blinded them to an appreciation of the close economic association that had developed between white and black. White dependence on black labour was the most significant social and economic fact in South African history in the nineteenth century.[48]

In October 1937 John Mulgan of the Oxford University Press, wrote to de Kiewiet informing him that they were planning a series of works on British dominions, inviting him to write the book on South Africa. As Mulgan originally envisaged the series, only about a third of each book would be given over to a historical survey, and the bulk of the text would deal with the social, economic and political background to the current situation, "always with reference to the past history and the environment of the country". What had been lacking in the histories thus far written on the dominions was "adequate emphasis on economic history, or . . . sufficient regard to the social and economic history of the outside world". So the book on South Africa would, Mulgan elaborated in a later letter, start with "a short economic history of South Africa, or rather its history with the emphasis on the economic aspects and relating it to the main trend of world economic history which influenced it". The latter half or two-thirds of the book would be devoted to "chapters on the political, social and economic aspects of the country as it is – that is more or less to show how people live and work there, what their economic activities and prospects are, what their political and – in South Africa's case – racial and national problems amount to". It was hoped that the series "would give an intelligent visitor a comprehensive and accurate account of the country, and at the same time would be valuable to students of economics and history here and in the different Dominions".[49]

De Kiewiet agreed to undertake the project, and in discussing it with Macmillan wrote as follows: 'I am going to try to discuss the natives as they really are, indissoluably part of the whole society. That will get rid of what is arrant nonsense, the usual treatment of white progress and conditions in three chapters and the 'Oh and then of course there is the Kafir' sort of final chapter . . . Maybe I had better keep the story sober, and not break any obvious lances. It after all is to be an explanation, something of a textbook, and thus should not belabour men and matters too hard. Anyhow, even a quiet and modest account will be shocking enough."[50]

De Kiewiet was a liberal in the widest sense of the word. Not only did he hold "left-wing" views, but he was above all determined to be as fair in his judgements as he possibly could, to see all sides of the question. "The principal difficulty with any writing on contemporary South African problems", he wrote, "is the extent to which the writer can use, or should use, his critical judgement. The great inequities in social and racial policy tempt one to sharp and critical comment. Sometimes it is even impossible to describe aspects of the native problem without revealing the danger and folly of white policy. My difficulty is therefore avoiding turns of phrase and descriptions which will give the colour of an indictment. But so much of South African life is an indictment that a pure impartiality will not be possible. Wage legislation that would be unobjectionable in New Zealand becomes a two-edged sword in South Africa, and so on."[51]

In the end there was far less on contemporary developments than had originally been contemplated. The work was published during Britain's darkest days of the war and de Kiewiet was exhorted to keep the work as short as possible as there was a scarcity of paper. De Kiewiet felt that there should be a chapter "about South Africa's place in the Empire", but under the circumstances he dispensed with this, and agreed that he would make do with "a very short summary statement by way of conclusion". In the end, not even this was published.

The strong "empire theme" of the series, however, came out in the preface, where he states that the book is "part of the history of the British Empire". It was a time of great crisis for the empire as it faced the threat from Germany in the early days of the Second World War. "The Empire is many things", he wrote, "even as it contains many races. Some things may undergo change. Change has been the essence of the Imperial process. But other things lie beyond the reach of war. They are the imperishable and timeless things . . . The Empire is more than a political system; it is more than an economic structure. It is a spiritual achievement, with the enduring qualities of spiritual achievements, whether in literature, art, science, or in the relations of human beings on the face of the earth."

In the event, only the book on South Africa was published. The publishing firm abandoned its plan for a series on the various dominions. The book appeared in July 1941; it had been reprinted three times by 1950, and continued to be regularly reprinted until 1968. In 1966 a paperback edition was issued. Despite all these reprints, and encouragement from Oxford University Press for de Kiewiet to prepare a new edition, he made no changes to the original text. As time went by he became increasingly tied up in university administration and less involved in history. His last work on South Africa was published in 1956. *The anatomy of South African misery*, a more polemical work, did not entail any further historical research but was the fruit of a series of lectures he delivered.

A history of South Africa: Social and economic enjoyed a flourishing life and became a widely recommended textbook for non-specialist students both in South Africa and abroad. It was the first serious attempt to draw the various disparate social and economic threads of South African history together and to weld them into a eminently readable and coherent tale at a time when political history still reigned supreme. A. J. P. Taylor in reviewing it said:

"The scholarship and penetration give the reader that exhilarating intellectual pleasure which one gets only once or twice in a decade; a mature mind has been stretched to the full and one's own mind has to be equally exerted."[52]

The fact that it was the Oxford University Press, and not de Kiewiet who decided on the emphasis that the work was to be given may suggest that this aspect of liberal historiography did not have its origins in de Kiewiet's mind but was the brainchild of a publisher. But of course de Kiewiet was chosen for the task because of the work he had already done, which was very much in line with what the Oxford Press wanted. It was Eric Walker who had recommended de Kiewiet to the Oxford University Press, and Walker knew that de Kiewiet had, under the guidance of Macmillan, developed an interest in economic history, and that in the chapter that de Kiewiet had written for volume 8 of *The Cambridge History of the British Empire*, he had demonstrated some considerable insight into social and economic issues among blacks in the nineteenth century.

In his *History* de Kiewiet moved away from the imperial policy that had dominated his first two books. In much of his work, by tackling broad social and economic themes, he was following up ideas that Macmillan had first put forward in *The South African agrarian problem* and *Complex South Africa*. Like Macmillan, de Kiewiet elevated racial contact between white and black to a dominant theme in South African history in the nineteenth and twentieth centuries, and he was vitally interested in the question of how the blacks became part of the white community and economically interdependent. De Kiewiet believed "that the leading theme of South African history is the growth of a new society in which white and black are bound together in the closest dependence upon each other".[53]

Macmillan and de Kiewiet, among others, have been singled out for criticism by the radicals of the 1970s for stressing cooperation and ignoring conflict. But perhaps this criticism has been somewhat harsh and sufficient allowance has not been made for the time in which they wrote. The versions of the past handed down by Theal and Cory were the "accepted" tradition, and they laid stress on conflict between black and white, particularly on the frontier, and with regard to cattle. Macmillan and de Kiewiet saw the conflict as being essentially over land. They believed that the theme of race conflict had been overplayed, and they emphasised that there had been much co-operation. Although recognising the importance of race, they did not see it as the motor of history. The radicals of the 1970s would be saying much the same thing, but they would again be giving prominence to conflict, this time conflict between classes rather than races.[54]

But if there were similarities with Macmillan, and in many ways de Kiewiet was simply following where his mentor had already trod, there were also differences. Like Macmillan, de Kiewiet saw trekboer frontier values as being responsible for the backwardness of Boer agriculture. But far more than Macmillan, he also stressed ecology and climate as significant factors in this respect. "South Africa has lived to a dangerous extent upon that part of its capital which is represented by its soil, grass, trees and water. Together natives and whites have dissipated huge resources. The grass-burning that reddened the late winter horizon sent up in smoke the organic matter that should have quickened the soil. When protected by a cover of vegetation, the virgin veld could not be harmed by the most violent deluge that poured upon it. Baked hard by grass fires, trampled down by innumerable hoofs, and laid bare by the grazing of countless mouths, the same veld was helpless before the devastation of thunderstorms. Streams that once came gently from the ground became muddy torrents after each rain. In South Africa rain rarely falls with the gentleness of an English drizzle. Clouds pile in over-topping formations, the heavens crash, and a deluge descends upon the earth. Paths made by stock driven to and from water, cracks produced by drought, valleys that have lost their vegetation are defenceless before the force of rushing water, and become the gullies and 'sloots' that carry off the precious soil . . . The improvidence of men found a cruel ally in drought."[55]

De Kiewiet was also less sympathetic to the missionaries than was Macmillan, and did not lay stress, as did Macmillan, on the "backwardness" of African societies.

One cannot help feeling that there were perhaps more similarities between Macmillan and de Kiewiet, and historians of the 1970s, than the latter care to admit. Macmillan and de Kiewiet both saw the imperial factor as being essentially a beneficial, liberal force, and this is perhaps a major area where there is a significant difference. The discussion of the roots of segregation is another area of difference. The early liberals were not interested in pre-colonial African societies, and in their histories although Africans were given more prominence they were still seen as passive characters, and did not receive the same attention as whites. They assigned a prominent place in history to the role of the individual and to ideas. In all this they differed from many of the radicals of the 1970s.

But, on the other hand, they both examined social and economic history, moving away from the political history that had up to then been so dominant. They were more concerned with the lives of ordinary people, with processes, and they focussed on industrialisation. De Kiewiet concentrated particularly on mining, and labour was seen as a critical area. Both men believed that material considerations were very important, although they would have rejected the radical view that they always outweighed other factors. But like the later historians, they also gave attention to the operation of the environment in their accounts.

The radicals of the 1970s, though, were reluctant to recognise this. Christopher Saunders has gone so far as to argue that even in the major issue between liberals and radicals, namely the relationship between economic growth and segregation (later apartheid) the difference between de Kiewiet and the radicals was more apparent than real. He maintains that although de Kiewiet was convinced that economic growth and segregation were incompatible and that the former would undermine the latter, he was thinking of the long term and appreciated that, in the short term, industrialisation and segregation were not necessarily incompatible.[56]

De Kiewiet has been praised for his "masterly style". Christopher Saunders said that de Kiewiet came to believe that "the way one said something affected what was said, and that all great history was great literature at the same time". In both *The imperial factor* and the *History of South Africa*, Saunders says de Kiewiet "showed an ability to include rich detail without overburdening his text, and to hold the reader's interest by the sheer power and eloquence of his prose. Macmillan's sentences tend to be long and complex. De Kiewiet was economical in his use of language, and he knew how to vary the length of his sentences, to carry the reader and the argument forward. He used short and pithy sentences to particularly good effect in his *History* . . . Published as long ago as 1941, it remains the greatest single work of historical synthesis to have appeared in this country to date, and at the same time the work of history which most deserves the encomium, 'literary masterpiece'.[57]

But not everyone was equally enthusiastic about his style. Another liberal historian, Phyllis Lewson, was critical of his "fine writing". She accused him of overwriting, as when he spoke in *The anatomy of South African misery* of how "the splendid stepping ox, the pride of every farmer who had a well-trained team, became a lumbering beast that impeded progress".[58] There is no doubt that on occasion "fine language" can be made to obscure or to cover up the failure to provide a reasoned explanation. The liberals have been accused of doing this. De Kiewiet's oft-quoted statement that "South Africa has advanced politically by disasters and economically by windfalls",[59] has been cited as an example of the way in which an epigram has been used as a substitute for an alternative explanation.[60]

J. S. MARAIS

An Afrikaans-speaking historian who was strongly influenced by Macmillan was J. S. Marais. Like Macmillan, Marais came to the conclusion that the history of South Africa was the tale of race relations, contact between race groups of different civilisation, and their gradual coming together into a single, although heterogenous community. He saw race as the real problem in South African affairs. In *The Cape Coloured People 1652-1937*, published in 1939, he wrote that the "Coloured do not appear to differ from us to-day in anything except their poverty, and that they share with our large army of poor Whites. As far as 'civilised standards' are concerned, all that need be said is that many of the Coloured live in a more 'civilised' way than many Europeans in South Africa. The prejudice against them is therefore not based only on their poverty . . . The unfortunate truth is that the South Africans' colour prejudice is, indeed, based on colour, or to speak more accurately, is derived from an unshakable belief in the essential inferiority of the Coloured man's 'blood' ".[61] This book is a social history in the same mould as the work of Macmillan, and specifically analyses the origins, development and fate of South Africans of mixed descent; his work is, however, as much concerned with policy towards the Coloureds as it is with the history of the Coloureds themselves.

Marais was also among the first historians to challenge the vision of the frontier that Theal had bequeathed to South Africans. In *Maynier and the first Boer republic*, published in 1944, he made a minute examination of the documents in the Cape archives relating to the turbulent events on the eastern frontier in the period 1778-1802, and effectively demonstrated that Theal's boast that he wrote "without fear, favour, or prejudice, to do equal justice to all", was not true. In making his claim, Theal said that he could "without laying myself open to the accusation of vanity, confidently place my work before the public . . . as a true and absolutely unbiased narrative". Marais demonstrated quite clearly with regard to the period 1778-1802 that Theal's work could not stand up to the cold scrutiny of facts; he showed that Theal was heavily prejudiced in favour of the white settlers on the frontier.

In particular, Marais directed his attention to the person of H. C. D. Maynier, Graaff-Reinet's second landdrost and later Resident Commissioner on the frontier, reviled by generations of Afrikaner historians as an intolerable liberal who caused the Boers great inconvenience and suffering by refusing to heed their complaints but having a ready ear for the grievances of Khoikhoi and Xhosa. Marais wrote of Maynier that he "has been perhaps the most misunderstood figure in South African history", and that it was Theal who had been responsible for this, having portrayed Maynier in such unflattering terms as a negrophile who could see no wrong in anything Khoikhoi or Xhosa did and no good in anything the Boers did. In the case of Maynier, Marais claimed, Theal "plays the part of the Public Prosecutor. He is concerned to obtain a conviction, and denies to the jury the opportunity of hearing the defence. The culprit's case is allowed to go by default. And the reason for such unprofessional conduct? Can it be that the defence was so unpalatable that it turned the stomach of the white settlers' apologist?"[62] A second impression of this slim volume appeared in 1962.

But although Marais was a liberal in the sense that he defended the humanitarian Graaff-Reinet landdrost against the picture of him drawn by Theal, and gave attention to the Coloured people of the Cape, he was also a liberal in the wider sense that he attempted to see all sides of the question, to do equal justice to all points of view, and this quality of his work comes out most clearly in his last major work, *The fall of Kruger's republic* (Oxford, 1961), in which he traces the events leading up to the Second Anglo-Boer War of 1899-1902. *Maynier and the first Boer republic* was a most detailed study, which it no doubt had to be if Theal were to be judged on the specifics of the way he had interpreted the documents. This work on the four years preceding the outbreak of war in October 1899 is equally detailed in its concentration on the quarrels and negotiations that preceded the outbreak of hostilities.

The most valuable and original part of the book is that which deals with the development of the situation after the arrival of Milner as High Commissioner in April 1897. This is no white-washing of Milner or the mining houses, and his analysis of events met with the approval of Afrikaner nationalist historians. His interpretations of the developing situation is not so very different from that put forward by Afrikaner nationalist writers, although it is not written from that point of view. In fact van Jaarsveld believed that his conclusions confirmed those arrived at by G. D. Scholtz a decade earlier, namely that Chamberlain's, and even more so Milner's, fear that an armed and Afrikaner-dominated Transvaal would eventually lead to the creation of an independent Republic of South Africa, played a crucial role in bringing about the war. Marais was, however, taken to task for not acknowledging Scholtz's work or any other Afrikaans works that had made a contribution to the subject. His sympathetic treatment of Paul Kruger and his understanding for the position in which the Boers found themselves, was approved. Van Jaarsveld criticised Marais for almost being too objective, in the sense that he refused to make any judgements, or to lead his readers.[63]

But other historians did not agree that Marais had been too objective. They were in fact to argue that "there were several small distortions in the narrative". He was accused of being too harsh in his statement with reference to the period at the end of August and early September 1899 that Milner "preferred war to a peaceful settlement". It was argued that although both Chamberlain and Milner were prepared to push matters to the point of war, this was not the same as saying that Milner "preferred war", or that he secured the recall of the British commander in South Africa, General Butler, because Butler had "made no secret of his view that peace should be maintained".[64]

Marais was also criticised for his minute treatment of Chamberlain's role in the Raid. Leonard Thompson complained that Marais "presses his material in the form of an indictment of Chamberlain for his complicity in the Jameson Raid", which he felt was "perhaps an error of judgement" as the "facts are convincing enough" and this issue had already been exhaustively covered by Jean van der Poel and Ethel Drus who had come to the same conclusion as Marais.[65] Jeffrey Butler too was unhappy with Marais's choice of words such as "indictment", "guilty" and "charge" in describing Chamberlain's role in the Raid.[66]

E. A. WALKER

Like many of the other historians dealt with in this book, Eric Anderson Walker is not easy to categorise. In some ways he fits into the framework of the British school.[67] Leonard Thompson, in referring to Walker's "great contribution" to South African history, says that he adopted an anti-Afrikaner bias, and that his work was "marred by a reluctance to admit that His Majesty's Government has ever erred".[68] Although there is much truth in this verdict, there are perhaps weightier reasons why he should be included in the liberal school rather than the British school, although he differed significantly from liberals like Macmillan and de Kiewiet. One of the reasons for his inclusion in this category is that he had fairly close associations with these men. In 1924 he was external examiner for de Kiewiet's M.A. dissertation,[69] and he recommended it for a distinction. In the preface to the various editions of his *A history of South Africa*, Macmillan was among those whose assistance he acknowledged. As adviser to the 1936 volume 8 of the *Cambridge History of the British Empire*, which covered the history of South Africa, Walker had a further opportunity of familiarising himself with the work of Macmillan and de Kiewiet, who each contributed three chapters to this epic work. He clearly approved of de Kiewiet's handling of economic issues in this volume, for when the Oxford University Press approached Walker about their plans for a book on South Africa in which the emphasis would fall on social and economic factors, Walker recommended de Kiewiet for the task. It was "particularly on the advice of Professor Eric Walker" that the Oxford University Press approached de Kiewiet.[70]

Walker is, however, included in the liberal school not primarily because of the company he kept, but because of his biographies of the Cape liberal politicians, de Villiers and Schreiner, and by reason of the fact that as far as the frontier is concerned he held the characteristic liberal view that it was on the country's frontiers, first of all in the Cape interior and then later in the Boer republics, that the Afrikaner's distinctive racial attitudes had been formed, attitudes which had been carried forward anachronistically into the twentieth century. He developed this theme in *The frontier tradition in South Africa*, a lecture he delivered at Oxford University in 1930. He also easily accepted liberal revisions of South African history, such as J. S. Marais's reassessment of H. C. D. Maynier.[71]

But in other ways he differed markedly from Macmillan and de Kiewiet. His work did not show the same concern for blacks, he did not share their preoccupation with social and economic issues, his history was, above all, white-centred and political.

* * *

Born on 6 September 1886 at Streatham in Surrey, Eric Walker grew to be a man of "splendid height and physique and amazing good looks". A fraction under two metres tall, he had to have his clothes custom-made, while a bootmaker constructed a special last for his shoes.[72]

He won a scholarship to Oxford, going up to Merton College in October 1905. He developed a passionate interest in rowing that was to keep him actively engaged in coaching once he had past his prime as a rower. Walker rowed for his college, and although he rowed in one of the Trial Eights in 1906, he narrowly missed his Oxford Blue.[73]

In 1908 he began his teaching career as a lecturer at Bristol University. While he was there he was invited to join the Leander Rowing Club. He considered this a great honour, so much so that when he died in 1976, his family, convinced that the membership of this club meant more to him than all his academic qualifications and honours, "entwined his brilliant pink Leander tie among the red roses and carnations on his coffin".[74]

In 1911 Walker set sail for Cape Town in the Kenilworth Castle, where he became the first King George V Professor of History at the University of Cape Town, remaining there until 1936.

In this period he was continually breaking new ground. His first publication on South Africa was his Historical atlas of South Africa, published in 1922. It enjoyed great success. Since it was not reprinted, it soon became a valuable piece of Africana. But apart from its value as a collector's item, it was an extremely good atlas, particularly when viewed from the perspective of the preoccupations of historians in the decades between the 1920s and 1950s . Its coverage of the Cape Colony and the extension of the colony to the north and east in the nineteenth century was especially well done.

The widow of Lord de Villiers, Chief Justice of the Cape Colony from 1873, and president of the National Convention of 1908-1909, made available to Walker the papers of her husband.[75] These formed the basis for Lord de Villiers and his times: South Africa 1842-1914, published in 1925. This lucid work ranks as one of the earliest scholarly works on South African history, and the first in the field of biography. It is written in a pleasant and engaging style. The narrative flows easily, although one could perhaps have wished for more personal asides on de Villiers.

De Villiers had a great desire to serve South Africa, and by so doing also to serve Britain, and he was very proud of his British citizenship, as may be gathered from the manner in which he anglicised the Johan Hendrik of his christening to John Henry.[76] His pride in the British connection obviously appealed to Walker, as did de Villiers's great passion for the ideal of a South African federation under the British flag, with its implication of harmonious cooperation between the British and Dutch/Afrikaners. But at the same time de Villiers disapproved of Rhodes's morality in the case of Lobengula's overthrow and the Jameson Raid, and after the raid his sympathies lay very much on the side of the republics. One reviewer complained that de Villiers was unable to see the merits of the Uitlander side of the question, and implied that Walker had adopted the same views as de Villiers, writing that "if it be a merit in a biographer to be in some sort a hero-worshipper, Professor Walker has that merit, though sympathy with his hero's point of view leads him upon occasion to fall short of the impartiality of the historian."[77] This is rather harsh. Walker did not eulogise Rhodes, but on the other hand, he did not treat him with undue severity in this book or any of his other works.

123

And he *did* recognise that the Uitlanders had grievances, even if the statement in the 1928 edition of his *History* that the Uitlanders had "real grievances" was toned down in the 1957 edition to the Uitlanders had "grievances".[78]

The Great Trek was published in 1934. This was also a notable pioneering achievement. In spite of the fact that the Trek held pride of place among Afrikaner nationalists as a major axis of their history, prior to Walker it had never been treated as a whole. Nor, until the 1940s, when H. B. Thom wrote on Gert Maritz and C. F. J. Muller analysed the attitude and reaction of the British government towards the mass migration, had any academic study of the movement been undertaken. Walker's work was thus a first in both respects. It enjoyed great success, and by 1965 had gone into five editions. This book saw Walker at his most engaging and stylish best. His descriptions of the fortunes of the Voortrekkers at Vegkop, Blaauwkrans and Blood River are strongly evocative of the atmosphere of the Trek. Walker himself "always said that it was his best and most readable book", and in 1946 when he was recovering from a severe mental breakdown, he read it to his daughter as therapy.[79]

The Great Trek is based mainly on printed documents. He did not aim at providing an exhaustive study of all aspects of the Trek, and there were numerous features that he did not deal with at all. He did not analyse the problems the Trek posed for British statesmen, and thus missed out on a vital aspect, for it was the British reaction that largely influenced the further course and direction of the movement. By only taking note of events up to 1848, he further limited his opportunity of seeing the Trek in its broadest context. To him the Great Trek was above all a journey, a flight "from the oncoming nineteenth century". Like Afrikaner historians he saw the Great Trek as "the central event in South African history".[80]

In 1936, the same year in which he left South Africa, volume 8 of the *Cambridge History of the British Empire* was published. Walker was the adviser to this volume which dealt exclusively with South Africa in 32 chapters, and contained a comprehensive bibliography. Although there was naturally enough no finely drawn line, on the whole the account of events was taken up to about 1921. Most of the chapters dealt with political developments with the dominant theme being the political struggle between Boer and Briton. The exceptions included chapters on "The native inhabitants" by I. Schapera, "Economic development, 1795-1921" by Arnold Plant, "Social and economic developments in native tribal life" by de Kiewiet, and a chapter on cultural development by C. L. Leipoldt. The liberal contribution to this volume was noteworthy, and Walker, Macmillan and de Kiewiet each contributed three chapters. De Kiewiet's chapter on "Social and economic developments in native tribal life", although only 21 pages long, has been singled out as breaking new ground in a significant way, in that he analysed the origins of black poverty and sketched, albeit briefly, the road towards African proletarianisation in the nineteenth century, taking into account factors such as changes in the ecology, and the beginnings of the migrant labour system.[81]

The *Cambridge History* became a standard reference work on South African history, and its bibliography was particularly prized as the fullest statement existing on South African historical literature.

In the mid-1930s Walker again turned to biography. *W. P. Schreiner: A South African*, which appeared in 1937, saw Walker at his best. Where he was not under pressure to fit in "all the facts", as he was in his general histories where he had to cover much ground, his style is relaxed and easy, he has leisure to turn a neat phrase or give colour to a particular event or mood. The biography on Schreiner is an immensely readable book. As in his biography of de Villiers, Walker shows great understanding and sympathy for his liberal views, approving of Schreiner's devotion to serve both South Africa and the British Empire. Even in the darkest hours of the Anglo-Boer War, Schreiner, who was prime minister of the Cape Colony on the outbreak of war, and who had striven mightily to avert the conflict, believed that "a man may yet serve loyally both dear old England and the South Africa that is even dearer to her sons".[82]

Walker sees the times in which Schreiner lived through the eyes of the main characters. He writes with confidence as he describes their attitudes and the motives for their actions. His touch is sure as he moves through the political decisions and considerations that impelled the actors. But when it comes to a larger interpretative question, such as explaining why Schreiner failed to become the great man that his contemporaries thought he had the capacity to be, Walker refuses to advance any reasons, or to help his readers come to some conclusions on the matter.

Walker's significant contributions to South African history had been written before he left South Africa. This includes his best-known work, which first appeared in 1928 and which he continued to revise right up to the 1960s. He began work on *A history of South Africa* around 1921.[83] In a tribute to Walker in 1976, Professor Colin de B. Webb wrote that when Walker came to the Cape in 1911 the study of South African history "as an academic discipline, was still in its infancy. By the time he left in 1936 to take up a post in Cambridge it was a flourishing and respectable university subject."[84]

This was obviously not the result of Walker's labours alone, but Webb regards the turning point in this change as the publication in 1928 of *A history of South Africa*. This work of "immense erudition, brightened by crackling humour", was "more scholarly, comprehensive and readable than any previous work of similar size, it provided a text-book which could be used in the universities for a far more rigorous undergraduate study of South African History than had been possible before." Webb went on to say that it was "a measure of Walker's greatness that, within its own genre, his 1928 *History of South Africa* remains unsurpassed except by his own revisions of the original. Though rival single-volume textbooks have appeared (in Afrikaans as well as English), Walker's *History* continues to be used to this day [1976] and our schools and universities are manned by generations of teachers who have qualified as South African historians with Walker as their guide." Other academic historians were working at the same time as Walker, such as A. F. Hattersley and Macmillan. But, as Webb notes, "their achievements were to differ. Hattersley became the historian of Natal and of British Settlement; Macmillan became the historian of race relations; only Walker became the historian of South Africa."[85]

There can be little quibbling with Webb's assessment. Certainly in the early 1970s, Walker was still the textbook most used in the English-speaking South African universities. As an introductory survey to students, de Kiewiet's interpretative analysis, A History of South Africa: Social and economic, or Arthur Keppel-Jones's "concise, vivid and allusive" outline,[86] South Africa: A short history, which by 1975 had gone into a 5th edition, might be recommended to provide a general overview of South African history, but for more detailed study Walker was the primary source for students. Both these other works dealt with the broad sweep of the South African past, whereas Walker provided a detailed scholarly narrative. It was essentially a political history written from a white perspective; it was so detailed and concerned with the narrative that processes tended to be ignored. Because it was so packed with information, it was not as easy to read as the other histories he wrote.

The tendency to give as many "facts" as possible was in some ways a substitute for meaningful interpretation, and was a characteristic of his general histories, including The British Empire: Its structure and spirit (London, 1943) which covered the entire history of the Empire from the voyages of the Cabots to the declaration of war against Japan in 237 crowded pages.

Walker, like most other writers before him, gave a prominent place in his South African history to relations between Briton and Boer, the movement towards self-government and the consummation of Union, but he always kept the world outside in view as he chronicled the events. He broke with tradition by seeing South Africa as a single unit not only after Union in 1910, but treating it as such from the beginning. He thus provided a better conception of its component parts, tracing "the interplay of the parts which was always more significant than the doings of any one of them".[87] He also gave what was until then the best exposition of the development of "native" policy in South Africa.

The History of 1928 took the narrative to 1924. In 1935 the book was revised and a chapter added that dealt with events up to 1935. Despite the changes this was not called a second edition; this only appeared in 1940, some five years after Walker had left South Africa. Since at least 1920, Walker had apparently been looking for a suitable opportunity to return to England, for in that year he applied for a chair of Colonial History at Oxford.[88] He did not get the position, but in 1936 he was more successful and in August he sailed for England to take up the post of Vere Harmsworth Professor of Imperial and Naval History in the University of Cambridge.

The second edition proper of the *History* took events up to the decision of the South African government to enter the war against Germany in 1939. This last chapter was very heavily packed with facts, but dealing with such contemporary events, Walker's touch was not as sure as it was when chronicling events in the nineteenth century. Although his main characters like Smuts and Hertzog stand out well enough, others like Jan Hofmeyr, Oswald Pirow, Tielman Roos, Dr Malan and Colonel Stallard do not, and they are sketched in very thin and pale lines in comparison with the nineteenth century figures like Sir Benjamin D'Urban and Moshoeshoe.[89]

In the 1940 edition, slight changes were made to the discussion of the events surrounding the Great Trek, as also the eventful years immediately preceding the Second Anglo-Boer War. In this edition, as also in later revisions, Walker was to give special attention to incorporating the findings of the latest research on the Jameson Raid and the build-up to the war. In the 1940 edition, although he was not in a position to categorically state that Chamberlain had been implicated in the raid itself, he made it clear that the British Colonial Secretary could not escape some moral responsibility for it. The two new works which he cited on the Jameson Raid were H. Marshall Hole's *The Jameson Raid* of 1930 and J. L. Garvin's three-volume *The life of Joseph Chamberlain*, published between 1932 and 1934.[90] He made use of new works that had appeared such as Macmillan's *Cape Colour Question* and *Bantu, Boer, and Briton*,[91] as well as H. A. Reyburn's 1934 and 1935 articles on the eastern Cape interior in the early nineteenth century.[92] In the 1947 reprint of the second edition, Walker has included material from J. S. Marais's *Maynier and the first Boer republic*, published in 1944 as well as P. J. van der Merwe's *Die Kafferoorlog van 1793*,[93] but, for the most part, the second edition is almost identical to the first and whole chapters are reproduced without any changes whatsoever. Even the most contemporary of the chapters in the 1928 edition, that dealing with events between 1910 and 1924, was left virtually untouched.

In England, Walker drove himself very hard. During the height of the war he was "up nearly every night as an air-raid warden", while he had a very heavy work-load at Cambridge.[94]

In July 1944, General Smuts, then prime minister of South Africa, asked Walker to come out to South Africa for a few months "to edit the history of the war in South Africa". He agreed, but before he could do so the accumulated pressures became too much for him and he suffered a mental breakdown. He was admitted to St. Andrew's mental hospital in Northampton with "a severe involutional melancholia". Electric shock therapy, psychotherapy, further treatment in London, and a move to Virginia Water mental hospital in Surrey did not bring about any lasting improvement in his condition, and he suffered until the middle of 1946. In July of that year a leucotomy operation was performed. Walker "never looked back". The result of the operation, his daughter Jean said, "was truly a miracle". Within three months Walker was lecturing again, and he returned to his Cambridge post, only relinquishing it in 1951.[95]

Shortly after his retirement, Walker and his wife paid a six-months' visit to their daughter in South Africa. The aged professor, now 65, embarked on a lecture tour of South African universities, lecturing also in Southern Rhodesia. During his sojourn in South Africa an honorary doctorate was conferred on him by the University of the Witwatersrand.[96]

The Walkers returned to England, and in 1957 a third edition of the *History* appeared, by which time the author had reached his three score years and ten. In this edition the title was broadened to *A history of Southern Africa* to reflect the fact that it included recent historical developments in the two Rhodesias and Nyasaland. Besides taking notice of developments north of the Limpopo, the main difference is that the work has been extended chronologically. Thus while the 1940 edition ended with the Union entering the war against Germany, two additional chapters have been added dealing with events between 1939 and 1955. These two chapters add a further 230 pages to the total length of the book. The 1928 edition contained 536 pages, and ended in 1924; the second edition consisted of a text of some 677 pages that chronicled events up to 1939. The third edition comprised 924 pages of text.

In dealing with events up to 1939 Walker made very few changes. The basic structure laid down in 1928 remained unaltered. A few changes occur in the first chapter on the "discovery", and there is a minor rearrangement of material dealing with events between 1871 and 1881.[97] Apart from the occasional short paragraph added with reference, for example, to works like Eddie Roux's 1948 *Time longer than rope*[98] or a couple of pages inserted to take in the conclusions of Jean van der Poel's *Jameson Raid* of 1951 regarding the complicity of Chamberlain and other leading figures in the raid,[99] the changes are mainly stylistic. In later impressions of the third edition which were printed in the 1960s, J. S. Marais's *The fall of Kruger's republic* (Oxford, 1961) and L. M. Thompson's *The unification of South Africa, 1902-1910*, (Oxford, 1960) have been used.[100]

The bibliography has been extended, but in the later impressions of the third edition more recent works which have been used, such as Marais's work, have not been taken up in the bibliography. In revising his work Walker made very little use of Afrikaans works. Although Marais' 1961 work and Thompson's work of 1960 are noticed in later impressions of the third edition, D. W. Krüger's *The age of the generals: A short political history of the Union of South Africa 1910-1948* of 1961 is not. It is not unfair to say that Walker failed to utilise many important works in revising his history.

That Walker's conception of South African history should not have changed between 1928 and 1957 is a major criticism of his work. Later impressions of the third edition (with corrections) continued to be printed until the end of the 1960s, with the result that students relying on Walker in the late 1960s were obtaining in fact a view of South African history (as far as events up to 1924 are concerned) laid down as early as 1928. This is, of course, a reflection on the state of historical writing itself, that no comparable general history of the country in English was published to compete with Walker's work, which enjoyed a virtual monopoly.

Walker was criticised for presenting a history in which whites held the centre of the stage. South African history as he saw it was the history of the white man in South Africa. But he was quite prepared to acknowledge that this perspective was possibly only a temporary one. In his introduction to *A modern history for South Africa*, published in 1926 and aimed primarily at matric pupils, he explained that "Histories of South Africa used to be written mainly to explain the growth of self-government in the Cape Colony and the quarrels of the British government and colonies with the republics. Later, men made the movement towards Union or the development of the Afrikander people the central fact and rewrote their histories accordingly. Perhaps tomorrow men will say that the dealings of Europeans here with the half-castes, natives and Asiatics are the really important things and will study our past from that point of view." From such a statement, written about the same time as he became aware, in the aftermath of the 1922 strikes, of the emergence of what he saw as an economic clash between Europeans and non-Europeans, one might have expected him to devote more attention to the role of blacks in South African society. But he did not.

Although he saw the 1922 disturbances as marking "a violent stage in the awakening of European South Africans to the fact that their economic and social problems were only other aspects of the Native problem" and described that awakening as "the chief fact in South African history since Union", he placed the emphasis on the whites and their reaction to the new problems with which they were suddenly confronted.[101] In this respect, he did not ask new questions of the past.

In the preface of the 1928 edition, Walker wrote that since "in a sense, all South African history is current politics," he had "written with the utmost restraint, of set purpose abstaining from pointing morals and adorning tales, especially in dealing with the history of the last forty years . . . For that period above all, I have been content to follow Bacon's advice and, within the compass of my knowledge and understanding, 'to represent the events themselves together with the counsels, and to leave the observations and conclusions thereupon to the liberty and faculty of every man's judgment'."

It was not a claim he repeated in the preface to the two later editions of his work, and, in fact, it was in his handling of modern developments that he was particularly criticised for not adopting a balanced approach. A major criticism of his work was that he refused to admit that the British government had ever been wrong in what it did in South Africa. This is why L. M. Thompson classified him among the British school of historians. It is his chapters dealing with events after 1939 in particular that have been singled out for attack. His sources were paltry, his research superficial, the more balanced view he had of the eighteenth and nineteenth centuries is missing. These chapters have come under fire on account of their tangled themes, unsystematic narrative, inaccuracies and distortions, contradictions and ir- relevancies, "palpable absurdities" and "heavy bias".[102]

Without making allowance for the different circumstances obtaining in South Africa and New Zealand, he declared that as a result of "archaic" agricultural techniques, a South African farmer "could feed only one-tenth of the number that one could feed in mechanised New Zealand." According to Walker, the Cape Coloureds were "disheartened at having been degraded from the proud status of British subjects to that of Union citizens". Jan Smuts is his hero, and B. J. Liebenberg believes that the reason for this is that Smuts in 1939 was in favour of the Union's joining the British Empire in the war against Nazi Germany. He also approved of certain things that Smuts had to say about Britain and the Empire. Thus, according to Walker, it was Smuts who "saved South Africa from what Deneys Reitz called the shame of neu- trality by bringing her into the Axis war". It was Smuts who said: "When I speak of England, I take off my hat . . . I choose the country under which we suffered forty years ago, but which, when we were at her mercy, treated us as a Christian nation should."

There can be little doubt that Liebenberg had hit the nail on the head when he suggested that Walker quoted Smuts so often because he approved of his pro-British views. Thus Smuts is again quoted saying that the "world needs the British system", that the British had a "mission to mankind of goodwill, good government and human co-operation, a message of freedom and human happiness". Smuts said, again quoted by Walker, that at the end of the Second World War in Europe there would be only the mighty power of the Soviet Union, and the United Kingdom, "a poor country now in material things, but rich in 'a glory and an honour and a prestige' such as no other land had ever had".[103]

* * *

If the 1957 edition of Walker's *History* was disappointing, the new edition of volume 8 of *The Cambridge History of the British Empire* in 1963 was doubly so. In the 1936 edition Walker was the adviser, and the general editors of the volume were A. P. Newton and E. A. Benians. In 1963 Walker was the general editor. Not having seen the need for any drastic revision of his *History* in 1940 or 1957, it was hardly likely that as an old man in his mid-seventies he would suddenly preside over a radically restructured edition of the *Cam- bridge History*. It is therefore no surprise to find that the changes between the 1936 and 1963 editions are very small.

Despite the promise in the preface that the "new edition incorporates the results of recent research" and that "many chapters contain a fair number of revisions and corrections", the changes are in fact slight. Professor I. Schapera has rewritten his chapter on "The native inhabitants", although still retaining the same framework and subheadings as in 1936; C. L. Leipoldt's final chapter on "Cultural development" has been rewritten by Professor Oswald Doughty and Walker himself. In chapter 21 the sections on the Jameson Raid and its results, in the original edition written by Cecil Headlam and J. H. Hofmeyr, have been rewritten by Walker. Thus, as in his *History*, one of the areas that Walker did indeed keep up to date was the Jameson Raid. The only other change of major note was in chapter 24, where Professor Kenneth Kirkwood rewrote the section on Rhodesia. For the rest, the changes do not amount to much more than a paragraph added here and there, or a note to the effect that recent research had thrown new light on a particular issue. The bibliography, which was seen as a particularly strong point in the 1936 edition, has been freshened up with a few new titles, but has not been systematically revised.[104] For people hoping that new questions of the past might be asked, and that the strongly white-centred approach of 1936 might have changed, the 1963 edition fell far short of their expectations.

This edition marked the end of the Walker "era". His significant contribution to the study of South African history had been made between the appearance of his historical atlas in 1922 and the publication of his work on Schreiner in 1937. The revisions of his *History* added very little to what he had already said about South African history up to 1924, and although he made sallies into post-1924 South African history, he will not be remembered for them.

Walker's daughter Jean said that her father "had maintained his wonderful recovery"[105] and he continued living in England until 1968. However, her mother's increasing blindness and deafness, and loss of interest in life, together with the strain that this placed on her father, made Jean decide to bring her parents to South Africa in 1968 to live with her in Durban. In August 1968 Walker was one of 13 persons to whom the University of Cape Town granted honorary degrees to mark the celebration of the university's Golden Jubilee. Natal University was to confer an honorary doctorate on him on 8 May 1976, but he died on 23 February that year and the degree was awarded posthumously. At his funeral the organist played his three favourites: the Twenty Third Psalm, Pack up your troubles in your old kit bag, and the Eton Boating Song.[106]

A MISSION-INSPIRED LIBERAL TRADITION

There is one other group of writers whose work falls into the liberal tradition. There are very few academically trained historians among them, and in fact not many of them have written histories. What they have done, however, is to express a particular view about the past that coincides closely with the liberal standpoint. The writers who belong to this tradition, what for want of a better name may be referred to as a mission-inspired liberal trend, are black, but not all blacks belong to this tradition. Black historical writers do not form a separate school any more than do white historical writers: Their work has not been characterised by a particular approach and it covers the whole spectrum of South African historiography, so that it may quite easily be slotted into some of the other categories established, particularly the liberal and radical schools.

Academically trained black historians have made a contribution to the study of South African history in Masters and Doctoral theses at various universities. The topics of these studies are, for the most part non-controversial, dealing, for example, with the history of black educational institutions, various aspects of policy at the Cape, the land question and ethnic histories.[107]

The number of such works is, however, small. Most blacks who have articulated their views about the past have done so not in historical works based on research, but in political writings and autobiographies which convey an *attitude* towards the past. The people, both black and white, who projected a black image into the study of history, or whose political writings or autobiographies had some relevance for the study of history, were not generally professional historians. Few of them had received much or indeed any formal training in history as a discipline. They included among their numbers a medical doctor like S. M. Molema, who was also an African National Congress (A.N.C.) official; a journalist and secretary of the A.N.C. like Sol T. Plaatjie who had "never received any secondary training";[108] a Presbyterian church minister like James Henderson Soga; and a trade union leader such as Clements Kadalie, founder of the Industrial and Commercial Workers' Union. These writers were themselves actively involved in black politics – they were office bearers in the A.N.C., the founders of black trade unions, members of political groups founded to resist the whittling away of the few remaining black rights. Their writing, therefore, has a strong propagandistic element. In this sense, there are striking parallels with early Afrikaner nationalist histories. This is not to suggest that history written from a black point of view has been uniform. Like white histories, it has undergone numerous changes in the past 60 or so years, and these changes closely mirror the development of South African society.

* * *

The missionary tradition of black historiography is a Christian liberal-humanistic approach to the past. The writers of these histories were the products of mission schools, in particular those at Lovedale and Fort Hare in the Cape, Adams College in Natal, Kilnerton in the Transvaal and the German mission station at Pniel. Several of the black intellectual elite established contact with one another at these institutions. To take an example from Adams College (known as the Amanzimtoti Institute prior to 1935); Z. K. Matthews, the first graduate of Fort Hare, in the 1920s became the head of the high school here, and came into contact with Albert Luthuli – then one of the teachers and later to become a Nobel Peace Prize winner – and with John Dube of the Industrial and Commercial Workers' Union. Others who passed through Adams College included J. K. Ngubane, Joshua Nkomo, Sir Seretse Khama and Chief Mangosuthu Buthelezi.[109] Among prominent blacks connected with Lovedale were S. M. Molema, Professors D. D. T. Jabavu and Z. K. Matthews, and I. B. Tabata.

It was the missionaries who transcribed African languages to writing, particularly with a view to making the Bible available to their charges in their own language. As early as 1857 the Bible was translated into Tswana.[110] The intellectual black middle class that emerged from these institutions had a firm grounding in Christian principles and accepted the Western lifestyle. Their writings are politically moderate, exhibit racial tolerance, and are very much in line with Cape liberal thought. They favoured the qualified franchise and equal rights for all "civilised" men. The histories they wrote were black-centred, but they accepted the world as it was, viewing it with "white liberal eyes"; they came strongly under the influence of white historians like Macmillan, portraying the blacks as backward, the whites as civilised. There was thus a strong sense of subordination in their writing. A general feeling of hurt at their lack of political rights comes out strongly, and they are very much opposed to racism, but there is no trace of anti-white feeling as such. They adopt a far more positive attitude towards the role of Britain in South Africa, seeing this influence as beneficial to blacks, protecting them against the racism of the Afrikaner. They held the missionaries in general and Dr John Philip in particular in high regard. There is hurt at the way the British let them down at Union in 1910, granting independence to whites without insisting on black political rights. Land ownership is a major theme in their work, and they give much attention to the Native Land Act of 1913, which robbed many blacks of the opportunity of making their living in an independent manner, forcing those who were not working on white farms into the mine compounds and urban townships. They wrote largely for their fellow blacks, to give them a sense of identity, so that they would know who they were, where they came from, in the hope that they would be inspired to "collect and record the history of their people". But part of their message was also addressed to a wider audience. Dr S. M. Molema had the British public in mind when he stressed how the blacks in South Africa had supported Britain against the Boers, but in the end it was the Boers to whom the British gave the vote, and the blacks who were handed over to the Boers without the vote. Molema also intended his history as a guide for the white rulers of South Africa: "To members of the governing race," he wrote, "some knowledge of the governed race, their mind and manners, seems necessary. For, knowing with whom one has to deal often decides how to deal. Much of the misunderstanding and contempt between nationalities, too, is largely due to want of acquaintance with each other. In such cases, of course, the weaker nation suffers."[111]

One work in this tradition that deserves mention is *The south-eastern Bantu* of J. H Soga. Like his father Tiyo Soga (1829-1871), who was a well-known Xhosa essayist and churchman, John Henderson Soga composed hymns and also engaged in translation work. He is best remembered however, as a historian. He completed his *Abe-Nguni Abo-Mbo Nama-Lala* in 1926 but the Lovedale Press could not be persuaded to publish it. At the request of the editorial board of *Bantu Studies* he translated it into English and it appeared in 1930 as *The south-eastern Bantu*. In the course of writing this history of the Xhosa, Soga travelled extensively interviewing Xhosa chiefs and recording numerous oral traditions and genealogies. What made it different from other ethnic histories was that it told the complete tale of the Xhosa, and that its arrangement and treatment copied the models of European history writing.[112]

Jordan K. Ngubane makes the point that the missionary education of these black writers largely determined the way in which they put their case: "They employed the so-called constitutional methods – calling public meetings, making protests, organizing demonstrations, passing resolutions, and sending deputations to white men in positions of authority. Since Dr Philip had used most of these methods and produced excellent results, his black pupils saw no reason why they should not try them. But there was another side to this story. The leaders of African nationalism at this stage did not believe that the issue of self-determination could become a matter of practical politics in their own lives. They wanted to buy time to nurse the unity they had created until it became an effective striking force. While moving towards this goal, they were willing to do all they could to agitate for reforms without provoking a head-on collision with white authority."[113]

The ideal of these writers was to uplift and educate the blacks, so that they could eventually obtain political equality with the whites in a non-racial unitary state. They hoped that the Cape "colourblind" franchise would be extended to the whole country, so that all blacks could share in the democratic process. They were optimistic about the future. Chief Albert Luthuli wrote about when he was at Adams College in the 1920s: "In the days when Professor Matthews and I were young teachers at Adams the world seemed to be opening out for Africans. It seemed mainly a matter of proving our ability and worth as citizens, and that did not seem impossible. We were, of course, aware of the existence of colour prejudice, but we did not dream that it would endure and intensify as it has. There seemed point, in my youth, in striving after the values of the Western world. It seemed to be a striving after wholeness and fulfilment. Since then we have watched the steady degeneration of South African affairs."[114] For these people, 1936 was a great shock, for in that year the white government of General Hertzog removed persons of colour from the Cape's common voters' roll.

THE ROOTS OF RACIAL ATTITUDES

An important element in what came to be known as the "conventional wisdom" of the liberal school of history, was clearly evident in Macmillan's work, and this was that it was on the borders of the Cape Colony that the Afrikaners, as a result of their Calvinism and the nature of their racial contacts, developed their racial attitudes, which they took with them to Natal and the Transvaal when they left the Cape on the Great Trek. In the interior they nurtured these frontier attitudes, and after 1910 they were able to reindoctrinate the colonial south where other more enlightened, British attitudes, had come to prevail. Walker, Macmillan and de Kiewiet's shining examples had been Cape liberal politicians like Lord de Villiers and W. P. Schreiner and liberal missionaries like Philip. The British government in South Africa had made mistakes, but they had always acted from the highest motives. They mourned the fact that these liberal elements had been defeated in South Africa and that the "frontier" had triumphed. They searched the past to find where the wrong turning had been taken, how had the frontier won?

Eric Walker, in an address delivered in Oxford in 1930, stressed the continuity and persistence of frontier attitudes in South Africa. He told his audience: "You will not understand South Africa unless you realize how strong and widespread that [frontier] tradition is. The frontier tradition is enshrined in most of our history books," he told them. The frontier point of view ran right through the works of Theal and Cory, "and has percolated downwards by way of school textbooks, newspapers, and politicians with a taste for historical illustration".

The basic issues on the frontier had always been land, labour and security. As far as the Voortrekkers were concerned, the "impelling motives common to them all were the desire for land, for security, for labour, and for the maintenance in its purity of their principal doctrine, the self-evident and eternal inequality of white and non-white, ex-master and ex-slave, Christian men and barbarian tribesmen". He said that "avowed Nationalists to-day look instinctively to the frontier tradition for much of their inspiration", that politicians were trying to solve problems in 1930 with the frontier values of a bygone age. Referring to the situation in South Africa at that juncture of time, he said that "South Africa is seeking to solve the riddle that her frontier past has set her, and the men with whom the answer lies at the moment are precisely those on whose minds the frontier tradition has the strongest hold."[115]

In 1937 the psychologist, I. D. MacCrone, who later became vice-chancellor of the University of the Witwatersrand, wrote *Race attitudes in South Africa*, which had a long introductory section on the historical development of race attitudes. His name, rather than anyone else's, has come to be associated with the view that Afrikaner racial attitudes came from their "primitive" Calvinism and religious attitudes formed on the frontier to differentiate between

Christian and heathen, and which attitudes were later associated with colour. His analysis led him to the conclusion that "the attitudes themselves, as they existed towards the end of the eighteenth and at the beginning of the nineteenth centuries, are very similar to those which we find displayed on all sides at the present time". He admits, however, that the attitudes, although remaining the same, may be rationalised differently: "The emphasis is now laid upon the white man and his 'civilization' rather than upon the Christian and his 'religion'."[116]

This became a major tenet of faith of the liberals in South Africa. As they saw it, the Afrikaner's racial attitudes had been formed by his contacts on the frontiers in the eighteenth and early nineteenth centuries; his prejudices were thus an anachronistic throwback that the Afrikaner had carried with him into the twentieth century. The liberals blamed this "irrational heritage"[117] for increasing the tension and conflict that accompanied South Africa's industrial revolution. A basic and unquestioned premise of the liberals thus became that racism was an outmoded way of thinking that had developed on the frontier, and that the Afrikaner's attitudes were not appropriate for a rapidly industrialising South Africa for they acted as a brake to more rapid economic progress. The Afrikaner with these outdated ideas controlled the state and thus was able to organise matters in accordance with his own ideological prejudices to the detriment of economic development. The liberals' main hope for the future was the belief that the economic progress that was taking place was the enemy of racial oppression and segregation, and that economic "realities" would inevitably help break down the barriers of segregation.

Thus in *The anatomy of South African misery* de Kiewiet wrote that: "In South Africa the laws of Parliament are at war with the laws of economics. Apartheid is at variance with many of the essential requirements of a growing modern industrial society. In the modern world it is a dissipation of wealth not to use the energies and skills of the whole population, or to inhibit the full development of the productive powers of any class in the population. Economic development and the more effective utilization of the native labour force are inseparable."[118] No matter how strong the political forces in favour of apartheid were, they would in the final analysis succumb to the imperatives of industrialisation, which could not tolerate inefficiency and waste. "That the laws of economics and the requirements of industrial efficiency are at war with the laws of Parliament is a notable cause for hope," he wrote. And the reason for this was to be found in the fact that, "by the side of the liberal spirits in politics and intellectual life, there exists a virtual fifth column of engineers, economists, industrialists and business men. They are not organised and have no leadership. Their actions were often irresolute and expedient. Their power is less in themselves than in the coercion implicitly exercised by investments, science, technology and the market place. Whatever their politics or timidity, their faces are perforce set against waste, inefficiency, and unproductivity."[119]

*   *   *

The above were by no means the only liberals, and many historians adopted approaches that were to a greater or lesser extent in line with liberal thinking. Among those who added to liberal thinking about the past was H. A. Reyburn. His claim to recognition rests on a number of very good articles published in *The Critic* in 1934 and 1935, in which he challenged some traditional conservative views concerning the early nineteenth century frontier.[120] In the late 1950s, Marais frequently cited Reyburn to his undergraduate students. Another liberal whose major contribution to the study of South African history rests on a number of very good articles is H. M. Robertson, whose publications in the *South African Journal of Economics* mainly in the 1930s and 1940s added a new dimension to the study of South African history by focusing on economic development in van Riebeeck's time, and even more significantly, with regard to the way that economic contact between the colonists and the Xhosa developed during the period of Dutch East India Company rule.[121] Other liberals who focused on social and economic issues were Sheila van der Horst in her major work, *Native labour in South Africa* (London, 1942), where she examined the changing nature of exploitation of African labour, a topic that historians were to explore further in the 1970s. A liberal who made her mark in the political history sphere was Jean van der Poel. Her two major contributions were her penetrating analysis of the complicity of Joseph Chamberlain and the imperial authorities in the Jameson Raid and her work, together with Sir Keith Hancock, in making available selections from the correspondence of General Smuts.[122] Among the later liberals who shared the views of the early liberals was the Rhodes University economist Desmond Hobart Houghton. His book *The South African economy* was first published in 1964. By 1976 it had gone into four editions.

But without the stimulus of Macmillan, who left the country for England in 1932, and de Kiewiet who was abroad, the liberals who followed them did very little to build on their ideas. It was only in the 1970s that the socio-economic themes pointed to by Macmillan and de Kiewiet were again taken up and explored further. One of the principal reasons for this failure to develop the ideas of the early liberals was that liberal historians were pre-occupied with political history in the wake of the National Party victory at the polls in 1948. They devoted most of their energy to analysing why liberalism in South Africa had failed and Afrikaner nationalism triumphed.[123] Those who followed in their footsteps did not, for the most part, question the tenets of liberal historical thought as formulated prior to the 1940s.

The emphasis on the origins of the "native problem" by English-speaking historians took on an ever-greater political flavour. Liberal historiography was generally critical of government policy towards the blacks, with the result that the conservative Afrikaners, who were largely in control of education, ignored their work. Liberal views never found their way into school textbooks, as various South African governments ensured that the textbooks reflected and defended government policy and thinking. The victory of the Nationalist Party at the polls in 1948 and the coming of a republic in 1961, rendered the English-speaking section of the country a politically powerless minority, whose frustration and disappointment led to self-examination and a search for an identity in the new situation. They looked back into history to see where the wrong turnings had been made, whether by the English-speaking section of the population or by the British government before that, in the way that it had given independence to the country in 1910. It was generally assumed by both English liberal and Afrikaner historians that the British in South Africa after 1806 had acted in a way sympathetic to the blacks, to protect them against the real or imagined racism and oppression of the Afrikaners. Much of the English literature that was concerned with the imperial factor, saw the years immediately preceding the establishment of the Union in 1910 as a lapse in this British concern for the blacks. The Afrikaner was critically analysed in an effort to lay bare the source of his racial attitudes and apartheid. Apartheid in particular came under the microscope. The liberals gave ever more attention to the blacks, continuing to dispel the idea that they were somehow not a central part of the history of South Africa but were peripheral to it. The emphasis, however, remained on interaction between white and black; there was little attempt to analyse black societies in their own right before they interacted or came into contact with the whites.

But there were important events taking place in the rest of colonial Africa in the aftermath of the Second World War – the forces of nationalism were growing apace and the era of decolonisation in black Africa began with the independence of the Gold Coast as Ghana in 1957. Other colonies in British Africa moved quickly to take over the reins of government, and in French and Belgian Africa too, a major reassessment of the relationship between metropole and colony was underway. The newly independent states prepared to rewrite their histories, to go beyond the colonial histories they had inherited from their European rulers, and to search for the roots of African society before contact with Europe – they tried to find links between these early pre-colonial societies and the post-independence societies, in a bid to show that the colonial era had not fundamentally changed African society, that in the long history of Africa the colonial era had simply been an episode, and a fairly short one at that. The shift in interest in the rest of Africa to a study of pre-colonial communities, also had its effect south of the Limpopo, although South Africa was not part of this colonial revolution.

In the 1950s and 1960s as decolonisation in Africa gathered momentum, books and university courses on Africa mushroomed. *The Journal of African History* made its appearance in 1960, graduate schools of African history were established in Britain and the United States, and in Africa itself schools of African history were to be found, *inter alia*, in Dar es Salaam, Nairobi and Ibadan. All this contributed to what T. O. Ranger called "a revolution in the study of African history".[124]

THE OXFORD HISTORY

With interest in the rest of Africa being focused especially on pre-colonial Africa, South Africa tended, in this respect at any rate, to fall behind what was being done elsewhere in the continent in the 1960s. Among a number of liberals there was, however, concern at this state of affairs. Leonard Thompson visited Ghana for its independence celebrations in 1957, and in 1961 took up a post in African history at the University of California in Los Angeles. In 1962 the anthropologist Monica Wilson went to California on sabbatical and she and Thompson planned the two-volume *Oxford History of South Africa* which appeared in 1969 and 1971.[125]

The *Oxford History*, which represented the summation of liberal thinking about South Africa at the end of the 1960s, was a major landmark in South African historiography. In some ways it made significant advances on what had gone before, but in other ways it seemed to have advanced very little since the ideas formulated in the 1920s and 1930s.

If there had been any lingering doubt, the *Oxford History* for all time dispelled the myth that South African history had begun when the Portuguese discoverers rounded the Cape in 1487 – it demonstrated that Africans had indeed had a history before the coming of the white man. It thus pushed back the frontiers of South African history by going beyond the starting dates of more traditional histories. Macmillan and his ilk had already done much to elevate other race groups to a role in South African history, but even they had reserved the major roles for the whites. This was one area in which the *Oxford History* advanced, and reflected the shift in thinking that had accompanied the era of decolonisation in the rest of Africa. Whites no longer hold the centre of the stage. About a third of the first volume that deals with events up to 1870 is devoted to the pre-colonial era, and about half to the movement of black peoples between 1778 and 1870. The whites become known as "settlers", against whose depredations and penetration the blacks fought. There are no separate sections on the two main axes of Afrikaner historiography, the Great Trek and the Anglo-Boer War. They are interwoven into the story and given no prominence. Black reaction to white domination is more important.

As the first major synthesis of South African history that gave attention to pre-colonial societies and to the role of blacks in South African history, it inevitably became a target of attack from both the left and the right of the political spectrum. Ronald Hyam "questioned whether this *History* has more than a marginal claim to call itself history at all". These mutters to the effect that it was not really a history, were partly based on the fact that the *Oxford History* had used an archaeologist, an anthropologist, a linguist, and even a journalist, in its bid to present its picture of the past. The *Oxford History* was an attempt to do for South African history what had been done elsewhere on the continent in the early 1960s, and to examine African societies themselves in their own right, but it was severely hampered in its efforts to do so because the anthropologists, archaeologists and historical linguists were unable to provide the answers to the questions that the historians wished to ask of early pre-colonial societies. Anthropologists tended to produce a static, ahistorical picture of African societies, with little sense of their internal dynamism. Thus a sense of history was missing from Monica Wilson's chapters on the pre-colonial history of black societies, which are portrayed as isolated and static. In the discussion of Nguni society before the Mfecane, for example, much attention is devoted to social structure and there is little indication of change over a period of 500 years. The reader is never clear about what instant in time is under discussion.[126]

This criticism was not levelled at the fact that an attempt was made to bring other disciplines into the study of the South African past, but rather that it was not an integrated, interconnected narrative. Donald Denoon writes that "it is necessary to insist on the self-evident points that history is not anthropology, that an historian is not an anthropologist, and that professional expertise in one discipline is no guarantee of proficiency in another".[127] Shula Marks makes the same point. She writes that "though the attempt to introduce the findings of social scientists to South African historians is well overdue, the deliberate decision of the Oxford editors *not* to integrate the different contributions, with their cross-cutting methodology and objectives, has meant that the essential interconnectedness of developments has been lost. An interdisciplinary approach on the part of the historian does not mean commissioning non-historians to 'do their thing'. The obligation devolves on the historian himself to be aware of the findings of his colleagues in the related fields of anthropology, economics, sociology, and political science, and to make use of these within his own essentially historical framework. I do not mean this in any rigid way, but for the historian chronology is of the essence: without this we are able to understand neither synchronous connections nor the changes in society over time. *The Oxford History*, which can as sensibly be read from the middle in either direction as from beginning to end, as a result lacks a certain sense of overall historical development."[128]

In the above quotation Shula Marks did not mention archaeology as one of the disciplines whose findings historians should use. But she has on other occasions spoken of archaeology. There was very little work being done on the Iron Age in South Africa. Shula Marks has made much of the fact that in this respect South Africa had by the end of the 1960s and even beyond that, lagged behind what was being done north of the Limpopo, saying that "archaeological evidence is based on random finds and isolated excavations rather than on either broadly based regional surveys or carefully selected sample digs."[129] But she also later warned that we should not overestimate what we can learn from this discipline, writing that "the attempts which were made in the rest of Africa in reconstructing African history from archaeological evidence, ethnography, oral tradition and historical linguistics has not always been particularly convincing" and there is a limit "to what mud floors and bits of bone and pot can tell us about social relations of production, political power and exploitation – let alone man's hopes and dreams and fears".[130]

Archaeological researches, at any rate until the late 1960s, tended to concentrate on tools and physical artefacts and sorting them into categories, rather than on the people who made them. There were, therefore, very few areas where the social scientists and the archaeologists could speak to each other in meaningful terms, and archaeology made only a limited contribution to lifting the veil.

Although Shula Marks singled South Africa out as being particularly badly off as far as archaeological research is concerned, the position in the rest of Africa was not all that rosy either. In 1981 Robert Collins reflected that, with few exceptions, archaeologists and linguists had made little attempt to link up with history. "To be sure they have made great strides within their own disciplines, and that is their primary responsibility," he admitted, "but as an adjunct to history, I find them drowning in their own terminology as isolated and special in the world of learning as mathematicians."[128] Thurston Shaw of the University of Cambridge replied to this. What he had to say is probably very true of other disciplines besides archaeology, and demonstrates the difficulty of using and integrating data from various fields, as Shula Marks complained that the *Oxford History* had failed to do. He said that "there is much more information about the African past waiting to be revealed by archaeological methods than by historical. That is why there ought to be more archaeologists in African universities than historians, instead of the other way around – which is yet another example of a foreign academic tradition being imposed upon Africa rather than one rooted in its own soil." What was required were more archaeologists, not necessarily simply historians who were prepared to use archaeological data. He went on to say that very often when historians used archaeological or ethnographical data they got them wrong, and that historians "need to train themselves as real archaeologists instead of trying to handle archaeological data without fully understanding it. . . . If they wish to make use of archaeological concepts and entities they must learn the language, and learn to use it correctly." Shaw adds a warning about using data from different disciplines: "I believe we need to be more careful about combining evidence from different disciplines," he writes. "Perhaps we forget too readily that different disciplines – such as those of archaeology, history, linguistics, and ethnography – use different kinds of data, different methods of collecting them, follow different rules in interpreting them, ask different questions and get different kinds of answers. In other words, these different disciplines are handling different 'dimensions'. Now we know that in handling scientific equations it is important to be clear what dimensions we are using and to get them balanced on each side of the equation; otherwise we go wrong. In our desire to solve some difficult equations about the African past, have we been so keen to find solutions that we have fudged the balance of the dimensions, and seen equivalents when they are not really there?"[132]

Oral tradition is somewhat unsatisfactory for the more distant centuries and only becomes a more reliable source for events after about 1800.

Although the *Oxford History* was not altogether successful in its integration of and use of other disciplines, it did point the way and it encouraged breaking down the barriers that separated history from the other social sciences. In this sense the authors had come under the influence of the French *Annales* school, which had an interdisciplinary approach and which concentrated on social history and the writing of a total, integrated history of the ordinary people, peasants and labourers, giving particular attention to their material culture. Besides broadening the subject matter of history, it thus also broadened its methodological base. It was the radicals who were to continue along these lines in the 1970s and to carry this forward in a fresh and challenging way.

The *Oxford History* was attacked for its concentration on interaction between white and black, which it was asserted had obscured the fact that very different kinds of societies had developed *independently* in the interior prior to the era of mineral discoveries; its reading of the role of the imperial power in South Africa had been wrong; it had failed to give attention to the uneven way that capitalism had spread through the country; and it had stressed race as the determining factor in South Africa, whereas the moving forces were classes – class formation and conflict.

It was the *Oxford History's* adherence to the old liberal principles formulated 20 to 30 years earlier that brought forth the most criticism. In many respects the *Oxford History* demonstrates how little change there had been in liberal thinking since the days of Macmillan and de Kiewiet. The patent concern with the present and the future are clear at every stage. It is heavily moralistic, bemoaning wrong turnings that had been taken in the past, but still hopeful that if these trends are reversed, all may still by well. K. R. Hughes writes that the liberal tradition "is long on morality and short on explanation." He describes the authors as "continually, and furtively, looking over their shoulders at the white racist reader. It is important to demonstrate to him that conflict between races is not inevitable and consequently racial harmony and partnership are paraded before the reader whenever possible. . . The liberal tradition. . . is so much concerned with the evils of separation . . . that it does not enquire much into the character of that connection."[133]

Many of the old stereotypes, including the theme of interaction, were repeated. The *Oxford History* did not re-examine them. Its major premise, set out in the first sentence of the preface to the first volume, is the "belief that the central theme of South African history is interaction between peoples of diverse origins, languages, technologies, ideologies, and social systems, meeting on South African soil". In terms of this, more attention was given to showing that Africans could and did respond to the new challenges presented by the appearance of colonialism, that they were not simply passive, but were capable of initiatives of their own, that their responses were every bit as important in the making of South African history as were the actions of whites.

But on the other hand, by seeing South African history in terms of interaction, they did not admit the possibility in the pre-colonial era of the growth in the interior of independent societies, or social formations as the revisionists were soon to be calling them. And this was one major prong of the objections of many historians to the *Oxford History*. Another was the adherence of the *Oxford History* to that other stereotype of the English-speaking academic liberal tradition, that Afrikaner racial attitudes had been formed on the frontiers of the Cape Colony in the eighteenth and early nineteenth centuries and that economic progress and prosperity would help break down the barriers of segregation which they maintained hampered further and more rapid development. The liberals were accused of accepting this premise as true without examining it.

In an essay written in Cape Town in 1975, Harrison Wright singled out for criticism the liberals' preoccupation with the present. Because they had written "at least in part to serve contemporary liberal ends", he believed that they had "tended to link together past and present particularly closely". Liberal history, he asserted "is liable to look too much to present problems for its subject matter and to be too simplistic in its search for origins. It is liable to be so committed that it is narrow in its judgements. It is liable, in short, to be didactic and oversimplified."[134]

Harrison Wright was not the first to criticise the *Oxford History* on these lines. In a review of the first volume in 1969, van Jaarsveld highlighted a number of areas which other critics also singled out, although his point of departure was an essentially conservative one, as indeed was that of Harrison Wright.[135]

Van Jaarsveld questioned whether old historical terms like Bushman and Hottentot could legitimately be replaced by terms like San and Khoikhoi, which were not generally accepted. He noted that although Theal was sharply criticised, the views of Marais were adopted uncritically. He objected to what he believed was an anti-white, and in particular anti-Afrikaner bias. The sources were used one-sidedly to project the liberal ideals of equality into the past – the blacks are defended, while the Afrikaners are portrayed as the racists, the guilty ones. The new image of the past came down to this, he maintained: South Africa is and always was a land of non-white peoples. The whites were "settlers", a minority group who with superior technological aids were able to subject the majority, take their land and cattle and turn them into slaves or labourers in a new white-dominated (and in particular Afrikaner-dominated) society. He saw the book more as an element in the propaganda campaign against the Afrikaner than as an attempt at a new scientific insight into the past. Taken as a whole, the image presented of the Afrikaner is a caricature. The Brit could not forget that the Afrikaner had opposed him for so long, transformed South Africa in keeping with his own ideas, inflicting a humiliating defeat on British and Cape liberalism. Van Jaarsveld saw it as an anti-apartheid book, conceived from an integrationist, liberal and equality-seeking perspective. At all times the reader was being persuaded that integration, mixing, cooperation was really at the core of the South African past, thus exactly the opposite of segregation and separate development. In this last criticism, although writing from a different viewpoint, van Jaarsveld is in agreement with other critics of the book who have made the point that the theme of interaction (and cooperation) is overstressed to the exclusion of factors such as conflict. Van Jaarsveld also touches on another area to which Harrison Wright was later to give prominence in his criticism of both the liberals and the radicals who came after them. This was in connection with the way in which nineteenth century blacks were credited with motives and insights that were very modern and not at all in keeping with the nineteenth century. Van Jaarsveld believes that too much credit is given to the supposed insight of chiefs like Dingane and Mzilikazi, as if they were able to see events from a broad South African perspective. Thus Leonard Thompson says of Shaka's devastation of Natal, without providing any evidence, that the Zulu chief, "being aware that the firearms of the white people in the Cape Colony constituted the most formidable threat to his kingdom, . . . used a depopulated Natal as a buffer zone between them".[136]

Van Jaarsveld, with some justification, felt that all too often whole arguments were built up from a single example. Thus, on the evidence of a single source, Monica Wilson claimed that after Andries Stockenström (senior) and 14 of his companions had been killed while amicably talking to a Xhosa leader in 1811, " 'all Kafirs who resisted were shot; their kraals burnt down; and their cattle seized. No prisoners were made and the wounded and infirm were left to perish'."[137]

* * *

Another work that marked a turning point in South African historiography as far as the study of blacks was concerned was Leonard Thompson's *African societies in Southern Africa.*, which appeared in 1969. This was a collection of historical, anthropological and archaeological articles which focused attention more pertinently on pre-colonial African societies, or pre-conquest societies as Thompson prefers to call them. In the late 1960s, Thompson stated that historians "have tended to ignore, or to treat very summarily, the history of the African peoples before they were subjected to white over-rule. The pre-conquest African societies are therefore a forgotten factor in southern

African history".[138] In the 1970s historians were to devote attention to this, and to rescue the "forgotten factor" from limbo.

A third work that heralded a new era in South African historiography was John Omer-Cooper's *Zulu aftermath* of 1966 which dealt with the rise of the Zulu kingdom and the widespread repercussions that followed its expansion.[139] Omer-Cooper was a South African who had gone to Nigeria; he later went to New Zealand. Although this work deals with the rise of the Zulu kingdom and is thus not primarily concerned with interaction, it is still to a certain extent dominated by the desire to show that Africans had a past of their own and also that they were not simply the objects of white actions and policies, but that they did respond effectively to the changes in their environment. As such it shares much the same preoccupations as the *Oxford History*. The attention given by Omer-Cooper to the Mfecane, focused the attention of historians anew on the disruptions in the South African interior. Among the first to take up the theme after him was William Lye.[140]

In the years following the appearance of these books historians were aided by the strides that were made as South Africa caught up with the rest of Africa in the fields of archaeology and anthropology. New work and new questions that these disciplines asked enabled historians engaged in writing the history of South Africa to make an important contribution to our perception of these societies.

The *Oxford History* was a landmark as much for what it did not do as for what it did. It was criticised by conservatives for relegating the history of the whites to the sidelines and for its liberal political assumptions; those holding more radical views also criticised it, and it was the latter's re-examination of the basic tenets of faith of the liberals that led to the largescale rewriting of South African history in the years following the appearance of the *Oxford History*.

By the time that the *Oxford History* appeared, north of the Zambezi River the great expectations that people in the newly independent states had held were rapidly dissipating in the face of economic realities. The dawning realisation that political independence was not a panacea for the country's ills, that the roots of the lack of development and poverty had not been automatically removed when their political subjugation ended, and that the economic inequalities had survived the colonial era, led to a greater concentration by scholars on neo-colonialism and economic imperialism. These problems were approached very much from a neo-Marxist point of view. This led to new questions of the past being asked and the political aspects of the transfer of power were pushed into the background. The situation of an industrialised South Africa contrasted sharply with the poverty and underdevelopment in many of the independent countries and more attention was given to an analysis of the South African process of industrialisation, fresh questions were asked of "the imperial factor" in South Africa and the way in which it had operated.

NOTES

1 W. M. Macmillan, *The Cape Colour Question*, London, 1927, p. 11.

2 E. A. Walker, *The frontier tradition in South Africa: A lecture delivered before the University of Oxford at Rhodes House on 5th March, 1930*, London, 1930, p. 20.

3 Macmillan, *My South African years: An autobiography*, Cape Town, 1975, pp. 3–7.

4 Ibid., pp. 52–60.

5 Ibid., p. 48.

6 Ibid., pp. 64–65, 70–71.

7 Jeremy Krikler, "William Macmillan and the working class", paper delivered at the University of the Witwatersrand History Workshop, 9–14 February 1987, p. 8.

8 Macmillan, *Autobiography*, pp. 57–61.

9 Ibid., pp. 83–85. See also Krikler, pp. 9–10.

10 *Autobiography*, pp. 87–106.

11 Krikler, p. 13.

12 Ibid., pp. 14–15.

13 Naidoo, *W. M. Macmillan: South African historian*, M. A., Unisa, pp. 62–72.

14 *Autobiography*, pp. 129–130.

15 Ibid., p. 146.

16 Willam Beinart and Peter Delius, "Introduction" in William Beinart, Peter Delius and Stanley Trapido (eds), *Putting a plough to the ground: Accumulation and dispossession in rural South Africa, 1850-1930*, Johannesburg, 1986, pp. 2–6.

17 See chapter 5.

18 *The agrarian problem*. See also Krikler, pp. 17–18.

19 *Autobiography*, p. 146.

20 *The agrarian problem*, p. 23.

21 *Complex South Africa*, p. 120.

22 Ibid., p. 16. See also *Times Literary Supplement*, 19 June 1930, p. 507.

23 Krikler, p. 23

24 *Autobiography*, pp. 185–186.

25 *The rise and fall of the South African peasantry*, London, 1979, p. 147.

26 *Putting a plough to the ground*, p. 5.

27 *Autobiography*, p. 162.

28 *The Cape Colour Question*, pp. 95–96.

29 Ibic., p. 283.

30 Ibid., p. vii.

31 More recently, Ordinance 50 has been regarded in different terms. Susan Newton-King, for example, sees it as "an attempt to increase the labour supply available to the colonists." See "The labour market of the Cape Colony, 1807-28" in Shula Marks and Anthony Atmore (eds), *Economy and society in pre-industrial South Africa*, London, 1980, p. 197. See also P. H. Kapp, *Dr. John Philip: Die grondlegger van liberalisme in Suid-Afrika*, Archives Year Book for S.A. History, 1985, vol. 2.

32 *The Cape Colour Question*, p. 288.

33 *Bantu, Boer, and Briton*, p. x. The references are to the 2nd ed. which appeared in 1963.

34 Ibid., p. vii.

35 Ibid., p. ix.

36 Jeff Peires, *The House of Phalo: A history of the Xhosa people in the days of their independence*, Johannesburg, 1981, p. 180.

37 *Bantu, Boer, and Briton*, p. 26.

38 Ibid., pp. 29–30.

39 *Autobiography*, p. 146.

40 F. A. van Jaarsveld, *Omstrede Suid-Afrikaanse verlede: Geskiedenisideologie en die historiese skuldvraagstuk*, Johannesburg and Cape Town, 1984, p. 46. Van Jaarsveld devotes some considerable space to Macmillan.

41 See, for example, Belinda Bozzoli (ed.), *Town and countryside in the Transvaal: Capitalist penetration and popular response*, Johannesburg, 1983; Beinart, Delius and Trapido, *Putting a plough to the ground*; Timothy J. Keegan, *Rural transformations in industrializing South Africa: The Southern Highveld to 1914*, Johannesburg, 1986.

42 F. A. van Jaarsveld, *The Afrikaner's interpretation of South African History*, Cape Town, 1964, p. 141.

43 Christopher Saunders, "The writing of C. W. de Kiewiet's, 'A history of South Africa social and economic' ", *History in Africa*, 13, 1986, pp. 323, 329. Unless otherwise indicated, the information in this section comes from the above publication, and Saunders' larger work on de Kiewiet, *C. W. de Kiewiet: Historian of South Africa*, Centre for African Studies, Communications of the University of Cape Town, no. 10, 1986.

44 Saunders, *C. W. de Kiewiet: Historian of South Africa*, p. 6 n. 16; C. F. J. Muller, F. A. van Jaarsveld, Theo van Wijk, Maurice Boucher (eds), *South African history and historians: A bibliography*, Pretoria, 1979, p. 167.

45 For a review of this book see *Times Literary Supplement*, 4 April 1929.

46 De Kiewiet, *The imperial factor*, p. 5.

47 Shula and Marks and Anthony Atmore, "The imperial factor in South Africa in the nineteenth century: Towards a reassessment", *Journal of Imperial and Commonwealth History*, 3(1), 1974. For a review of *The imperial factor* see *Times Literary Supplement*, 7 August 1937, p. 566.

48 De Kiewiet, *The imperial factor*, pp. 2–3, 14.

49 Quoted in Saunders, "The writing of C. W. de Kiewiet's, 'A history of South Africa social and economic' ", pp. 324–325.

50 Ibid., p. 326.

51 Ibid., p. 327.

52 Saunders, *C. W. de Kiewiet*, p. 36, quoting from the *Manchester Guardian*, May 1941.

53 De Kiewiet, *A history*, p. 79.

54 Saunders, *C. W. de Kiewiet*, p. 39.

55 De Kiewiet, *A history*, pp. 188–189.

56 Saunders, *C. W. de Kiewiet*, p. 43.

57 Christopher Saunders, "Our past as literature: Notes on style in South African history in English", *Kleio*, 18, 1986, pp. 50, 52.

58 Ibid., pp. 52–53. Saunders cites Phyllis Lewson's article, "The language of the historian", *English Studies in Africa*, 13(2), 1970, p. 356.

59 *History of South Africa: Social and economic*, p. 89.

60 Stanley Trapido, "South Africa and the historians", *African Affairs*, 71(1972), p. 445.

61 J. S. Marais, *The Cape Coloured People 1652-1937*, London, 1939 and reprinted by the Witwatersrand University Press, Johannesburg, 1957. The quote is taken from pp. 281–282 of the 1957 reprint. Marais's other major works include *Maynier and the first Boer republic*, Cape Town, 1944 and *The fall of Kruger's republic*, Oxford, 1961.

62 Marais, *Maynier*, p.v. See Chapter 2 (Theal) for more details of Marais's work on Maynier.

63 Review of Marais by F. A. van Jaarsveld, *Historia*, 7, 1962, pp. 65–67.

64 The quotes are from Marais, pp. 289,319. For the review in question see *Times Literary Supplement*, 13 October 1961, p. 680.

65 *Journal of African History* 3(1), 1962, pp. 148–150. The works Thompson is referring to are Jean van der Poel, *The Jameson Raid*, London 1951 and Ethel Drus, "The question of imperial complicity in the Jameson Raid", *English Historical Review*, 68, 1953, pp. 582–593 and "A

report on the papers of Joseph Chamberlain relating to the Jameson Raid and the inquiry", *Bulletin of the Institute for Historical Research*, 25, 1952, pp. 33–62.

66 Jeffrey Butler, *The Liberal Party and the Jameson Raid*, Oxford, 1968, p. 268. See also Marais, p. 94.
67 L. M. Thompson, "South Africa" in R. W. Winks (ed.), *The historiography of the British Empire – Commonwealth: Trends, interpretations, and resources*, Durham, N.C., 1966, p. 214.
68 L. M. Thompson, "Afrikaner nationalist historiography and the policy of apartheid", *Journal of African History*, 3(1), 1962, p. 130.
69 Saunders, "The writing of C. W. de Kiewiet's, 'A history of South Africa social and economic' ", p. 324.
70 Ibid.
71 Walker, *A history of Southern Africa*, 3rd ed., 1968 impression, p. 117.
72 Jean Walker, *'Skin deep': The autobiography of a woman doctor*, Published by Dr J. F. Midgley J. P., 1 Disa Avenue, Kommetjie, Cape, 1977, pp. 7,41.
73 Ibid., p. 7.
74 Ibid., p. 162.
75 Ibid., p. 33.
76 Walker, *de Villiers*, p. 3.
77 *Times Literary Supplement*, 22 January 1925, p. 49.
78 *History*, 1928 ed., p. 440; 3rd ed., 1968 impression, p. 434.
79 Jean Walker, p. 98.
80 *The Great Trek*, 4th ed., London, 1960, p. 1. For an analysis of Walker's contribution to the study of the Great Trek see C. F. J. Muller, "Die Groot Trek", *Die hervertolking van ons geskiedenis*, Communications of the University of South Africa, B. 19, Pretoria, 1963, reprinted in B. J. Liebenberg (comp.), *Trends in the South African historiography*, Unisa, 1986, Pretoria pp. 58–91.
81 Saunders, *C. W. de Kiewiet*, p. 21.
82 *Schreiner*, p. 198.
83 *History*, 1928 ed., p. vi.
84 Webb's tribute appeared in the 1976 issue of *Janus*, the journal of the Historical Society of the University of Cape Town. It is reprinted in Jean Walker, pp. 164–165.
85 Quoted in Jean Walker, p. 164.
86 *English Historical Review*, 74, 1959, p. 175.
87 *History*, 1928 ed., p. vi.
88 Jean Walker, p. 163.
89 For a review see *Times Literary Supplement*, 31 August 1940, p. 427.
90 *History*, 2nd ed., 1947 reprint, p. 453 n .2.
91 Ibid., pp. 155 n. 3 and 158 n .2.
92 Ibid., pp. 156 n .3 and 160 n .2.
93 Ibid., pp. 122–124.
94 Jean Walker, pp. 89,95.
95 Ibid., pp. 93–101.
96 Ibid., pp. 110–111.
97 The last part of chapter 10 of the 1940 ed., "Moshesh and Waterboer, 1854–1871", is included in the 3rd ed. as part of Chapter 11 entitled "Gold, diamonds and confederation, 1861-1881". Chapter 11 of the 1940 ed. is called " 'My confederation policy', 1871-1881".
98 *History*, 3rd ed., 1968 impression, p. 658 n. 1.
99 Ibid., pp. 440–456.
100 Ibid., pp. 441 n. 2, 447 n. 1, 456 n. 2, 531 n. 6.
101 See also Walker, *The frontier tradition*, p. 23.
102 See B. J. Liebenberg, "Eric Walker's interpretation of recent South African history", *Historia*, 11, 1966, pp. 171–190.

103 Ibid. The quotes come from Walker, *History*, 3rd ed., 1968 impression, pp. 69, 707, 731–732, 745, 822.

104 For reviews of the 2nd ed., see *Times Literary Supplement*, 20 September 1963, p. 69 and *Journal of African History*, 5(2), 1964, pp. 327–328.

105 Jean Walker, p. 110.

106 Ibid., pp. 151–153, 161–162.

107 M. C. J. Mphahlele, *The Methodist venture in education at Kilnerton, 1886–1962*, M.Ed. University of the North, 1971; M. O. M. Seboni, *The South African Native College, Fort Hare, 1903–1954*, D.Ed. Unisa, 1959; E. P. Lekhela, *The origin, development and role of missionary teacher-training institutions for the Africans 1850–1954*, D.Ed. Unisa, 1970; L. D. Ngcongco, *Imvo . . . and Cape 'Native' policy, 1884–1902*, M. A. Unisa, 1974; S. S. M. Lekhela, *An historical survey of Native land settlement in South Africa from 1902 to the passing of the Natives Trust and Land Act of 1936*, M. A. Unisa, 1955; K. K. Ncwana, *Amangakwana ngeminombo yezizwe zase-Mbo (Origin of the Abambo tribes)*, Lovedale, 1953; A. Z. Ngani, *Ibali lamagqunukhwebe (History of the Gqunukhwebe tribe)*, Lovedale, 1947; W. M. D. Phophi, *Phusuphusu dza dzimauli: A history of Rammbuda's tribe, northern Transvaal*, Cape Town, 1956; V. Poto, *Ama Mpondo: Ibali nentlalo (The Pondo: Their history and customs)*, Lovedale, n. d.

108 Sol. T. Plaatjie, *Native life in South Africa, before and since the European war and the Boer rebellion*, London, 1917, p. 11.

109 D. E. Burchell, "Adams College Natal, c. 1920–1956: A critical assessment", *Journal of the University of Durban-Westville*, New Series 1.

110 Van Jaarsveld, *Omstrede verlede*, p. 124.

111 S. M. Molema, *The Bantu past and present*, p. vii. Other works of relevance are Z. K. Matthews, *Freedom for my people*; Sol. T. Plaatjie, *Native life in South Africa*; J. H. Soga, *The south-eastern Bantu*; D. D. T. Jabavu, *The life of John Tengo Jabavu*.

112 Jeff Peires, *The House of Phalo*, pp. 178–179.

113 Ngubane, *An African explains apartheid*, London 1963, p. 80.

114 Albert Luthuli, *Let my people go: An autobiography*, London, 1962, p. 42.

115 E. A. Walker, *The frontier tradition in South Africa*, Oxford 1930, p. 22.

116 I. D. MacCrone, *Race attitudes in South Africa: Historical, experimental and psychological studies*, Johannesburg, 1937. The quote is taken from p. 135 of the Johannesburg, 1957 reprint.

117 This phrase was coined by Shula Marks in "Towards a people's history of South Africa? Recent developments in the historiography of South Africa" in R. Samuel (ed.), *People's history and socialist theory*, London, 1981, p. 299.

118 De Kiewiet, *Anatomy*, p. 65.

119 Ibid., pp. 69–70.

120 H. A. Reyburn, "Studies in Cape frontier history: I, Land, labour and law; II, Trouble on the Baviaans River; III, Stockenstrom and Slagter's Nek; IV, Tooverberg, V, Reprisals; VI, From Amalinde to Somerset Mount", *The Critic*, III and IV, October 1934 to February 1936.

121 His best-known articles are "150 years of economic contact between black and white", *South African Journal of Economics*, 2(4), 1934 and 3(1), 1935, "The Cape of Good Hope and 'systematic colonisation' ", *South African Journal of Economics*, 5(4), 1937, "The economic development of the Cape under Van Riebeeck", *South African Journal of Economics*, 13(1-4), 1945 and "The politico-economic background of Jan van Riebeeck's settlement", *South African Journal of Economics*, 20(3), 1952.

122 J. van der Poel, *The Jameson Raid*. Together with W. K. Hancock, she was editor for *Selections from the Smuts papers*, 5 vols, Cambridge, 1966–1973. Her other works of note were *Basutoland as a factor in South African politics, 1858–1870*, Archives Year Book for S. A. History, 1941, vol. 1 and *Railway and customs policies in South Africa, 1885–1910*, London, 1933.

123 For a detailed analysis along these lines see Jeffrey Butler and Deryck Schreuder, "Liberal historiography since 1945" in Jeffrey Butler, Richard Elphich and David Welsh (eds), *Democratic Liberalism in South Africa: Its history and prospect*, Middletown (Connecticut), Cape Town and Johannesburg, 1987.

124 T. O. Ranger, "Towards a usable African past" in C. Fyfe (ed.), *African studies since 1945: A tribute to Basil Davidson*, London, 1976.

125 Monica Wilson and Leonard Thompson (eds), *The Oxford History of South Africa*, vol. 1, *South Africa to 1870*, Oxford, 1969 and vol. 2 *South Africa 1870–1966*, Oxford, 1971.

126 R. Hyam, "Are we any nearer an African history of South Africa?", *The Historical Journal*, 16(3), 1973, p. 622; D. Denoon, "Synthesising South African history", *Transafrican Journal of History*, 2(1), 1972, p. 112.

127 Denoon, "Synthesising South African history", p. 110.

128 S. Marks, "Liberalism, social realities, and South African history", *Journal of Commonwealth political studies*, 5(3), 1972, p. 245.

129 David Birmingham and Shula Marks, "Southern Africa" in Roland Oliver (ed.), *The Cambridge History of Africa*, vol. 3, *from c. 1050 to 1600*, Cambridge, 1977, p. 598.

130 Marks, "Towards a people's history?", p. 304.

131 Robert Collins, "Synthesis and reflections: African history is a precarious profession" in D. I. Ray, P. Shinnie and D. Williams (eds), *Into the 80's: The proceedings of the Eleventh Annual Conference of the Canadian Association of African Studies*, vol. 1, Vancouver, 1981, p. 242.

132 Ibid., pp. 116–117.

133 K. R. Hughes, "Challenges from the past: reflections on liberalism and radicalism in the writing of Southern African history", *Social Dynamics*, 3(1), 1977, p. 47.

134 H. M. Wright, *The burden of the present: Liberal-radical controversy over Southern African history*, Cape Town, 1977, pp. 35,58.

135 F. A. van Jaarsveld, "Ons verledebeeld: Geskonde oue of vertekende nuwe?" in *Geskiedkundige verkenninge*, Pretoria, 1974, pp. 166–186. This originally appeared in *Standpunte*, 22(6), 1969, under the title "Vergruisde of vertekende beeld?", pp. 1–21.

136 Ibid., pp. 175–176, citing the *Oxford History*, vol. 1, p. 346. For further discussion of African reaction, see pp. 206–207.

137 Van Jaarsveld, "Ons verledebeeld", p. 183, citing the *Oxford History*, vol. 1, pp. 237–238.

138 Leonard Thompson (ed.), *African societies in Southern Africa*, London, 1969, p. 1.

139 J. D. Omer-Cooper, *The Zulu aftermath: A nineteenth-century revolution in Bantu Africa*, London, 1966.

140 W. F. Lye, *The Sotho wars in the interior of South Africa, 1822–1837*, Ph.D., University of California (Los Angeles). 1969 and "The Ndebele kingdom south of the Limpopo River", *Journal of African History*, 10(1), 1969, pp. 87–104.

W.M. Macmillan

J.S. Marais

C.W. de Kiewiet

E.A. Walker

L.M. Thompson

T.R.H. Davenport

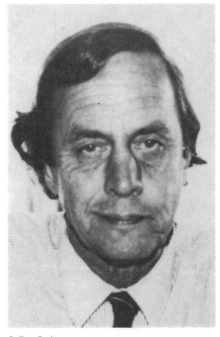

M. Wilson

S.B. Spies

R. Ross

T. Keegan

H. Giliomee

D. Denoon

153

W. Beinart

S. Marks

D. Yudelman

D. O'Meara

5 A radical approach to the past

A NON-ACADEMIC RADICAL HISTORIOGRAPHY

Although the radical academic historical tradition that emerged in the 1970s owed much of its immediate impetus to the shortcomings of the *Oxford History*, it also owed something to a non-academic radical historical phase that formulated new questions of the past in the 1940s and 1950s. Like the missionary-inspired liberal tradition, this writing saw history essentially from the point of view of the subordinate sections of society. The roots of this tradition lay in the growing black resistance to the South African government, and a number of the writers in this tradition, but by no means all of them, were black.

During the Second World War the African working class expanded enormously. It is estimated that between 1939 and 1952 the African urban population virtually doubled. One result of this was that there was a great ferment of political activity among blacks.[1] The coming to power of the Nationalist Party in 1948 seemed to make the fulfilment of black aspirations for a better deal even more remote. Black resistance increased and signs of Marxist influences were more in evidence. An early example is E. Roux's *Time longer than rope: The black man's struggle for freedom in South Africa*,[2] written "from a standpoint of humane indignation"[3] and which contains much data about Clements Kadalie's Industrial and Commercial Workers' Union (I.C.U.). First published in 1948, this work by a one-time professor of botany at the University of the Witwatersrand and leading member of the Communist Party of South Africa between 1923 and 1936, has with the passage of time steadily gained greater acceptance among a wide spectrum of people as a realisation of its merits becomes more apparent. In a perceptive article in 1980, the Cape Town mathematician K. R. Hughes wrote that if he found himself in the

155

position of having to recommend *one* book to overseas friends, despite the fact that the book had been published as far back as 1948, he always recommended *Time longer than rope*, "a book whose analysis is superficial, judgements faulty, reporterage inaccurate and yet bears all over it the stamp of a first-class mind."[4]

In the 1950s the government struck a number of major blows at African resistance to white rule. The banning in 1950 of the Communist Party of South Africa, which had been founded in 1921, was part of the government offensive. The majority of black writers were by no means communists, or even communist sympathisers; among the older generation their Christian upbringing in most cases made them keep communism at arm's length; some of them saw the Communist Party as a white party, with little to say to blacks of the country, while others again, already fighting against totalitarianism in South Africa, were not inclined to embrace another totalitarian system. Thus the view was expressed that the Communist Party could not tolerate any movement that it did not dominate – if it could not control an organisation, it killed it. The Communist Party was associated with white ruling groups. The few blacks who had joined the Communist Party, it was maintained, had simply completed the membership forms which had been publically distributed, without having the faintest notion of what communism was about. The dominant "conscious element" in the Party was the *petit bourgeois* intellectual whites, who supported the ruling white political parties whenever there was a political crisis.[5] A movement to have the communists expelled from the African National Congress was only narrowly defeated in 1945 and 1947.[6]

Although black leaders and writers were by no means staunch supporters of the Communist Party, they were affected by the 1950 Suppression of Communist Act, since it was directed not only at the Communist Party, but at any group or doctrine that aimed at bringing about "any political, industrial, social or economic change ... by the promotion of disturbance or disorder, by unlawful acts" or "encouragement of feelings of hostility between the European and non-European races of the Union".[7]

This is however not to deny that even among those who had no particular love for the Communist Party, when the Communist Party was forced to go underground it gained stature as a leader in the fight for freedom. This was not confined to South Africa of course, and in the rest of Africa as well, Russian support for decolonisation made black nationalist leaders, struggling against their colonial rulers, more amenable to communism. Marxist terminology became more popular, but those who used it were not necessarily communists.

In the 1950s there is a change in the histories being written. The whites are no longer seen as heroes who won the country for Christianity and civilisation, but as outsiders, interlopers, conquerors and exploiters who dispossessed the original owners. Black historians no longer distinguished between the exploitative Afrikaner and the liberal English – they were all whites who had shared in the rape, plunder and exploitation of the country. The missionaries were not friends of the blacks but agents of capitalism and white control. The Cape liberals were not really liberal, they had only wanted the black voters to obtain a pro-British majority in the Cape parliament – after the republics had been destroyed the liberal English worked with the reactionary Hertzog to eliminate the black vote. The British were not spared, in some ways they had been worse than the Afrikaners. The emancipation of slaves in 1834 came about because British capitalists discovered they could make better profits from "free" labourers than from slaves. The British were always ready to come to the aid of the Afrikaners when they landed in difficulty. It was the British with their regular soldiers who could be kept in the field almost indefinitely, which a Boer commando with its need to conduct farming operations, could not, that posed the biggest threat to the blacks. Had it not been for the British, the Boer Voortrekkers would have been wiped out. Blacks in history who had collaborated with whites were labelled traitors. The Anglo-Boer War was a war between English and Afrikaner exploiters fought on someone else's land.

The celebration in 1952 by the whites of 300 years of white settlement since Jan van Riebeeck and his men landed at the Cape, was countered by resistance from blacks, who argued that there was nothing to celebrate but much about which to grieve. In a speech, S. M. Molema exhorted his listeners "to remember the salient, the dominant fact of South African history, namely that all the monuments, all the celebrations and all the feasts of the White man have a diametrically opposite meaning to the Black man, because every monument of the White man perpetuates the memory of the annihilation of some Black community, every celebration of victory the remembrance of our defeat, his every feast means our famine and his laughter our tears. Such are the Great Trek celebrations and the Voortrekker Monuments; such are Dingaan's Day, Kruger Day and Union Day, and such are the approaching Van Riebeeck celebrations".[8]

Massive rallies on 16 April 1952 protesting against the van Riebeeck celebrations, encouraged the executives of black organisations to organise the Defiance Campaign in the middle of the year. In all this heightened political activity, two works were published which were to have an important role in opening up new ways of thinking about South African history.

Three hundred years: A history of South Africa appeared under the pseudonym "Mnguni". It was published by the New Era Fellowship of Lansdowne in the Cape as part of its opposition to the celebration of 300 years of white settlement in South Africa. In this book the history of South Africa is seen as the history "of 300 years of struggle between oppressors and oppressed". For many years there was much speculation about the identity of "Mnguni", and it was suggested that the author may in fact not be a black person. This has recently been proved correct. In 1980 Jaca Books of Milan brought out a new and expanded 438-page edition of the original *Three hundred years* which consisted of 176 pages. The title of the new edition was *Storia del Sudafrica*, and in it the editor is identified as Hosea Jaffe, a prolific left-wing pamphleteer who had been born in Cape Town in 1921, studied engineering at the University of Cape Town and went into exile in the 1950s; he obtained a degree at the University of London, and later settled in Europe where he taught in various schools and colleges. He continued to write, and his most recent publication is *A history of Africa*, published in London in 1985.[9]

Another book that appeared in 1952 in Cape Town and which left its mark on South African historical writing was *The role of the missionaries in conquest*, the author of which was given as Nosipho Majeke. It was thought that this was a pseudonym for a white, and this has since been established. The work was in fact written by Dora Taylor, who lived in Claremont in Cape Town and was the wife of J. G. Taylor, who was at the time senior lecturer in the Department of Psychology at the University of Cape Town. She went to London in the early 1960s and died there in the late 1970s.[10] *The role of the missionaries in conquest*, like *Three hundred years*, was aimed at furthering the liberation struggle. It was written from a Marxist point of view, and because it portrayed the liberals as part of the oppressive South African system, it was not a work that found much favour in liberal circles, any more than did *Three hundred years*.

In the introduction to her book, Taylor writes that the story of South African history, "if truly told, is one of continuous plunder of land and cattle by the European invaders, of the devastation and decimation of people, followed by their economic enslavement. It is a story of treacherous deeds, rapacity seasoned with sanctimonious hypocrisy, of treaties that were not treaties but the cynical legalising of plunder, of the policy of 'divide and rule' carried out with systematic cunning in order to turn one tribe against another, one people against another".

Jaffe's pamphlets of the 1940s are of significance not so much for their "crude polemics" as for the fact that he anticipated the neo-Marxists and radicals of the 1970s, in particular in putting forward the view that segregation and capitalism were bedfellows rather than enemies. Jaffe was one of the first writers to move away from old terms like Bushmen (whom he refers to as !ke) and Hottentots (whom he calls Khoi-Khoin). He anticipated tendencies in radical writing by seeing the United Party as representing the Chamber of Mines, and maintaining that the coming to power of the Nationalists in 1948 did not mean a significant change: "In no fundamental, and in very few details," he wrote, "did and does this regime differ from the Nazism of General Smuts."[11]

Dora Taylor also anticipated later research by portraying the missionaries as imperial agents. It was the missionaries who were responsible for the policy of segregation. The Moravians and the early London Missionary Society missionaries, including van der Kemp at Bethelsdorp "followed the

158

principle of segregation from the outset . . . The segregated mission reserve was the particular contribution of the missionary to the pattern of South African society. It was part of the liberal myth of 'protection'. It is trusteeship in its earliest form. In other words it is the beginning of the herrenvolk lie of the inferiority of the Non-European. 'Protection' and 'inferiority', the idea that the Black man is 'different' from the White – these have become part of the machinery of oppression."[12] Ordinance 50 was not a purely humanitarian effort brought about unselfishly by Dr Philip. It had a strong economic motivation, and, in putting forward this view, Jaffe and Taylor were way ahead of Shula Marks and Susan Newton-King, although the latter two were later to flesh out the theme and clothe it in a class analysis.[13] Taylor said that while Ordinance 50 granted the Khoi legal equality and lifted the restrictions on the free movement of labour, it was also "a segregatory law, with especial application only to 'Hottentots and other free persons of colour'; it consolidated those sections of the existing labour laws, based on old Dutch slave laws, which were essential to a Masters and Servants relationship; that is, any breach of contract on the part of the servant was to be punished as a *criminal* offence."[14]

Taylor also anticipated other work done later in the 1970s on the role of Britain in South Africa. She wrote that "the missionaries made a great show of 'protecting' the Griqua against the Boers, but actually it was the Boers who were being protected by the British in all their land seizures." Time after time when "the Dutch were in danger of being defeated by the Africans, the British came to their assistance. It had happened in the Cape Colony when a united force of Khoikhoi and amaXhosa – Ndlambe's warriors – had pursued the Dutch as far south as George; and again, when Dingane had put Retief and his party to death as his answer to their arrogant request for his country, the British at Port Natal had joined forces with the Dutch." Treaties the British had signed with African chiefs also helped the Boers: "Any such 'alliance' between an African chief and the British, by persuading him to accept their 'friendship' – and consequently their interference in his affairs – neutralized his power and therefore saved the Boers from possible annihilation."[15]

It was not only Marxist writers who took up a new attitude. Although Albert Luthuli, who won the Nobel Peace Prize in 1961, was educated in the liberal tradition at Adams College, he became disillusioned with white liberals, as they had accomplished nothing, and black rights continued to be whittled away. He became more militant, seeing black education as aimed at making the blacks permanent wood cutters and drawers of water. The Bantu Education Act of 1954, followed by The Extension of University Education Act in 1956, creating separate ethnic or tribal colleges, came as a severe blow to Luthuli. He described the first of these Acts as "a specialised type of education designed exclusively by Europeans exclusively for Africans.

It is not, as were former educational systems in South Africa, designed simply by adults for children."[16]

*   *   *

In the rest of black Africa the beginning of the end of the colonial era was signalled by the independence of the Gold Coast as Ghana in 1957. In the following 10 years one colony after another became independent. In 1960 the massacre of blacks in the township of Sharpeville introduced a new bitter note into African frustration and anger, while the coming of the republic at more or less the same time, also seemed to cut blacks off from help from the outside world, and to make them feel even more alone in their bid to improve their situation.

The fight for freedom that the A.N.C. had led with constitutional methods of peaceful protest, gave way to a liberation struggle, a struggle that its black participants believed would have to be violent to end white rule. Freedom became the central issue. Statements like that of Kwame Nkrumah on the occasion of Ghana's independence in 1957, that this independence meant nothing while other parts of Africa remained in chains, did much to encourage South African blacks, as did the growing strength of the Afro-Asian bloc in the United Nations.

A number of black writers either left South Africa voluntarily or went into forced exile, continuing their writing from abroad. The A.N.C. and Pan African Congress (P.A.C.) opened information offices everywhere in the world, and the pamphlets they produced, although hardly scientific history, take the whites before the international community, where they are charged with racism, oppression, exploitation, militarism and police-state activities. History is invoked to bring notice of their misdeeds before the world. But this is no impartial trial and the verdict of guilty is usually delivered at the same time and in the same breath as the charge.[17]

Although much of this recent work, represented in numerous pamphlets, does not really meet with any standards of genuine historical enquiry, it does demonstrate the strong link between national and historical consciousness. In this sense it is similar to some of the Afrikaner propagandistic work that appeared early in the century as Afrikaners sought to put British imperialism in the dock and find it guilty. Just as the Afrikaners used history to put their case forcefully, so too are the blacks using history to present their case. The wheel has come full circle. In the early part of the twentieth century, Afrikaner pamphleteers and writers of history were likewise not always trained historians; they too were politically active in the fight against British imperialism. They saw history as in the process of being made. Their history was also a summary of historical grievances and a charge sheet against the British. As history was formerly interpreted solely from a white or Afrikaner point of view, today it is seen from a solely black point of view. Just as the Afrikaners struggling to free themselves from the yoke of British imperialism saw their history as in the process of being made, as uncompleted, blacks now see the past in the same way. Thus African history is still being made, the struggle is an ongoing one and history is part of that struggle, not a passtime that is written reflectively by fully trained professionals sitting in ivory towers.

An interesting example of the way the tables have been turned is provided in the British annexation of the Transvaal in 1877, and the successful rising of the Boers of Paul Kruger to cast off the colonial yoke at the end of 1880. In 1952 Dr Molema saw the position of the blacks after the coming to power of the National Party in 1948 in similar terms. He could not understand how the Afrikaners could act as they did towards blacks in the light of their own struggle for freedom against the British imperialists. He warned that "as the Dutch-Afrikaner had the British dictator and tyrant to thank . . . for awakening him from his complacency to form a united front, so the African, the Non-European of 1949 to 1952 can now, and will assuredly thank the Dutch-Afrikaner Nationalist for arousing him from his stupor of disunion to grope for his equally unprivileged brother to form a Non-European United front, and having exhausted all constitutional methods of obtaining redress, to launch a determined campaign of Civil Disobedience and Defiance of Unjust Laws."[18]

A book published in 1980 in Sri Lanka, in putting the case of the blacks, quotes a statement made by Paul Kruger on the eve of the Boer rising of 1880. It reads: "With confidence we lay our case before the whole world. Whether we win or die, freedom will rise in Africa like the sun from the morning clouds."[19] These same words are now used to justify black actions.

From *The rise of Azania, the fall of South Africa* by David Dube (Lusaka, 1983), it appears that black student organisations have relinquished the idea of South Africa as a multi-racial land: it is a black land belonging to blacks alone. Blacks will write their own history alone, only they can decide who will be the new heroes of the South African past for whom monuments will be built in the future.

In his column "My view", in the Johannesburg *Star*, Nimrod Mkele in reflecting upon the penchant in black Africa for changing names after independence and eliminating the names bequeathed from the colonial past, wrote: "Once Azania arrives we will have our work cut out for us relabelling the map of this southern tip of Africa, for the Boers have littered our countryside with fonteins, bergs, burgs, vleis and strooms while the English have left us with a legacy of their own imperialist history – Port Elizabeth, East London, Grahamstown, Durban and ad nauseum." He went on to say that "the job of place name change will not be that hard, for Africans still use the names a lot of places were known by before the white man imposed his own. Bloemfontein will thus become Mangaung. Pietermaritzburg will revert to its original name Mgungundlovu and Kingwilliamstown will be Qonce."

He suggests too that Mamelodi wa Tswane may well be an improvement on "the unromantic sounding Pretoria".[20]

Some of the recent history, however, purports to have a serious historical content, but one hesitates to place it in the category of academic radical works. One recent work which attempts to analyse South African history in Marxist terms is Bernard Makhosezwe Magubane's *The political economy of race and class in South Africa* (New York and London, 1979). It is a disappointingly superficial work which tends to draw direct parallels between the generalised statements of Marx, Hobson and Lenin, and specific situations in South Africa's past. There are some very "woolly" arguments, such as his "philosophical reason" for referring to South Africa's whites "as settlers and not as white South Africans". He argues thus: "Before the Africans became 'Kafirs', 'Natives', 'Bantus', and now 'Blacks', they were citizens and owners of the land later usurped by their European conquerors. Both the statelessness and degradation of the African people emerged in one and the same historical process – in the act of conquest, the forcible robbery of their means of subsistence. Their indigence today is a result of the most cruel lawlessness known to human history. Having taken this into account, the whole meaning of being called Kafir, Native, Bantu, or Black, rather than being called African, changes the moral and legal status of the white settlers' claim to the South African state."[21]

LABELS AND INFLUENCES

Nowhere does the artificial division of historians into various "schools" create more problems than in discussing trends in historical writing in the past 15 or so years. The historical writing that emerged in the 1970s has variously been labelled "revisionist", "radical", or "Marxist". None of them is totally satisfactory. Part of the difficulty is that although the writers thus described all approached history in a way that betokened a sharp break with "the conventional wisdom" as handed down by historians before them, there were major differences between the various practitioners of the new history. As Frederick Johnstone has observed, "This is a new school in the broad sense of meaning a body of work within a new and radically different paradigm, though not in the narrower sense of implying as well a unified consensus on all issues."[22]

A discussion of the terminology could quite easily itself be the subject of a substantial article, but it would not take us very far along the road to understanding what recent trends in historical writing are all about. As Johnstone has written: "The labels are not so important and each has its virtues and limitations." Of the three terms, radical, revisionist and Marxist, the first two "are rather unspecific theoretically", but he admits that, "on the other hand, some of the new work is only partially or tangentially Marxist". He feels nevertheless that, "Talking about a Marxist school is in many ways more appropriate, since the distinctive feature of this work has been that, in one way or another, it has taken the approach of historical materialism and class analysis."[23]

There should be no serious quarrel with this. Some of the historians and others whose work in the 1970s and 1980s made a major contribution in breaking with traditional views of the past, and who are mentioned in this chapter, do not embrace a Marxist perspective. Nevertheless, they have benefited significantly from the opening up of new themes by the Marxists. Without this they would in all likelihood not have been in a position to make the advances that they have done. So although their work may perhaps not be described as Marxist, they owe much to the way the Marxists have formulated their questions of the past. In this chapter both the terms Marxist and radical will be used.[24]

It is preferable not to use labels at all, and to avoid becoming embroiled in drawing fine distinctions between work that contains both "radical" and "liberal" elements. This is particularly relevant in the mid-1980s, when the lines of distinction are far more blurred than they appeared to be in the early and mid-1970s. There are self-proclaimed liberals and radicals, but what, asks the Rhodes University historian, Jeff Peires, do we do about "those who do not categorise themselves as liberals or radicals, but simply as historians?" He goes on to say that "the fact is that most honest and capable academics report the truth as they see it, and that some of their findings are 'liberal' and some of their findings are 'radical'."[25]

Along the same lines, Robin Law said that he did not mean to undervalue the Marxist contribution to history, but rather to suggest "that such contributions are likely to be valuable independently of rather than because of a commitment to a distinctively 'Marxist' standpoint. "Historians", he wrote, "need to utilize the insights of Marx and other theorists eclectically, with no hesitations about reformulating or jettisoning even what Marx himself may have regarded as fundamental."[26]

There is little to be gained from indulging in arguments about who belongs to which school, along the lines that attended the debate following the publication of Harrison M. Wright's book *The burden of the present*.[27] Wright, for example, categorised Barry Kosmin and Colin Bundy as radicals, but in reviewing the book, Jeff Peires, with some justification, stated that he did not consider either of the two to be radicals.[28] Wright was not prepared to accept this, and countered by saying that the "only evidence that Peires gives to show that Colin Bundy and Barry Kosmin are not radicals is to state that he does not consider them to be so". Wright argued that it was all a matter of opinion, and as further "proof" that he was correct, he referred to a 1975 statement by Terence Ranger in which he stated his opinion that Bundy was a radical; he also cited the fact that both Bundy and Kosmin acknowledged a debt to Arrighi, who was an early inspiration for the radical cause.[29]

Another attempt at labelling, this time with regard to the various stages through which radical writing is supposed to have gone, was made by David Yudelman, which he describes as "only fractionally facetious". One may accept this as a fairly useful analysis, without necessarily subscribing to the specific breakdown of categories and persons included in each of them. Yudelman discerned a number of stages through which writing of what he calls the Left has gone through. The first phase, that of the "Elder statesmen", from the mid-1960s to the early 1970s, was "characterised by the theoretical contributions of the early Harold Wolpe and Martin Legassick and the empirical contribution of Rick Johnstone". The second phase, from the mid-1970s to the early 1980s, was "characterised by the Sussex School of Poulantzian disciples, particularly the Gang of Four: Rob Davies, David Kaplan, Mike Morris and . . . Dan O'Meara." Stage three is the "Third Wave", which has existed since the time of stage one but "has only recently asserted itself fully. It has produced most of the best empirical work but has remained a largely inarticulate underswell on theoretical issues, and has generally neglected to make its differences with the Elder Statesmen and the Gang of Four groups explicit. One might number people such as the converts from liberalism, Shula Marks and Stanley Trapido, among the precursors, Charles van Onselen among the second generation and William Beinart, Peter Delius and Tim Keegan among the latecomers. In some ways, the Third Wave underswell can best be characterised as quasi-Marxists or Fellow Travellers – never entirely happy with the theoretical reductionism of the Elder Statesmen or Gang of Four, they nevertheless avoided confronting them directly."[30]

*　*　*

It was on the whole not academics working in South Africa who took the lead in approaching South African history anew. There was a body of South Africans living abroad, mainly in the United Kingdom, who had become exposed to wider intellectual influences than their colleagues back home. A number of them were attached to the School of Oriental and African Studies of London University, where Shula Marks was prominent in directing their attention to fresh possibilities. They re-examined and reinterpreted the role played by Britain in South Africa, did research into the very much neglected period of South Africa's industrialisation, and queried the traditional beliefs about the origins of South African racial attitudes and policies; they analysed the concept of the "state" and its role in society, defined and studied white and black working classes; they studied pre-colonial black societies in their own right and not merely where blacks interacted with whites. In line with trends in historical research in Europe in the wake of the rise of socialism after the Second World War, they moved away from Rankean-type history with its heavy concentration on political and national history, on the lives of leaders; they investigated societies, concerned themselves with the commonplace events of life, with the lives of ordinary people caught up in patterns of change, and social and historical processes, like urbanisation and proletarianisation. This sort of social history included much of what in earlier days would have been regarded as the separate field of economic history. The so-called writing of history "from below" is a total approach to the past. What is generally known as "people's history" has brought about new insights that were denied to those writing exclusively about historical personalities, the state and politics.

These efforts have also gone hand in hand with attempts to bring history to the notice of the "ordinary" man and woman. At the University of the Witwatersrand in 1978 the first History Workshop was held to popularise history, to help stimulate a historical consciousness among people, to break down the barrier between the professional writer of history and the workers who were the subject of his studies. Encouragement was given to the idea of people writing their own history, in their own areas and situations. The workshop was adjudged a worthwhile undertaking and by February 1987 four such workshops had been held. To the extent that these workshops, with their historical plays, visual and other material, aim at creating a historical consciousness and imparting information about the past, they are accepted by conservative critics, but in general the latter are sceptical of the motives behind the efforts to make workers aware of their history and give them an identity within that history. These attempts have been criticised as aiming to prepare the working class, which in this context means the black working class, for revolution.

In this connection it is interesting to note that at the Fourth History Workshop in February 1987, charges of elitism were levelled at the professional historians by political and trade union activists, who accused them of distancing themselves from the struggles of the workers. Popular organisations, it was maintained, should be recognised more by the historians who were writing history from below, they should have a "say" in the way history was presented. The academic historian concerning himself with the history of the workers should realise that "one has a great deal to learn from the people whose history one wishes to interpret". The people themselves, it was argued, "should have a voice in shaping the direction of research and interpreting its results".[31]

Another series of workshops that should be mentioned is that of the University of Cape Town, which has seen the production of numerous papers on the history of the mother city, many of them focusing on the lives of the subordinate classes.

Instead of histories comprised of masses of facts "that were left to speak for themselves" the radicals wanted to get behind the "facts", to understand *what it was all about*, to lay bare the patterns and processes of history. And in the attempt to reduce the mass of data to some meaningful structure, they found Marxism a powerful tool.

165

This sort of social history is, of course, by no means the preserve of any particular group of historians, nor is it of necessity Marxist, although virtually all the meaningful work in this genre has thus far been done by those writing from a historical materialist point of view. Van Jaarsveld, in his pleas for renewal by Afrikaans-speaking historians, admits that by laying so much stress on the Afrikaners, Afrikaner historians have failed to do justice to the role of the blacks and the English, and he has exhorted them to tackle subjects like capitalism and the emergence of the working class, black rural history and the process of black and white urbanisation. Afrikaner historians, he insists, will have to become more problem-orientated, to adopt an interpretative rather than a narrative approach, to choose synthesis and to seek explanations for the course of development over a long period of time with the help of the social sciences. Class, he has told his fellow Afrikaners, is not a concept they need shy away from simply because it is constantly on the lips of the Marxists. It is a legitimate historical concept that can be studied without linking it to a Marxist ideology.[32] His pleas have as yet borne no major fruit, but even outspoken critics of the radicals like van Jaarsveld have been obliged to recognise the significance of the new insights the Marxist approach has brought in its train.

In undertaking these studies they have demonstrated the importance of interdisciplinary cooperation, thus helping to broaden historical methodology by contact with the social sciences. They used archaeology, sociology and anthropology, and employed oral and experiental testimony. Oral testimony is important not only in the study of pre-colonial societies but also in those societies which, although they may generally be literate, contain important illiterate groups. In the nature of South African society it is clear that even where blacks for example can write, the tendency for African nationalists surrounded by hostile police elements and informers, may be to put as little as possible down on paper. Although this consideration is undoubtedly a very modern one, even before the Second World War there were reasons for either not relying on the written evidence, or not committing certain matters to paper. In the Katberg, documented by Jeff Peires, one informant said: "The stories you've heard are the stories we've heard. Funny things happened in those days. But I will tell you one thing. He wasn't such a fool as to leave anything lying around on paper."[33]

To date, the most noteworthy and systematic attempt to collect oral testimony is the University of the Witwatersrand's Oral History Project, which was launched in 1979 "to investigate the process of proletarianisation in the South African countryside from the mid-nineteenth century to the mid-twentieth century". This was embarked upon because it "was felt that the existing history of this period, based as it was solely on archival material, did not confront some of the fundamental changes that took place in the agricultural hinterland surrounding major industrial areas, such as the Witwatersrand".[34] By early 1987 there were some 500 tapes and transcripts of oral testimony in the African Studies Institute of Wits University, and this material had been used in a meaningful way to enrich a number of studies. A recent example of a work that integrates oral testimony into the overall structure of the analysis is Tim Keegan's *Rural transformations in industrializing South Africa: The Southern Highveld to 1914* (Johannesburg, 1986).

*   *   *

There is a wide variety of opinions among radicals. Many of the radical works have come from political scientists and sociologists, rather than from trained historians. But although there are great differences among them, they have all been influenced to some extent by Marxist concepts, they mostly adopt a materialist approach to history, believing that the past should be seen in terms of a class struggle and the forces and relations of production. Class, not race, was the motor of history. Although there was not universal agreement on what constituted a class, G. A. Cohen's definition has a good measure of acceptance. He wrote that "a person's class is established by nothing but his objective place in the network of ownership relations, however difficult it may be to identify such places neatly."[35] To view class from a historical materialist perspective, thus, is to see it as a set of social relations which is structured according to the relation of the members of the society to the means of production. "Membership of the working class, for example, is defined according to the common lack of either ownership or control of the means of production, and the necessity to sell labour-power in exchange for a wage."[36] Basically, the radicals believe that racial discrimination in South Africa provided an excellent environment for the maximum development of capitalism, which they see as "a mode of production in which the economic surplus is subject to private appropriation and in which ownership of the means of production is severed from ownership of labour-power".[37]

The radicals did not see capitalism as the liberals viewed it, as a beneficial modernising force. They regarded it as a class exploitative system, with basic contradictory social forces. They viewed it in its global context, and even pre-colonial societies were drawn into it the moment they began trading with whites, who were part of that worldwide system.

The questions the radicals ask of their documentary and other historical evidence are those of Marxist political economy: "Who owns what? Who does what? Who gets what? Who does what to whom? Who does what for whom? How are who does what and who gets what linked to who owns what and who controls what? How is all this linked to what is going on in society and history?"[38]

Marx himself, however, did not feature very frequently in their arguments, which were based mainly on his modern interpreters such as Louis Althusser and Nicos Poulantzas, and the French anthropologists, M. Godelier, C. Meillassoux and E. Terray.[39] Marxist concepts were continually changing as new variations were conceived, revised, applied and discarded in favour of yet other applications. To some the development of theory was a priority, but the best work in the new tradition has been based on empirical research. It was, however, not only Marxism or neo-Marxism that gave inspiration to the radical historians, and they have also been influenced by modern socio-economic and anthropological thinking.

One of the influences with which they came into contact was the French *Annales* school. British social and socialist history was another, and British Marxists like Eric Hobsbawm and E. P. Thompson were important figures, as was André Gunder Frank, who developed a thesis of underdevelopment based on Latin America. Some radicals relied heavily for their theoretical framework on Eugene Genovese, whose study of American slavery, *The world the slaveholders made*, has revolutionised thinking on slavery.[40] The French Canadian George Rudé also featured prominently.

In France there was at the turn of the century a reaction against the Rankean-type history practised by the establishment of the Sorbonne, and after the Second World War the Rankeans were dethroned and the *Annales*-historians became the establishment. They pioneered the modern socio-economic and anthropological approach to history, which was an analytical rather than a hermeneutical approach. It dealt with structures and made comparisons, studying the collective rather than the individual, groups and processes rather than specific events; it was interested in material culture and the formation of classes. It studied social change and repetitive patterns of community life, making generalisations and delineating abstract social forces. Central to this was the process of social change in industrialising societies, with the focus on the ordinary man, the peasant and the urban worker. It was a total approach that did away with the borders between history and the social sciences, and it was not necessarily Marxist, although after the Second World War its practitioners were largely Marxists.

After the Second World War there was also a reaction in West Germany against Rankean-type history.[41] But it was above all from Britain that the new movement in South African history received its intellectual nourishment. Owing largely to those scholars associated with *Past and Present*, English-speaking historians became familiar with the way the study of history had been revolutionised by Marc Bloch and Lucien Febvre, Fernand Braudel, Emmanuel Le Roy Ladurie and the whole *Ecole des Annales*. In the United Kingdom it was only in the 1950s that the "new" history came there when a left-wing group around Eric Hobsbawm directed their attention to a fresh approach. A distinctive British input was the changes wrought in the study of sociology. A younger generation of sociologists became increasingly preoccupied with change, and turned more and more to historians like Hobsbawm and E. P. Thompson. The study of history moved closer to the social sciences, particularly sociology, so that history was sometimes called a social science, and there was talk of historical sociology or sociological history. The focus of attention was the pattern of change in society, with historical processes and anonymous forces that determined the lives of men and women.

André Gunder Frank's theory of the "development of underdevelopment", or the dependency theory as it is sometimes called, had an enthusiastic band of followers in South Africa in the 1970s in particular. Frank characterised Latin America as having been capitalist since its conquest – as part of the Spanish colonial empire it was integrated into the world capitalist system. The most backward of these regions in modern times were the highland area of Peru and north-eastern Brazil. At one time they had been the hub of economic activity. They were not backward because they were subsistence-orientated, feudal areas – their backwardness was the result of capitalism. According to this theory, developed by Frank for Latin America, the world capitalist economic system expanded to obtain markets and raw materials, drawing all countries into it, exploiting and making them captives of the system, disrupting the social and economic life of the pre-capitalist societies with which it made contact. The roots of underdevelopment began when pre-colonial economies were drawn into this worldwide system, which occurred as soon as they began trading with the outside world; they became dependent on the international capitalist system; exploitation of labour and the establishment of a class society followed, so that the initial adaptation made by the indigenous peasants was neutralised, peasant initiative destroyed. The result was poverty and the inability to modernise – they were placed in a position of permanent dependence – thus underdevelopment. Capitalism, so the argument ran, could not tolerate indigenous economic independence or indigenous economic competition, and the local inhabitants were transformed into a rural and urban proletariat, on whose labour the wealth of the capitalists rested. According to Frank, the only way out was a socialist revolution.[42]

Frank's analysis has been criticised on a number of levels. One of the better-known critiques is that of Ernesto Laclau who says that even if the world economy was in fact "capitalist" at the time of the conquest of Latin America, which he doubts, this does not mean that the Latin American colonies necessarily automatically became capitalist. He further queries whether the underdevelopment was necessarily the result of Latin America's involvement in the world economy. Were there not other reasons that accounted for the phenomenon?[43]

Immanuel Wallerstein, a noted sociologist, attempted to give Frank's thesis historical substance and apply it beyond the confines of Latin America. Walter Rodney did much to apply it to Africa with his book *How Europe underdeveloped Africa*.[44] E. A. Alpers, among others, examined the underdevelopment of East Africa in the light of the slave and ivory trade, which caused all traditional activities to be diverted from their natural course and subordinated to the great demand for slaves and ivory. This inevitably led to the underdevelopment of the region as agricultural and manufacturing industries were neglected in the hectic chase for slaves and ivory.[45]

In the study of South African history the underdevelopment theory has had a number of followers including Colin Bundy, Harold Wolpe and William Beinart.[46] The influence of underdevelopment theory can be seen in several of the articles in *Economy and society in pre-industrial South Africa* (London, 1980), edited by Shula Marks and Anthony Atmore.

The Althusserian brand of structuralism was a prominent strand of Marxist thought that found a strong echo in South Africa. This was not surprising given the predominant British influence on radical writing on South Africa. In the 1970s, Althusserian structuralism was very much in the forefront of Marxist thinking in Britain. The noted British Marxist historian, E. P. Thompson, was bitterly opposed to the development of structuralist Marxism and he attacked it vigorously.[47] Although he was later accused of having over-reacted to Althusser, the accusations were made with the benefit of hindsight, for in the 1970s it seemed as if this kind of structuralism was going to put down deep roots in British Marxist social and cultural thought. It is only by looking back on the decade that it can be seen that the hold of Althusser was largely a passing intellectual fashion. Another British Marxist historian, Eric Hobsbawm, gave Althusser less attention than Thompson did, expressing the view that Althusser "has practically nothing to say to historians".[48]

The arguments of Louis Althusser and his disciple Nicos Poulantzas had a significant influence, among others, on Rob Davies, Dan O'Meara, and Duncan Innes.[49] The work of those who followed Althusser and Poulantzas was theoretical in the extreme, and it was this branch of radical writing that came in for the most criticism. For structuralists the conscious activities of people were not important – they concentrated on the unconscious structures that determined those activities. Classes were structurally determined, not only at the economic level but also on the political and ideological levels. Classes were not simply groups of people with similar interests.

Althusserian structuralism was very concerned with the development of theory and was less interested in the "facts"–empirical data. The great danger from Althusser is his insistence on the primacy of theory, and his rejection of the idea that there can be any given "facts" independent of theory. "Facts" are produced by the theory. According to Althusser the Marxist problematic, which he defines as "a systematically interrelated set of concepts", is not derived from empirical data, the concepts are in some way prior to empirical data. It is only through the mediation of concepts that it is possible to apprehend "facts". The significance and indeed the content of "facts" are determined by the problematic. As Robin Law sums it up, according to Althusser, "Marx's theory is not 'true' because it can be successfully applied, but can be successfully applied because it is 'true'." Structural Marxists became so wrapped up in theory that they challenged one another's work according to the extent to which it did or did not follow orthodox Marxism, for example saying that a certain work was invalid because it gave primacy to the relations of distribution and not, as it should have done, to the primacy of the relations of production.[50]

It was the reliance on Althusser that was partly responsible for the fact that certain of the radical work was so theoretical. Belinda Bozzoli does not believe that Althusserian structuralism with its anti-historical bias, is a particularly appropriate model for South Africa, for Althusser maintained that wherever capitalism was dominant, it succeeded in imposing ideological control over society. In South Africa, however, the ruling class had been too weak to impose a common culture on the whole of society.[51]

The study of pre-colonial black societies formed an important part of the new drive in South African history, and perhaps the work that has had the most influence on Marxist thought in this regard was *Pre-capitalist modes of production* by B. Hindess and P. Hirst, published in London in 1975. Although differing in certain respects from Althusser they adopted his approach. Hindess and Hirst were not really interested in history as such or in dealing with the problem of applying Marxist concepts to historical research. They were only concerned with theory and conceptualisation. They wrote that "the field of application of these concepts is not history. We reject the notion of history as a coherent and worthwhile object of study."[52] An example of this attitude in the study of South African history is contained in the introduction to a recent study of Graaff-Reinet in the period 1852–1872, where the author states that he is not so much interested in specific events as in the process of structural change. He says that he did not choose the subject because of any deep interest in local history, in Graaff-Reinet itself or in "the period". Graaff-Reinet is thus simply a peg on which the author hangs his theories in an attempt "to arrive at some understanding of the rural political economy of the Eastern Cape in the pre-industrial era".[53] The structure is all-important, and the "facts" hardly seem to matter.[54]

The delegates attending the Workshop on Precapitalist Social Formations and Colonial Penetration in Southern Africa held at the National University of Lesotho in 1976, eagerly embraced the ideas of Hindess and Hirst, but by 1979 in the face of the criticism of people like Thompson and Law, and also a realisation that Southern African societies for the most part bore little relationship to the peoples studied by Meillassoux and others, there was a marked cooling off of enthusiasm for their views.[55]

Another trend of thought that has found an echo in South Africa springs from what Hobsbawm terms "social banditry". This applies to banditry which is not only criminal activity, but which is also a form of primitive rebellion. Social bandits are distinguished from other criminal elements in the rural areas by the fact that they have a special relationship with the peasant society of which they are members. Thus while the police would regard them simply as criminals, to other peasants they are seen in very different terms – as heroes, liberators or avengers, who are worthy of the support of the community.[56] This theme has been the subject of research, amongst others, by Charles van Onselen and Don Pinnock.[57]

EARLY DOUBTS ABOUT THE CONVENTIONAL WISDOM

The frontier

One of the first tangible signs of a rejection of the conventional picture of liberal South African history came in 1969 with *Class and Colour in South Africa 1850-1950* by H. J. and R. E. Simons, which told the story of the past from a point of view of black resistance to white power and policy, and analysed in class terms the reasons for the unsuccessful attempts to overthrow capitalist domination.[58] Frederick Johnstone in 1970 was one of the first people to point out that white supremacy seemed to be a vital element of South Africa's booming industry, thus challenging the liberal view of the *Oxford History* that economic growth was breaking down the bonds of racism.[59] At the same time, the sociologist Heribert Adam questioned the accepted belief that the forces of industrialisation would by themselves erode apartheid, which so many liberals maintained was simply an atavistic carryover from eighteenth century frontier attitudes and which thus had no place in a modern industrialising society.[60]

At the core of the heated debate that soon developed between liberals and radicals over the interpretation of twentieth century history was the question of the relationship between South Africa's racial policies and economic development. The liberals maintained that there are no internal conflicts within capitalism, that it is colour-blind and favours no single group above any other. Racism had been interpreted by the liberals largely along ideological lines, but there was now a shift towards exploring its economic function. The radicals' basic argument to counter that of the liberals was that capitalism had to have a cheap supply of labour, and that in South Africa the means of satisfying this need were racial oppression and the policy of segregation and apartheid. They thus saw the needs of capitalism as a vital factor in increasing segregation and oppression. Economic growth did not take place in South Africa despite outmoded racist practices and policies, as the liberals would have it, but *because* of such policies. So far from economic development breaking down apartheid, white dominance and the rapid economic development that had taken place was the reason for increasing segregation. In opposition to the liberals they argued that further economic growth would not prove how impractical apartheid is; on the contrary it would demonstrate its practicality. As they saw it, South Africa's problems did not lie with an anachronistic Afrikanerdom that was carrying into the twentieth century its legacy of racial prejudices inherited on the frontiers of the Cape colony in the eighteenth century, but with an exploitative capitalist system. Class, not race, was the determining factor in South African history.

172

The liberals, they maintained, had accepted the stereotype of the Afrikaner's "frontier mentality" without examining it sufficiently. They had asked questions about what had caused this mentality, but they had not questioned whether the Afrikaner had really developed the attitudes in question. The liberals, of course, were not alone in this. As David Yudelman pointed out, South Africa's critics have portrayed the country as unique, explaining modern apartheid in terms of a "mythical white Afrikaner tribe still metaphorically carrying its Bible in one hand and rifle in the other as it marches unwillingly into the twentieth century". There is much truth in his observation that "the Afrikaner, in general, has thus been credited with a far larger role in the evolution of contemporary South Africa than he deserves. This is partly the fault of Afrikaner nationalist mythology, which has portrayed him as the divinely ordained protector of the values of Western Christian civilisation and, like the American frontiersman, the hero of an epic story of pioneering survival." He went to to say that it was also the fault of English-speaking South Africans "who have portrayed the Afrikaner as the villain, the fanatic who created or at least perfected institutionalised race discrimination in the shape of apartheid".[61]

Although there was considerable difference of opinion among radicals as to where the roots of segregation, and later apartheid, were to be precisely located, they were in agreement that the origins should be sought in the twentieth century, and not on the eastern frontier of the Cape in the eighteenth and early nineteenth centuries. Under the influence of the radicals the traditional picture of what had really been happening on the Cape frontier was revised. Possibly the most important early radical statement was Martin Legassick's seminal paper on the frontier, "The frontier tradition in South African historiography", first delivered in the 1970–1971 academic year at the Institute of Commonwealth Studies in London.[62]

Legassick's study, which was strongly influenced by Genovese, challenged the traditional view of the frontier and its importance. He denied that the Cape frontier was comparable to the American frontier. He argued that race attitudes at the Cape were a legacy from Europe, that the colonists arrived with this as part of their intellectual baggage, and that these attitudes were not formed on the frontier. It was not the Boers on the frontier but the Dutch East India Company that determined the status of blacks from the beginning, giving preference to the whites. The colonial border community thus shared roughly the same views regarding people of colour as the inhabitants of the western Cape – the colour attitudes were not specifically a characteristic of the frontier. He pointed out that some of the *least* colour-conscious contacts took place on the frontier. The fact that some of the interaction was of a violent nature did not necessarily mean that there was more segregation here than there was for example in the more closely settled slave-owning areas of the western Cape. As he saw it, it was not race that primarily determined relations on the frontier, but class – we should look elsewhere for the origins

173

of segregation and apartheid. He believed, together with Genovese, whom he quoted, that "race relations are at bottom a class question into which 'the race question intrudes and gives . . . a special force and form but does not constitute its essence'."[63]

Legassick believed that the frontier did not foster white group consciousness at all. The basic social unit on the frontier was the large patriarchal family, and these family units sought isolation from each other on large farms, feeling crowded if they could see the smoke from one another's chimneys; the units were frequently at loggerheads over boundary disputes, which did not foster group consciousness; political factionalism was rife. There were few distinctly frontier institutions to bind them together. Most of their institutions were linked to the western Cape. There was thus little to give them a feeling of belonging to a distinct frontier society, with its own distinct mores. Family reunions and nagmaal *did* unite frontiersmen, but at the same time they united them with people in the western Cape, so that they did not promote a consciousness of being a separate frontier community. The one possible exception to this, Legassick admits, was the commando, and in the development of his argument that group consciousness and racism had been formed on the frontier, MacCrone had paid much attention to the commando system as it had operated against the San.[64] But, says Legassick, "it is hard to reconcile the 'unity of the white fighting group' with the fact that white burghers were wont to send their Bastard or Khoi servants on commando duty in their place; or with the evidence that the Griqua and Bastard frontiersmen of the Orange River valley dealt with San cattle-thieves just as harshly as white frontiersmen. Nor were the San treated universally as enemies. Further territorial expansion towards the Orange River was based on a change of relationships, guided by concerned local officials but implemented by the frontiersmen themselves."[65]

There was undoubtedly much violence on the frontier, and this may be partly attributed to the weakness of a government presence in the outlying districts. But, equally, there was much trade, and Legassick argued that war and trade were really only opposite sides of the same coin, that unequal trade, or competition, led to reprisals, theft and raids, and that the basis for the hostility was not simply race. There can also be no denying that although men of the stamp of Coenraad Buys were guilty of violence towards the Xhosa, they were presumably not motivated by racial hatred for they sometimes lived quite peacefully under the authority of the Xhosa chiefs, and Buys "married" quite freely among Xhosa women. As is well known, in the events attending the Slagtersnek rebellion, a number of these frontiersmen who had formed close associations with the Xhosa called for the help of the Xhosa against the Cape government.

Legassick concluded that "the stereotype of the non-white as enemy, therefore, does not seem to be explicitly a frontier product, whether one examines the San frontier, the Xhosa frontier, the pre-trek northern frontier, or the frontier that developed predominantly in the Transvaal." He warned that it was important "not to equate the greater violence, brutality and harshness of treatment of dependants in such areas, with greater racism". There is little doubt that Legassick was correct in stating that most of the cases of ill-treatment of Khoikhoi related to attempts to retain servants after the expiry of their contracts.[66] They were not ill-treated because of the colour of their skins.

Legassick thus threw doubt on the traditional liberal, and indeed also the Afrikaner belief, that the Afrikaner's racial attitudes of the twentieth century had been formed on the frontiers of the Cape in an earlier century. If the Cape was not the melting pot for the forging of South African racism, where were the origins of such attitudes to be sought?

The imperial factor

From the examination of the nature of relationships on the frontier, attention shifted to the Voortrekkers in their wanderings beyond the Cape, and to the slave-owners in the western Cape. In general, this research tended to indicate that white society had, in the words of Shula Marks, "never been as monolithic in its attitudes to people of colour as the textbooks imply".[67] Nor was white society in pre-industrial South Africa as strong as the general histories have tended to suggest. An important point that the liberals, with their attention riveted on "interaction" had missed, was that a number of evenly matched and *separate, independent* societies, or social formations had developed in the interior, and that they were more or less evenly matched. According to this view it was British intervention that tilted the balance. This view of matters had earlier been put forward by Jaffe and Taylor who reserved some of their bitterest attacks for the British, blaming British intervention on the side of the Boers for saving the Voortrekkers from being wiped out by the black chiefdoms in the interior.

One of the major areas to which attention has been given is, therefore, a reappraisal of the role of the imperial factor in South Africa. Most liberals saw this as beneficial, particularly with regard to the position of the blacks, portraying the British as protectors of the blacks against the Boers. Conservative Afrikaner historians have also tended to see the British in this role, emphasising how they "interfered" in a bid to thwart legitimate Afrikaner aspirations.

An important article written by Anthony Atmore and Shula Marks in 1972–1973,[68] made a significant contribution towards seeing the British role in South Africa in another light. Many of the areas in which they suggested that historians should direct their attention anew have been subjected since to more detailed research along the lines they indicated.

They rejected the interpretation that British intervention in South Africa had been negrophilist in nature. Although British intervention in South African affairs often wore "humanitarian garb", blacks had been subjected by the British in the interests of capitalism, which the authors saw as an exploitative, class-divided system. British intervention gave the whites the upperhand in the country. It was the British, not the Boers, who were the greatest threat to the independence of African societies, and the subjugation of most of the powerful African polities was undertaken by the British in the 1870s. And they were subjected to serve British interests which underwent a change following the discovery of diamonds beyond the Cape borders in 1867.

The liberal historians regarded the destruction of these independent African polities with equanimity, as having been necessary in the interests of "progress", "civilisation", the spread of Christianity and the advancement of capitalism, which they saw in positive terms as a modernising force. But British power was really extended over indigenous communities in the Transkei territories, the Zulu, the Pedi, Ndebele and Shona with British economic interests and aims in mind – to provide a source of cheap labour. The independence of the Africans had to be shattered before the state could move in with its taxes and control of land, forcing Africans into the towns where they became a cheap proletarianised labour force – in this way the blacks were brought into a single worldwide capitalist system. According to this view, the whites (or settlers in radical terminology) were allies of imperialism for the extension of the exploitative capitalist system.

According to Atmore and Marks, the main error of those who had examined the British role was that they had failed to take into account the changing nature of the British economy and the importance of economic interests in British calculations. The British in fact were primarily interested in transforming South Africa to serve British interests. Contrary to the liberal view, Atmore and Marks believed that the British to a large extent succeeded in their aims. Leonard Thompson in the *Oxford History* wrote that "any final assessment of the achievement of an imperial power must depend largely upon the sort of society it left behind when it withdrew". In his view the British had failed to secure freedom and justice, in that "in withdrawing from South Africa, Great Britain left behind a caste-like society, dominated by its white minority. The price of unity and conciliation was the institutionalization of white supremacy".[69]

Atmore and Marks believed that this verdict was incorrect because Thompson had misunderstood what British rule in South Africa was all about. "Britain's interests in South Africa," they wrote, "rarely had very much to do with freedom and justice particularly for the black man, though it always made useful propaganda. An imperial power should be considered successful if it has created a colonial society that generally well serves its – the imperial power's – interests; there is little doubt that at least until 1948 and probably even after that . . . Britain has found in South Africa's white governments entirely satisfactory collaborators in safeguarding imperial interests, whether one regards these as strategic or economic."[70]

176

The securing of a sufficient supply of labour played a major role in British considerations. This was important, for example, at the Cape after the abolition of the slave trade in 1807. Legislation, including Ordinance 50 of 1828, was seen as aiming to provide the colonists with such a supply. Historians had hitherto seen Ordinance 50 as the brainchild of Philip and British humanitarians to safeguard the Khoikhoi by giving them equality before the law. But Atmore and Marks argued that although the colonists were unhappy with the measure, what the ordinance did and in fact aimed at, was to incorporate the Khoi and the slaves emancipated after 1834 into the colonial economy "as semi-servile labourers subject to new forms of coercion".[71] This approach was not entirely new. Jaffe and Taylor had pointed the way, although in more direct and simpler terms. Others like Susan Newton-King have since subjected the ordinance to a more rigorous analysis. She has seen Ordinance 50 as part of "state regulation of the Cape labour market" and "an attempt to increase the labour supply available to the colonists".[72]

The key to British rule in South Africa was the search for reliable collaborators. Britain was content with informal control if she could find collaborators willing and able to serve her changing interests. Indigenous black societies broke down under the "weight of the demands of an increasingly industrialised Britain". And among these demands the most important was for labour, with pressure being exerted through taxation and land encroachment. Adequate supplies of labour could not be obtained without coercive measures, which only the state was able to provide. "The imposition of a 'market economy' in southern Africa was indeed inseparable from this demand for the assistance of the state to procure cheap, highly controlled labour," the authors concluded.[73] Black societies could not bear the strain of serving the interests of the imperial power – in other words, they were not successful collaborators. They were thus crushed and transformed so that their labour could be more efficiently exploited.

Neither did the white Trekkers in the interior make satisfactory collaborators as British interests in the later nineteenth century turned from raw cotton and textiles, to investment abroad and the creation of modern infrastructures in undeveloped regions overseas – by the 1890s London's role in the gold-based international money market betokened another shift in "interests." Atmore and Marks believed that "the conflict between Britain and Afrikaners, which culminated in the South African war and the reconstruction of the Transvaal, was basically the result of the failure of the Afrikaner societies to fulfil the role of collaborating groups to the satisfaction of the gold-mining industry",[74] which was largely controlled by British capitalists. Among the more important reasons for the opposition of the mining capitalists to Kruger, was the failure of his government to provide the mineowners with a cheap and pliable labour force.

These were some of the areas touched upon by Atmore and Marks. They were mostly tentative suggestions to encourage researchers to ask new questions of the past. Much of what they said was not totally new. It had been said as far back as 1952 by Jaffe and Taylor. But these were not academic historical works. Conservative historians dismissed them outright as anti-white treatises, and most liberals rejected Taylor's assumptions regarding British motives and actions. In 1952, white liberals were not prepared to concede that their view of British involvement in South Africa as a generally benign, "liberalising" influence might need revising. But 20 years later, a new generation of historians, having absorbed the intellectual currents of Europe, and being dissatisfied with the *Oxford History*, were eager to take a fresh look at South African history, and to view the British presence from an entirely new perspective, one which was very much in keeping with a resurgence of Marxism and socialism. Studies in the nature of capitalism and its worldwide operation seemed to fit in very well with the view that it was British capitalism, not British philanthropism, that had been the major formative influence in South Africa. Marks and Atmore reflected and helped give direction to these new concerns of historians, and in the years following the appearance of this article, studies were undertaken in a number of areas highlighted by the authors.

THE ERA OF INDUSTRIALISATION

The implications of many of the points raised by both Legassick, and Atmore and Marks, have been explored further. In particular attention has been devoted to the twentieth century, and to the process of industrialisation.

The view that the British brought an end to the independence of the two Boer republics in 1902 in the interests of mining capitalism and that the causes of the Jameson Raid and the Anglo-Boer War should be sought with the Rand capitalists, is not exactly new. J. A. Hobson in 1902[75] was saying much the same thing, and all Afrikaner historians of the period, and indeed since then, have come to a similar conclusion. But although their final assessments of the situation have not been very different, the terms in which recent writers on the subject have analysed British involvement are very different from those put forward by Hobson, J. S. Marais or G. D. Scholtz.[76]

There are a great number of variations in the arguments that have been put forward, but by and large the narrative follows these lines: Before the discovery of gold north of the Vaal River in 1886, the Transvaal, or South African Republic, was a poor, backward state run by the Boers. The inhabitants were either unwilling or unable to contribute to the upkeep of their republic in the form of taxes. The government was unable to pay its public officials in cash – the only commodity of which the state had an abundance was land, so that faithful duty to the state was rewarded by land grants. A relatively small group of men came to hold increasingly large amounts of land. They did not use much of it, and actual possession was in the hands of blacks and white bywoners, although legal title was retained by the governing elite. The situation changed after the discovery of gold. At first, the

Boers in the top echelons of government worked well with the mineowners, and they shared similar interests such as controlling a large black labour force and creating conditions that would erode the independence of the blacks and their ability to earn a living elsewhere than on white farms or the mines. Government officials were happy to assist the mines in recruiting labour so long as this did not interfere with the provision of a labour force for the farms. They also helped administer pass laws to give greater control over the movement of labour, but they did not do this very efficiently. The situation has been seen by these historians in terms of a class alliance between the Afrikaner elite and the mineowners, albeit an informal one. All this contrasts sharply with the traditional picture.

But a change in this class alliance came with the development of deep-level mining. The mineowners found the restrictions implicit in Kruger's government somewhat irksome. It was the landowner class that clashed with the mineowners, the result of which was the Jameson Raid and the Anglo-Boer War. The landowners, who were so important and influential in Kruger's government, could not satisfy the demands of deep-level mining; the capitalists wanted action that would enable them to obtain a larger supply of cheap labour. Railway freight rates were high, so was the price of dynamite, largely because of Kruger's monopoly system, and it has also been argued that the mineowners were opposed to the ease with which their labour force could obtain illicit liquor.[77] Like the African chiefdoms earlier, the South African Republic had to be destroyed and restructured to serve British interests. After the war the republic was replaced by a government that was both more sympathetic and better able to meet its demands.

The above, and over-simplified, account of research into complex issues, however, is not universally accepted. For example, the view that Kruger's government was either unwilling or unable to supply the mines with an adequate supply of cheap labour, has been recently challenged by Patrick Harries, who argues that after the Jameson Raid the Transvaal government took a number of important steps in this respect, enabling the mines to reduce African wages by 30%. Collaboration between capital and the state to create a cheap labour force did not have its origins in the postwar British administration in the Transvaal, but was a feature of initiatives taken by Paul Kruger's government after the Jameson Raid. "Viewed objectively," Harries writes, "the pre-war labour policy of the Transvaal government was not an obstacle to the development of the gold-mines. In terms of the supply of labour, the mine-owners had more to lose than to gain from a destructive, imperialist war. The incapacity or unwillingness of the Kruger government to supply the mines with labour cannot be seen as a cause of the Anglo-Boer War."[78]

As far as the liquor question is concerned, Charles van Onselen has advanced a new view of the relationship between influential Boers among the ruling elite in the South African Republic and the mining magnates. Van

Onselen explained that the Boer farmers in the Transvaal had an agricultural surplus, much of which found its way to De Eerste Fabrieken near Pretoria, which by the early 1890s had become known as the Hatherley Distillery. The mineowners found that the availability of alcohol was a powerful incentive in drawing labour to the mines, and once at the mines the more they drank the less the workers saved, so that they spent a longer time at the mines before going home. There thus grew up a firm class alliance between the mining capitalists and the rural Afrikaner farmers, supported and protected by "a significant section of the Afrikaner ruling class".[79]

But in 1896, when the mineowners were engaged in new deep-level mining and had more need for a stable labouring force, they became concerned about drunkenness and its effect on productivity. They thus agitated for prohibition laws by "exploiting divisions within the Afrikaner ruling class", bringing "to an end the formal class alliance which had existed between the Afrikaner rural bourgeoisie and the mining capitalists".[80] Here too, Patrick Harries argues that the 1896 prohibition on the sale of liquor to blacks demonstrates the government's willingness to help the mining industry, for it took this action despite the fact that it was "a blow to the fledgling local manufacturing industry".[81] In other words, the government did not always support the rural Boer population when its interests were in conflict with those of the mining industry.

Macmillan had pointed to the problem of undercapitalised rural agriculture[82], and this theme was now taken further and developed. Another reason why the South African Republic had to be brought to an end was that undercapitalised rural agriculture was unable to satisfy the need of the towns for cheap produce. Capitalisation and the transformation of agriculture were required. Kruger's pre-capitalist agricultural state had to undergo agricultural capitalisation in the interests of world capitalism. The war led to a change in property relations, and with an eye to the provision of food, agriculture was capitalised. Milner was the agent of capitalism who restructured the state to serve the interests of Britain and capitalism. This could not have been done without bringing an end to the republics and restructuring agriculture. According to Legassick, the Union of 1910 was a compromise between gold-mining capitalism and a capitalistic agriculture.[83]

As van Onselen has noted in another context, before 1899 the state was dominated "by an aspiring agricultural bourgeoisie . . . that gave preference to the accumulation of capital in the countryside", while after 1902 the state favoured "the pursuit of profit by urban industrial enterprise".[84]

After the war, mining capital was installed as the dominant factor with the aid of imperial intervention. The interests of the mining industry were served, and it all added up to a very different pattern of rural development than the republican government had envisaged. When Afrikaners were returned to power in 1907, for the most part they allowed that strategy to continue. Thus did the imperial factor in South Africa permanently transform relationships in the Transvaal. The Anglo-Boer War is seen in class terms and material interests, and the radicals could find little place for an independent role for men's ideas and beliefs in the models they created.

* * *

Before the Anglo-Boer War, because the Uitlanders did not have the vote, the mineowners had to use back-door methods to influence the government, like J. B. Robinson's approaches to Paul Kruger, with whom he formed a friendship. They had permanent lobbyists in Pretoria to keep a watch on things and sometimes give officials gifts.[85] There was thus a basis of co-operation before the war. This increased quickly after the war. The point has been made that the mining houses and the state started drawing closer to one another during the Reconstruction period and formed a good working relationship when Louis Botha's Het Volk Party came to power in 1907. It is asserted that from an early date the mineowners began to approach the state directly rather than work through the opposition political parties. Initially, a limited co-existence was achieved through personal contacts between some of the main figures in the government and the leading capitalists.[86] Dan O'Meara maintained that in 1902 in the Transvaal an alliance between the richer farmers (whom he asserts supported the Het Volk party) and the mineowners came about. He said that this alliance continued and that after 1910 it was simply transferred to the South African Party.[87] Although this view was shared by a number of radicals in opposition to the more traditional version of events which has it that Het Volk was the party that opposed the mine magnates, while the Transvaal Progressive Association had the support of the owners, O'Meara has advanced no evidence to support his view.

Although Botha and Smuts, in the first decade after Union in 1910, remained suspicious of individual mineowners, they accepted that the mining industry was the backbone of the South African economy, and that it provided the revenue for financing agricultural extension, rural credit and markets, and also jobs for dispossessed Afrikaners. Since gold mining was seen by the government in these terms, historians have made the point that as far as the mineowners were concerned, British investment in the mines was just as safe under an Afrikaner government as it had been under direct British rule,[88] thus confirming an impression expressed by Atmore and Marks in their reassessment of the imperial factor.

Afrikaner historians have generally seen the era of the Pact government as a clear advance on the road to the final triumph of Afrikaner nationalism, while liberal historians have stressed the establishment of the industrial colour bar as a break with what had gone before the Pact victory at the polls in 1924. Even most radical historians, although for different reasons, have agreed that 1924 is a turning point of sorts, discerning a shift in hegemony from imperial and mining capital to national, manufacturing and agricultural capital in an alliance with white labour.[89]

Others again have challenged this view, arguing that the Pact, whatever it may have said to the contrary, failed to reverse the outcome of the 1922 strike. The colour bar was only reinstated by The Mines and Works Amendment Act of 1926 insofar as the regulations issued under the act of 1911 became statutory law. The movement of black mineworkers into semi-skilled jobs which had not been specified in this legislation was not reversed or stopped. The wages paid to white mineworkers remained low. The view that the Pact government actually promoted the interests of the mining industry more than it promoted those of the white workers and the farmers was made by Rob Davies. More recently, David Yudelman, whose conclusions, although he attacks the radicals, are not really incompatible with their findings, also makes out a strong case for continuity between the Pact's policies and those of its predecessors. He shows that in spite of its rhetoric, the Pact government did not mount an onslaught on mining capital in order to serve the interest of national capital, but, on the contrary, treated the gold mining industry sympathetically.[90]

Another work, which although written from a radical perspective does not have a rigid theoretical basis, and which criticises both liberal and Marxist interpretations, is that of Marian Lacey, which deals with the development of South Africa's segregation policies between 1910 and 1932.[91] Lacey also demonstrates that although white trade union leaders supported the Pact, the government actually undermined skilled labour. She also shows how the ruling class manoeuvred to exploit Poor Whites but to do so in such a way that they did not make common cause with black workers.

The last word has not been spoken on whether 1924 represents a turning-point in South African history. If one looks beyond the sphere of mining there is still much to support the view that 1924 does indeed mark a sharp break with the past and the radicals' analysis does not take account of ideology and beliefs, for which they have generally been unable to find a place.[92]

According to historians writing about South African industrialisation, what made industrialisation in South Africa so different from the process in the United States and Western Europe was its dependence on minerals. Until 1930 at any rate the mineowners had no interest in encouraging the growth of an internal market or a local manufacturing industry – machinery and stores could be imported more cheaply. Locally grown wheat was not as cheap as the North American and Australian grain that flooded the market and came up the railway lines. This situation only changed when farmers organised themselves to control the market and capital was injected to improve production, which did not occur until the twentieth century.

As far as the manufacturing sector is concerned, Duncan Innes has calculated that before 1900 De Beers was responsible for half of the Cape's exports, but that this activity by De Beers did not in fact lead to the diversification of the colonial economy itself. De Beers imported the complex machinery it required. The growth of diamond and gold mining did not lead to a similar growth in industry, and capital was concentrated in a small number of activities that were associated with mining itself. For a long time little attempt was made to process goods that were available in Western Europe; control over banking and transportation remained in the hands of overseas capitalists. There were few links between mining and the rest of the South African economy until the Pact government's period in office.[93]

It was the Pact government, so the argument runs, that promoted industrial diversification – it was state intervention that provided the impetus for industrialisation. The government had to find jobs for its white supporters, and it set up Iscor with tax money from the mines, which were not so happy to be subsidising local industrial development. "We should notice", writes Donald Denoon, "that the growth of industry (including heavy industry) was a consequence of deliberate state intervention, in spite of the preference of mining capitalists for concentration upon mining alone. Mining did lead to manufacturing, but only after more than half a century, and only because the state insisted on diverting revenue."[94] The rise of a "local bourgeoisie" with enough muscle to push through a programme of protective tariffs for local industries, and a rise in the gold price in the 1930s, which put additional money into the state's coffers, enabling it to promote agriculture and local industries, worked together to enable South Africa to expand into secondary industry and not merely be a primary producer. Seen in these terms, for South Africa and other countries like her who expanded into secondary industry, the depression, in terms formulated by Geoffrey Kay "was experienced not as a temporary hiatus but as a sign that a particular phase of productive development was drawing to a close".[95]

*　*　*

Another prominent theme in recent historical writing on South Africa is a class explanation of Afrikaner nationalism and a study of the material base of Afrikaner society. In 1983, Dan O'Meara examined the class structure and class struggle inside the National Party. In concentrating on economic development in the period 1934-1948 he made the first serious examination of the material upliftment of the Afrikaner in these years and of the growth of a well-to-do class of Afrikaner. O'Meara tried to show how the Afrikaner underwent a fundamental change as a result of the economic progress of the 1940s: his class basis was broadened and he joined the ranks of the capitalists.

O'Meara gave attention to the pioneering role of Sanlam, which with the help of agricultural capital mobilised Afrikaner money. He dealt with the growth of Afrikaner companies like Federale Volksbeleggings and Volkskas, and traced the role that Afrikaner institutions like the Ekonomiese Instituut of the F.A.K., the Afrikaanse Handelsinstituut and the Afrikaner Broederbond in particular played in the 1930s and 1940s in making the Afrikaner financially strong.

He differed radically from more traditional writers on the subject, both English and Afrikaans, who had seen Afrikaner nationalism as a development that had its roots in a "frontier" attitude. These explanations, O'Meara believed, were incorrect because they emphasised the continuity of Christian Nationalism with the past, whereas as he saw it, the significance of the development of Christian Nationalism in the 1940s lay in its *break* with the past, a break which was carefully disguised by the symbolic structure of the ideology – the language remained the same and lulled historians into thinking that the phenomenon they were describing was the same. A new class alliance brought a new kind of Afrikaner to the fore – a capitalist, but he was still dressed in Voortrekker garb. O'Meara went on to say that apartheid was developed to serve the interests of the capitalist class among the Afrikaners. Although Legassick before him said much the same thing, what O'Meara added to the analysis was that the Afrikaner soon saw that economic apartheid was impractical. Apartheid had primarily to provide a stable labour market for agriculture and, in the second place, it had to protect the employment of white workers in industry in order to obtain their support for the Herenigde Nasionale Party.

According to O'Meara Afrikaner nationalism came to be characterised by a contradictory alliance of class forces: on the one side, the wine, wool and ostrich farmers of the Cape, together with Sanlam, who focused on economic issues; on the other, the group of small traders, teachers, church ministers and civil servants in the Transvaal, who were more ideologically inclined and who formed the Broederbond. This contradictory Sanlam-Broederbond alliance is seen by O'Meara as central to the development of Afrikaner nationalism, and, so O'Meara believed, threw doubt on the conventional picture that was drawn and which consistently underestimated the economic factors.

The work is not written in a clear style, it is full of Marxist jargon and sentence constructions that must be tortuously unravelled. His approach is strongly theoretical and Poulantzian and he rejects what he calls the empiricism of traditional historians. O'Meara's thesis is fascinating, but his primary research has been inadequate to support the broad claims he makes. He over-simplified, he failed to support his contentions with evidence. For example, he maintained that with the outbreak of the Second World War many farmers joined the Nationalist Party because they were deprived of a good market as a result of South Africa's entry into the war against Germany.

According to O'Meara, Smuts lost the 1948 election because by 1948 the United Party could no longer accommodate the increasingly divergent claims of the various capitalistic interests and it lost the support of the Transvaal farmers. Once again, he does not support his claims.

Like a number of other radical writers, he refuses to assign an independent role to people's hopes and value systems – these are reduced to purely material needs. He made no in-depth study of what the Afrikaners were saying as reflected in the correspondence columns of newspapers, branch minutes of political parties, correspondence between political leaders, activities of church synods, journals of schools, and so on. Without taking all these non-economic institutions into consideration there can be little basis for O'Meara's claim that the economic movement was the "essential element", the "real motor" of Afrikaner nationalism.[96]

All this does not mean that it has no value. It is stimulating, it comes up with the hypotheses that future researchers will have to take into account – in short, it opens up new avenues of inquiry and helps to jolt researchers out of the rut of traditional thinking. It raises fresh possibilities. After the appearance of this book no-one will be able to see Afrikaner nationalism in quite the same terms as before. Even Professor van Jaarsveld has agreed that it is a work no serious academic can ignore.[97]

Some considerable attention has been given to O'Meara's work because of its unique attempt to identify the constituent material elements of Afrikanerdom, but it was not the only book to study Afrikaner nationalism. Two other works on aspects of this phenomenon were T. Dunbar Moodie's *The rise of Afrikanerdom: Power, apartheid and the Afrikaner civil religion* (London, 1975), which analysed how Afrikaner nationalism interpreted the world for itself, and which, unlike O'Meara, concentrated very much on analysing Afrikaner nationalism in terms of its internal political development, focusing on the "conscious or implicit meanings held by actors themselves",[98] and Irving Hexham's *The irony of apartheid: The struggle for national independence of Afrikaner Calvinism against British imperialism*, (New York, 1981). A work that analysed Afrikaner political thinking prior to the emergence of Afrikaner nationalism was André du Toit's and Hermann Giliomee's *Afrikaner political thought: Analysis and documents*, volume 1, 1780–1850, (Cape Town, 1983).

* * *

A work which although it has been influenced by a number of people who have theorised about the nature of the historical process and which deals with industrialising South Africa, but yet is remarkably free of Marxist terminology, is Charles van Onselen's two-volume study of the Witwatersrand in the critical years between the opening up of the gold fields in 1886 and the beginning of the First World War. The author acknowledges his debt to people like Herbert Gutman, George Rudé, Eric Hobsbawm, Gareth Stedman Jones and Edward Thompson. His debt to Eugene Genovese and his major work *The world the slaveholders made* is evident in the first of the eight essays in van Onselen's work which is called "The world the mine owners made" and which provides a synthesis of the social and economic history of the region for the whole period.

This study, which is probably the best example of history writing "from below" to date, has an underlying theoretical basis, but this is hardly noticeable in the body of the work, which consists of detailed studies of certain groups or classes on the Witwatersrand. The second essay is about liquor, and the others deal with prostitutes, cab-drivers, domestic servants, washermen, the Afrikaner poor and criminal gangs – in other words, they were concerned with the activities of ordinary people.

It is a collection of essays and not a full-scale synthesis. The amount of work that has gone into tracing the connections between those in power and these selected groups of people makes it clear how difficult a fully-fledged synthesis along these lines would be to write.

Van Onselen sees his work as a corrective to those "timid historians" who, "in the midst of an industrial revolution . . . have tip-toed through the tree-lined avenues of the northern suburbs, peering into the homes and lifestyles of the 'Randlords', attempting to put a romantic gloss on the ceaseless pursuit of wealth at a time when, elsewhere in the city, the dusty streets were bursting at the seams with a seething mass of struggling humanity." He places the experiences of the down-trodden within the wider framework of the industrial revolution, to provide an "analytically informed chronicle of the warm, vibrant and intensely human struggle of people seeking to find a place of dignity and security within a capitalist world that encroached on them all too quickly". By "refracting their experiences through the process of class struggle", he was concerned to show how "the ruling classes gradually came to assert their control over the subordinate classes on the Rand and exercise a powerful influence over where they lived, how they spent their non-working hours, how domestic labour was allocated within their homes, and how they were to endure periods of unemployment".[99]

The connections are plausible and suggestive, they raise fascinating possibilities, but some of them are not altogether convincing. The firm class alliance that grew up between the mining capitalists and the rural Afrikaner farmers, supported and protected by "a significant section of the Afrikaner ruling class" is suggested rather than demonstrated, and changes in this relationship are likewise asserted rather than documented. Van Onselen thus raises possibilities and he shows how successful history "from below" can be, he makes us sensitive to possible links, but he has not established all his conclusions on a firm base. Although van Onselen has accused other historians of putting a "romantic gloss" on the way of life and activities of the Randlords, he in turn is open to the charge of putting a "romantic gloss" on the way of life of the subordinate classes with his vision of their struggle as one that is "warm, vibrant and intensely human".

* * *

The fact that so much of the recent work on South African history has come from political scientists and sociologists, very strongly influenced by Poulantzas, is partly responsible for the fact that a good deal of the history of the twentieth century emanating from the theorists has focused far more on power blocs and "fractions on capital" than it has on African workers –

where the working class does come into the picture, it is usually the white working class. Much attention has thus been given to a discussion of the nature of the state and the structure of white power. Although there are wide differences among them regarding the definition of the state, South African neo-Marxists influenced by the work of Poulantzas follow his argument, which insists that the state has no power itself, that it is the expression of class powers. The state is thus merely an instrument in the hands of a particular group or class. It is an independent abstraction. He believed that the state "institutions or the apparatuses do not 'possess' 'power' proper but do nothing but express and crystallise class powers".[100] He devised the concept of rival classes or "fractions of capital" which contend for the power of the state. The state organises society and tries to reconcile the conflicting interests of the various groups or "fractions of capital".

The debate centred around the question of how one should regard the question of the "relative autonomy of the state". The definition of the state is the subject of much disagreement. Rob Davies, for example, saw the state as a captive instrument of national capital, while Yudelman regarded it as an amalgam of the "continuous administrative, legal, bureaucratic and coercive systems", the institutions which give it continuity and durability, and distinguish it from individual governments which come and go. He saw the state as an active collection of individuals and institutions wielding public power in the interests of dominant pressure groups, encouraging elements which supported it and taking action against those elements which threatened it. Yudelman's conception of the state enabled him to avoid becoming involved in fractionalist hypotheses. As he defined it, the state thus plays an independent role in the power struggle rather than being a mere instrument of power.[101] His definition, however, is not one that finds favour among neo-Marxists, who feel that he rather overplayed the autonomy of the state. One of the more radical of the historians who does become involved in a discussion of fractions of capital, Dan O'Meara tended to equate state and government, which led him, in the opinion of other radicals, to over-estimate the importance of governments and electoral politics, despite the fact that he professed to adhere to the central role of class alliances. O'Meara was roundly criticised by certain radical elements for dating the capture of the state by "class alliances" in 1924 and 1948 for no other reason than the fact that in elections held in these years new governments came to power.[102]

BLACK SOCIAL FORMATIONS AND PROLETARIANISATION

Dissatisfied with the limitations of the treatment of black societies in the *Oxford History*, numerous historians made an attempt to come to grips with pre-colonial or pre-capitalist African societies. They were aided by the fact that the study of archaeology had caught up with what was being done in the rest of Africa. But there is much that archaeology has been unable to do, and huge gaps remain, particularly for the earlier periods. In practice this means that owing to the dearth of sources, pre-colonial history really does not go very far back into the pre-colonial past – it deals largely with the period just prior to contact with the first whites and during the early years of white relations with black societies – in other words the scope of the subject is governed largely by the availability of written sources. In this sense, it does not cover a period of history very different from that researched by the liberals.

Most of the black societies studied recently have been the subject of earlier research and the ground covered is not all that new, but, whereas earlier studies focused principally on black leaders like Moshoeshoe,[103] the migrations of blacks, and the interaction between peoples, historians such as Jeff Guy, Philip Bonner, Kent Rasmussen, Jeff Peires, William Beinart, Peter Delius and Kevin Shillington, to name a few, have since the 1970s been concerned primarily with the internal dynamics of the societies they have studied.[104] They have looked at these societies from a fresh vantage point, asking very different questions of their material from those asked by earlier historians. Most of the previous studies were silent about economic and political processes and the structure of society. In line with anthropological research, the liberals tended to treat the societies as static and unchanging, they showed very little appreciation of the internal changes that were constantly taking place.

As with those working on twentieth century themes from the industrial history of South Africa, researchers in the field of pre-colonial history also exhibit wide differences in approach, although most of them are primarily concerned with the material base of society. A particular influence has been the French anthropologists. The work of Hindess and Hirst, too, is high on the list. But there is an important difference, which is perhaps related to the fact that those who have made pre-colonial history their specialised field are historians rather than sociologists and political scientists. Possibly this is the reason why their work is far less theoretical than that on the twentieth century. They use the same terminology as radicals working in other fields, but this is particularly in their introductions, where they outline their viewpoint, but in the text itself there is very little of this. The theory has been internalised. The work, too, is based on the usual written sources, and although they have employed oral tradition, this is mainly to supplement the written documents and it is clearly subordinate to documentary sources. They have not totally abandoned historical narrative, but there is far more conceptualisation than in the earlier histories.[105]

* * *

The study of pre-colonial African societies is in many ways part of the tale of proletarianisation and industrialisation. To lay stress on the structure of

188

the white state, as certain radicals did, and the process of proletarianisation, is to stress the powerlessness of the Africans to control their own destinies – they are seen as captive to white agencies and to international capital. To a certain extent, this paralleled the trend in research in the rest of Africa after the disillusionment that gripped so many newly independent states after the initial euphoria of the 1960s. Africans north of the Limpopo began to focus on neo-colonialism and the way they were bound and limited by external agencies in spite of the fact that they had political independence. Shula Marks pointed out that, quoting Terence Ranger, this could lead to a dichotomy between those who stress " 'African activity, African adaptation, African choice and African initiative', and what he terms the 'radical pessimist' who in the face of the persistent and persisting poverty of the continent has stressed the international determinants of African powerlessness and who posits salvations only through 'world revolution'."[106]

Early radical studies on industrialisation concentrated on the mining industry's demands for labour and on the effects of this on African society. Later studies have sought to demonstrate that blacks were not passive ciphers in the process, but that their own experiences and the social relationships existing in their societies were very closely linked to their entry into the industrial labour market and in the institutions that were developed in the industrial setting.

An example of this is the study of the development of the system of compounds on South African mines. The need to cut labour costs was an important ingredient in the development of the migrant labour system with its pass laws and mine compounds. In the early days at Kimberley there was a shortage of labour, and although Africans needed cash they could obtain enough of it by producing commodities on the land to which they had access, or in the case of those close to Kimberley, by selling firewood. Their labour was in great demand, they did not *have* to work. Their wages were consequently high and they could insist on being paid in part at least with firearms. But after the abortive diggers' revolt of 1875 and a government more in sympathy with the industrial capitalists at the helm, the companies were able to obtain more control over the labourers who worked for them. It was not long before the diamond industry came into the hands of large companies as small-scale miners were pushed out by the rising costs that accompanied the new methods required for deep-level mining. There was a need for an overall marketing strategy in the face of falling profits. Control over labour was essential and it was obtained largely through the migrant labour system and the establishment of compounds. The institution of compounds gave control over labour, the theft of diamonds decreased because of the difficulty of engaging in illicit diamond buying; at the same time it hampered strikes for higher wages and agitation for improved working conditions. In terms used by Rob Turrell the change occurred between 1880 and 1885 when industrial capital replaced the earlier dominance of merchant capital.[107]

In the case of the young gold industry in the late nineteenth century (and for some years into the twentieth century) there was not the same need to combine as in the case of diamonds – the price of gold was fixed, it was not necessary to combine to regulate flow, theft was harder. But the mineowners had learnt from Kimberley that the compound system and contract labour made it easier to control and discipline labour to reduce absenteeism. They could not, however, transfer the system to white miners, who were skilled and who would leave the mines if forced into compounds. So, from the beginning, there was the division between unskilled African migrants from the rural areas and skilled white migrants from abroad.

The above scenario seems to imply African powerlessness. But among historians who relied less on Althusser, there was a movement towards examining the role of blacks in the way that proletarianisation proceeded in South Africa. They were not seen merely as pawns. The way in which they resisted proletarianisation and struggled to retain and obtain control over the various aspects of their lives and culture has received more attention. Recent writers have stressed African initiative in the emergence of the compound system. Shula Marks and Richard Rathbone have pointed out that "the evolution of the compounded migrant was not something decided upon and simply imposed by the mining industry of its own volition . . . it was as much a response to the resistance of African social formations to full proletarianisation as any thought-through scheme by mine magnates to cheapen costs".[108] This is a theme upon which Shula Marks has concentrated, returning to it in *The ambiguities of dependence in South Africa: Class, nationalism, and the state in twentieth-century Natal* (Johannesburg, 1986). In the introduction to this book which deals with Solomon ka Dinuzulu (son of Dinuzulu), John Dube of the South African Native National Congress and George Champion of the Industrial and Commercial Workers' Union (I.C.U.), she writes that capitalism in South Africa "had to come to terms not with the fragmented cultures of slaves, but with, in many instances, the still pulsating remains of powerful African kingdoms. The structures and social relationships of African precapitalist society profoundly shaped the struggles that actually crystallized in policies of segregation. The contests over the form and pace of proletarianization took place at a bewildering number of levels: between capital and labor, between and within branches of the state, between different capitalist interests, and between all of these and the precolonial ruling class of chiefs and headmen in the countryside, as well as between the latter and their subjects."

There was no single road from the pre-industrial system of farming to proletarianisation. What gave the African working class its specific character was the way in which African experience in pre-capitalist societies reacted and responded to mineowners, white farmers, and white workers. In the 1980s there is much focus on this aspect of proletarianisation, on the way rural people were integrated into the new urban setting of the townships.

People who came into the city from rural settings had to relate to other new urban dwellers whose former experiences in the country were different from their own. Pre-industrial communities frequently differed very much from one another. Apart from this, people in certain areas were proletarianised before others, so that when a new group arrived they might find "that the 'old hands' in the city are all of one group; that particular occupations are monopolised by members of another; that certain dwelling-areas are occupied by a third; that social life is controlled by a fourth, and gang life by a fifth . . . Added, therefore, to the cleavages reflected from within rural communities, are those complex divisions in the new city population *between* formerly coherent rural social groupings."[109]

* * *

Attention has been given to the way that blacks were forced off white-owned land, and in the "reserves" how they were reduced to a situation in which they were unable to make enough from their farming ventures to lead an independent existence.

As far as agriculture in traditional African society is concerned, Shula Marks and Anthony Atmore have made the point that in studying South African history we should see the nineteenth century "as it happened not as it turned out at the end". More specifically, they asserted that "the 'traditionalism' and 'stagnation' of contemporary African agriculture in the 'reserves' is a consequence, not a cause, of the way in which the peasantry was integrated into the developing capitalist economy of South Africa in the late nineteenth and twentieth centuries".[110]

Seen in its broadest context, these historians are trying to answer the question of how the rural African population of South Africa has been transformed from the pastoralist-cultivators of the pre-colonial era to, in the words of Bundy, "sub-subsistence rural dwellers, manifestly unable to support themselves by agriculture and dependent for survival upon wages earned in 'white' industrial areas or upon 'white' farms".[111] Some of the more traditional explanations for this change include the failure of the indigenous economy to adapt to a new situation where land was no longer so freely available, unwillingness to innovate and to learn more sophisticated farming methods from whites, the fact that farming was inextricably tied up with social customs and supernatural beliefs; it has been maintained that Africans did not respond in the same way as whites to market opportunities.

The liberals shared this view of matters. In the 4th edition of *The South African economy*, published in 1976, Desmond Hobart Houghton wrote that in South Africa "there may be said to be two different types of rural economies existing side by side in the same country. One is the essentially market-oriented farming, as practised by white farmers, and the other is the largely subsistence-oriented farming of African peasants in the reserves. The difference between the two is deep-seated and manifests itself in a variety of ways reflecting cultural differences and fundamental attitudes to the exploitation of the natural environment . . . The white farmers are scientific and experimental in their approach, while the African is traditional, and even the few progressive individuals are hampered by the communal system of land tenure and other social restraints . . . The differences between market-oriented farming and subsistence farming is so great that they cannot conveniently be treated together."[112]

There was a fundamental difference between this view and that propounded by the Marxists. Many of the radicals subscribed to Laclau's distinction between a "mode of production" and an "economic system". Laclau writes that "we understand by 'mode of production' an integrated complex of social productive forces and relations linked to a determinate type of the means of production." He defines an economic system as being designated by "the mutual relations between the different sectors of the economy, or between different productive units, whether on a regional, national or world scale . . . An economic system can include, as constitutive elements, different modes of production – provided always we define it as a whole."[113]

The distinction made between a mode of production and an economic system is an important one for Marxist analysis, because it enables them to represent South Africa as having a single economic system, in which the capitalist mode of production has destroyed the pre-capitalist mode of production practised by Africans in pre-colonial days.[114] Capital did not spread evenly through South Africa at the same rate, or in the same way, but even the most "traditional" African societies were being drawn into the worldwide capitalist system alongside white farmers. To the radicals there was no question of treating the two separately.

Of particular interest to the historians researching these pre-colonial societies is the effect of the penetration of mercantile capital, that is capital brought by traders and which is regarded as being entirely different from industrial capital, which came with the mineral era. While industrial capital was able to vitally affect and restructure relations of production, the ability of mercantile capital to do so by itself, so it is maintained, following the thesis outlined by Geoffrey Kay, is somewhat limited. It could only operate with the consent of a dominant group or class and it meets the producer only in the market place at the level of exchange. The surplus capital generated by merchants could not be used to reorganise production on capitalist lines.[115]

The discovery of minerals was responsible for some internal disruption in African societies. At the same time as the chiefs were trying to retain their control over land, labour, cattle and marriage, certain elements in the polity were trying to forge direct links with the colonial markets and to produce surplus for these external markets without the intervention of the chiefs. The road to black proletarianisation was closely connected to the ability of the chiefs to control the labour of the young men. This was an on-going struggle between the chiefs and the young men in question. The move towards producing a surplus for an external market changed the traditional system of distribution in African societies, greatly affecting stratification within the society and disrupting social relations. Chiefs used different methods in their bid to retain control – in some cases they manipulated the age of marriage and bride-wealth; young men were sent to work on the diamond fields by the chiefs in order to obtain guns.

Most of the work has been done on the Zulu, but Jeff Peires has been working on the Xhosa and Philip Bonner on the Swazi. Margaret Kinsman has ventured in to the precolonial history of the Tswana with two articles,[116] and, more recently, Kevin Shillington has taken an in-depth look at aspects of the Tswana experience. Because the radicals have devoted their attention largely to centralised states, they tend to deal with the rulers rather than the ordinary people, so that pre-colonial history still has a strong "political" overtone.[117]

There have been numerous studies on the Nguni, following on John Omer-Cooper's thesis that the Mfecane was the result of military innovations introduced by leaders like Shaka.[118] Other historians have devoted attention to stratification within Zulu society, to the changing pattern of production and the social relations attendant upon such changes, the role of cattle and also the regimental system. Of these, the regimental system to-date, has yielded the most promising results.

The traditional view that the rise of the Zulu state must be seen in terms of the military innovation of the Zulu regiment, which did not have deep roots in the past, has been revised in more recent years. Taking a "total" approach to the study of history, Jeff Guy has analysed the ecology of Zululand, and he comes to the conclusion that by the end of the eighteenth century Zululand was in the grip of an ecological crisis and that this contributed to the social changes that took place – the regimental system was introduced in order to rationalise the allocation of labour during this crisis. Guy and others have demonstrated that the emergence of the age regiment should be seen in terms of a revolution in production rather than a military innovation. Control over the age regiment gave the chief not only control over marriage, but also over the population increase and production. Guy suggested that, far from being only a military force, the army also gave the king wide powers over the exploitation of the physical resources of the region.[119]

Bonner in his study of the Swazi, Beinart in his work on the Mpondo, and Delius on the Pedi, have all demonstrated the responsiveness of blacks to change and how important the chiefs were in production and supervising the economy.

In the case of the Mpondo, raiding, defence and closer settlement (all a result of Zulu depredations) implied organisation from the top, and these changes in the early nineteenth century led to the chiefs increasing their

193

control. Mpondo adaptability is emphasised. When traders made their appearance among them, looking for ivory, hides, cattle, sheep and maize, the Mpondo readily accepted the new technology of iron hoes, ploughs and draught oxen to increase their production when they saw that there was a good return in it. They were not bound to continue with "traditional" methods. Beinart suggested that with the increase in the demand of the outside market for agricultural products, so did the chiefs' control over production decline. The cultivation of agricultural products did not require large organisation as did raiding to restock the chiefdom's cattle, and each homestead had access to the implements it required and could make its own arrangements with the traders. They no longer needed the chief's intervention to the same extent. This phenomenon is not confined to the Mpondo; studies in other parts of Africa have shown that, while the activities connected with the capture, transport and sale of slaves and the obtaining and transport of ivory, required largescale organisation that could only be accomplished by centralised control of a major chief over a large area, once ivory and slaves were no longer the staple products of trade, and peasants turned their attention to products like ground-nuts, they no longer needed the organisation of the chief to the same extent.

Among the Mpondo, the changes brought about by the Mfecane and the advent of mercantile capital in the form of the white trader, changed production and settlement patterns as well as social relationships. The Mpondo responded to the new market possibilities, but with the collapse of the market for cattle in the early twentieth century and the increase in migrant labour, stagnation and underdevelopment became the lot of the Mpondo. Beinart also demonstrates, though, that the Mpondo were not simply forced to go out as migrant labourers by the needs of capital, but that their entry into the wage-labour market was closely linked to the nature of productive relations in Mpondo society. In order to pay colonial taxes, to have access to the products of traders, for investment in agricultural implements, a wage labour system was desirable. Beinart shows that labour migrancy was not the result of poverty. The poorer families needed all the available male labour in the fields, and when they went out as labourers they took up short-term employment on the Natal sugar fields. This was far less remunerative than the contracts on the mines of the Witwatersrand, which the young men of better-off families could undertake since their presence in the fields was not so crucial. By the 1930s when observers spoke of the rigid traditionalism among the Mpondo and the manner in which they were clinging to their old ways, this was really not because of "traditionalism" but as a result of these other factors.[120]

Bonner demonstrated with his study of the Swazi that the state controlled the allocation of land and cattle, which gave the chiefs control over production and the lineages of the polity. With low population, simple technology and low soil fertility, it was control over people that was vital.[121]

Again this is not an observation that is unique and studies in other parts of Africa, particularly on the indigenous institution of slavery, have made the point that the need to bolster scarce human resources was a major factor in slavery in Africa.

Peter Delius showed that from the 1850s (that is long before the opening up of the diamond fields) the Pedi were already migrant labourers, and that this was linked to the aftermath of the Difaqane, when the Pedi were threatened by the Zulu, Swazi and Boers. The migrant labour system thus was not simply something devised by the capitalists. The Pedi needed guns to defend themselves, and because of their distance from suitable markets and their having nothing to sell except low-value grain, labour was their most profitable commodity. The many refugees who attached themselves to the Pedi discovered that the only way they could accumulate cattle for bride-wealth payments, was to sell their labour power on the colonial labour market. Changes in gun technology forced the Pedi to keep going out as migrant labourers to obtain the latest guns, so they became dependent on this outside technology. Delius also looked at the sort of situation that Beinart did, examining the responsiveness of the Pedi to economic change, and the vital role played by the chiefs in production.

One of the central themes developed by Delius in explaining the growth of the Pedi polity is that it was largely Boer attempts to exact taxes and labour from the Pedi that led some of their chiefs to move away to the Pedi heartland, and others who did not move away, to assert that the land upon which they lived belonged to Sekhukhune, the paramount chief, thus denying that the South African Republic had the right to demand taxes and rent of them. As the demands of the South African Republic for labour, tax and rent increased, so did those Pedi living in that grey area of borderlands which Delius refers to as land that fell under "a loose dual hegemony", become more inclined to stress their relationship with Sekhukhune as their paramount and protector in order to evade the exactions of the Boers. In other words, Delius overthrows the traditional view that Sekhukhune was deliberately expanding the Pedi domain. Delius portrays Sekhukhune, not altogether successfully, as being a reluctant expander, writing that "to some extent Sekhukhune was pulled in the wake of more militant subordinate chiefdoms and groups intent on exploiting the authority of the paramount in order to enhance their local power, to extend their independence of control, to resist exaction and to secure their right to the land upon which they had settled."[122] Delius also, and this time with more success, overthrows the traditional picture of the Pedi as the aggressor in relations with the Berlin Missionary Society missionaries, and shows that the missionaries in fact took the lead in attacks on the Pedi in order to have the polity crushed and the way opened for more successful missionary enterprise.

Although much of the ground dealt with by Delius has been researched before, what he adds to our understanding is that, whereas other researchers have seen relationships between the Pedi, the Boers and the British from the point of view of the white groups, Delius has placed the Pedi firmly in the centre of the picture; he is concerned with developments within the society, with the internal dynamics and changing power structures, with economic, political and ideological struggles.

* * *

As indicated above, part of this new literature seeks to demonstrate that Africans, contrary to popular belief, were able to respond with great effectiveness to changes in their economic and natural environment. They showed remarkable adaptability and a willingness to meet new situations. This is a very different picture from that painted earlier of static and unchanging societies unable to act effectively when they came into contact with whites moving into the interior. The new historians maintain that, on the contrary, the Africans initially responded with more success than did white farmers in many areas, particularly when they were dealing mainly with traders and merchants. The discovery of minerals and the arrival of industrial capital to replace mercantile capital changed much of this, and capitalism with its need for a cheap and easily-controlled labour force found it intolerable for Africans to enjoy economic independence, and even provide a measure of competition – the result was that they crushed African entrepreneurship.

In his study of a number of eastern Cape, Transkei and Ciskei regions in the late nineteenth and early twentieth centuries, Colin Bundy argued "that there was a substantially more positive response by African peasants to economic changes and market opportunities than is usually indicated; that an adapted form of the prevailing subsistence methods provided hundreds of thousands of Africans with a preferable alternative to wage labour on white colonists' terms in the form of limited participation in the produce market; that a smaller group of black farmers made considerable adaptations, departing entirely from the traditional agricultural economy and competing most effectively with white farmers."[123] Bundy argued that in the period immediately following the discovery of minerals, Africans on the whole responded more effectively to economic change than white farmers. Bundy demonstrated how the situation altered after the discovery of gold. Prior to the discovery of minerals, despite attempts by white farmers to have African squatter-peasants evicted from white farms, for many years the Cape government lacked both the means and the desire to do so – too many white farmers and other influential white groups with access to parliament were in favour of the creation of a black peasantry. For many farmers, to lease their land to these peasants was far more profitable than farming it themselves – once again, a class alliance, rather than a simple racial division.

But after the discovery of gold on the Witwatersrand in 1886 white farmers faced more competition for labour. The mines also needed labour and wanted

196

it as cheaply as possible. Sufficient labour could not be attracted while peasants still had access to land and could produce enough for their cash requirements. So both white farmers and mine owners were intent on destroying peasant independence. At the same time, many peasants were ousted from white land or forced to become farm labourers as the value of land rose and agriculture was commercialised or capitalised. Commercialisation of white agriculture was aided by huge subsidies and grants, tax relief and advantageous rail rates, all of which bypassed black peasants, who in the reserves were further disadvantaged by the fact that they were invariably far from the nearest railway lines. As more peasants were forced off white farms the pressure on the available land increased, which resulted in a deterioration in efficiency within a short while. The final disasters prior to the Native Land Act were the rinderpest and East Coast fever.

This is part of the research that seeks to examine the implications of the transformation of undercapitalised to capitalised agriculture, with the emphasis on black proletarianisation. Bundy's study was of the Cape, but other work having reference to the Orange Free State and the Transvaal at the turn of the century likewise suggests that Africans were successful farmers. White farmers had legal title to the land, but could not afford to commercialise agriculture, so they resorted to sharecropping, leasing the land to Africans for a share of the crop. After the Second Anglo-Boer War, white pastoralists with means stocked up with Texan and Australian cattle imported by the British; there was money available to undertake fencing. From now on commercial beef and dairy production was largely in the hands of whites, as was merino sheep farming. Few Africans had the land or the capital to engage in commercial wool-farming. Africans, however, did have advantages in agriculture. Whites did not have the capital for investment in agriculture, and Africans knew more about dry-land farming than did whites.

Whites concentrated on pastoralism and left agriculture to the Africans. Exceptions to this pattern were white agricultural enterprise in the western Cape, where wheat and wine were produced, and in the coastal belt of Natal and later Zululand, where there were sugar plantations.[124] But in other places where capital was in short supply and much of the countryside had been devastated, sharecropping was increasing and for some 10 years after the war it seemed to be the dominant form of agriculture in the Free State. Tim Keegan, among others, has argued that black producers were better able than whites in the conditions existing after the war to make the land productive – they had the necessary skills for peasant production. They could mobilise cheap family labour by making use of the patriarchal structures of precapitalist days; Poor White bywoners had no such opportunity.[125]

But in time the blacks were also pushed off the land. With the support of the government, which provided subsidies, tariff protection and laws to ensure a plentiful supply of cheap labour, white landowners were able to accumulate capital to develop their farms. The owners then began opposing sharecroppers and the white bywoners.

Although both white bywoners and black sharecroppers were pushed off the land, the whites were proletarianised far more rapidly, and far more completely than the blacks, who for a long time continued to have access to land in the homelands or reserves. One of the main differences lay in the different division of labour in the two societies. According to the radicals, the liberals had not seen this because they were blinded by the theme of interaction. If they had paid more attention to the fact that separate societies, independent of each other, had emerged in the interior, they would have understood much more about the process of proletarianisation and how it affected black and white in separate ways. As Shula Marks explained it: "The fact that in African society it was the women who did the agricultural work in the main meant that when the men were forced into town to earn money for taxes, they left their families behind in the countryside; when Afrikaners were displaced from the land as a result of the expansion of capitalist farm-ing . . . the women were amongst the first to move to the towns, for it was the able-bodied young men who were wanted for farm work. The outright expropriation of Afrikaners compared to the continued access which Africans were to have – under the migrant labour system – to a diminishing amount of land was to have the profoundest consequences for class struggles and consciousness in twentieth-century South Africa."[126]

In the mid-1980s the examination of change in the rural areas remains a principal theme. Two major works on the subject appeared in 1986, viz Tim Keegan's *Rural transformations in industrializing South Africa: The Southern Highveld to 1914* and *Putting a plough to the ground: Accumulation and dis-possession in rural South Africa, 1850–1913*, a number of articles edited by William Beinart, Peter Delius and Stanley Trapido. Themes that have been explored in earlier literature are taken a step further. The Native Land Act of 1913, frequently seen in the 1970s as having had a uniform, deep and immediate effect on independent African farming, has been subjected to closer analysis which suggests that the act was not felt everywhere to the same extent, nor was the effect immediate, except perhaps in the northern and eastern Free State, which is what Marian Lacey had said earlier. Attention has been given to the changing nature of tenancy at the turn of the century and early years of the twentieth century. The alterations in the pattern of sharecropping, rent and labour tenancy have been brought under the mi-croscope; white farmers gave increasing support to labour tenancy, believing that rent tenants on neighbouring farms were stock thieves. As more research into small areas is done, the possibility of a synthesis seems to recede, for each study adds to the complexity of the phenomenon being studied, with subtle shades of difference between one region and the next.

There is also some accent, as indeed there was earlier in the work of Beinart, for example, on the fact that around the turn of the century Africans very often still had a choice – they did not *have* to work for white farmers. There was still communal land available, rented farms or the possibility of taking work as migrant labourers. White farmers knew that too much pressure would result in the Africans moving to the reserves. But as time went by, opportunities for Africans in a number of regions became more circumscribed. The increasing density of settlement in African reserves reduced their room for manoeuvre.

Another noteworthy contribution to the study of relationships in the rural areas is Helen Bradford's 1985 University of the Witwatersrand doctoral thesis, *The Industrial and Commercial Workers Union of Africa in the South African countryside 1924–1930.*

It is to the existence of the reserves that researchers like Harold Wolpe, Martin Legassick and Marian Lacey have turned their attention. Wolpe was among the first to put forward the view that the mineowners were able to fix lower wages for labour migrants because of the existence of "native reserves" where Africans had access to land and family to support them.[127]

The mines favoured the retention and expansion of such reserves as it reduced their welfare costs, relieving them of the need to provide social security, as the migrant labourer could exist partly on the agricultural production of the reserve. This was much cheaper than allowing African families to settle around Johannesburg, where the employers would have been responsible for supporting the families as well as the workers. So it was the families of the workers who helped to ensure that the labour costs of the mines were kept down. According to this view, labour was drawn from the reserves and rural areas, with the state acting as an agent of capitalism, by introducing compulsory measures like tax, wage limits, pass laws, influx control, and a ban on trade unions, thus ensuring class domination.

Marian Lacey has argued that mining capital wanted the reserves to be maintained and even expanded as labour pools for the migrant labour system, but that the farming capitalists did not like the reserves because they kept labour away from their farms. The South African Party government favoured the mines, while the Pact government favoured the farmers. Eventually a compromise between mining and the agricultural sector was arrived at which paved the way for inter-party co-operation and Fusion. She demonstrates how a compromise was worked out between farming and mining. The National Party was 'converted' to a 'reserve' policy, while, on its side, the South African Party abandoned its defence of the Cape African franchise. This last must be seen in the context of the fact that the mining industry by this time was drawing more of its labour from the Cape and wanted the reserve migrant labour system to be fully implemented in the Cape, which the disfranchisement of the Africans facilitated.[128]

But this argument about the reserves is also being questioned in the 1980s. Martin Legassick has taken Lacey to task for applying too literally Wolpe's argument that the reserves were intended to keep wage costs down by providing a rural subsidy to workers. He warned that this must be treated with caution, saying that in modern South Africa the reserves (homelands) play almost no part in subsidising workers' wages, yet this has not changed the fact that capitalism is still based on the existence of homelands. Legassick argued that "the migrant labour system serves to cheapen labour independently of what the rural end produces. Perhaps, then, the conflict between mineowners and farmers was more over convenient access to and control over 'their' labour supply than over the issue of 'subsidization' ".[129]

Studies have been made of the structure of Cape liberalism in the nineteenth century. Historians have queried whether the basis of Cape liberalism was really humanistic, and whether the Coloured franchise created an open society. Stanley Trapido says that historians have accepted Cape liberalism at its face value, and have thus failed to analyse "the conditions which made liberalism in the Cape possible, the purpose which different liberals gave to the institutions which were created, and the changing circumstances which constantly reshaped liberalism in the Cape".[130] He was intent upon showing that although the rhetoric attached to liberalism did not change, the alliances between various groups and their aims and purposes did. His examination of the factors that gave rise to liberalism and sustained its growth led him to the conclusion that of vital importance was the fact that certain groups at the Cape, like government officials, missionaries and merchants, had an interest in the creation of a stable peasantry, and that while this was the case the black franchise was safe. This is much the same conclusion as Bundy came to.

The discovery of minerals changed this, and these same classes were now no longer interested in the establishment of a stable peasantry; Africans were increasingly seen as a labour force that should be proletarianised as soon as possible. In the 1880s a new class alliance came into being at the Cape, aimed at inhibiting the growth of free peasantries and turning the peasants into a labour force; the franchise came under attack. Afrikaner nationalists were also opposed to the existence of a free African peasantry and to the franchise. They joined up with English-speakers at the Cape who had some interest in mining, and also English farmers. The conflict between those whites in favour of the existence of an African peasantry and who supported the African franchise, and those opposed, has often been seen as being one between Afrikaners and English. But the radicals insist that it was not so, that it was class that determined the battle lines, not ethnicity.

This view of liberalism is not one that latter-day liberals like Rodney Davenport have allowed to pass unchallenged. While Davenport agrees that liberals did share "a common class base" which was eroded after the mineral revolution, he feels that to concentrate on this "diverts attention from the problem of what liberalism was really about." He writes: "The most distinctive feature of nineteenth-century liberalism in the southern African experience was a concern for the rights of other cultural groups or individuals which, being relatively rare, was often seen as suspect, as a 'dishonest masquerade under the cloak of religion'." He admits that liberals were often paternalistic, but the choices confronting them were not easy ones, and he believes that they were, "for the most part, intelligent people who agonised humanely and with integrity about difficult situations", such as whether or not it was in the best interests of the Africans to have access to "white man's liquor", or whether, although this could substantially alter the balance of political power, the Cape's low franchise qualifications should be extended to the blacks in the Transkei who were totally unschooled in the ways of electoral systems.[131]

THE PRE-INDUSTRIAL CAPE

One gap in recent historiography is that those who have been working on the period of industrialisation following upon the first discovery of minerals in the late 1860s, have failed to link up their findings to the pre-industrial period in the Cape and Natal, to see what influence social relations in the colonies had on the way capitalist South Africa developed. Having decided that Afrikaner racial attitudes were not formed on the Cape frontier in pre-industrial times, radicals and liberals tended to write off the Cape as insignificant for an understanding of the process of industrialisation.

Robert Ross in particular has contested this relegation of the Cape to a minor role in the development of South African society. In the same way as Shula Marks directed attention to the manner in which pre-capitalist structures affected the form and nature of segregation, so has Ross asserted that it was not the mineral revolution that made Cape agriculture market-orientated. He follows up on Leonard Guelke's thesis on the trekboers and early Boer society, in which he argued that although the availability of "free" land enabled people without money to be independent farmers, albeit at what was largely a subsistence level, this did not mean that they were not market-orientated. On the contrary, they were prepared to grab at market opportunities.

Ross argues that prior to the mineral era agriculture and pastoral production was already "largely geared to the market, and indeed to export trade". In the settler-dominated rural areas relations of production "were unmistakably capitalist in character". He also says that in most of the Cape "the majority of the labourers were already thoroughly alienated from any independent access to the means of production. In other words they were proletarianized." This proletarianization and the "considerable levels of commercialization" did not thus all come about as a result of the mineral revolution. Pre-industrial relations of production "were at least quasi-capitalist". Capital accumulation in the sense of the appropriation of power and resources by one class to the exclusion of others, with the state's help, was not an exclusively post-industrial phenomenon.

Ross believes that the pattern of agriculture that developed at the Cape became the model for South African agriculture as a whole: "The South African white agricultural system is a specific historical construction which was developed in the Cape Colony", he writes, "and was then extended further and further north . . . With few exceptions the South African countryside as a whole, outside the African reserves, became what it had long been in the Cape, namely a land not of plantations, not of smallholders, but of large owner-operated farms worked by a harshly exploited black labour force."[132]

Some of the new work has focused on slavery at the Cape in the eighteenth century.[133] Much of this has been done by historians who most certainly could not be included under a Marxist umbrella, but who differ quite fundamentally from each other as well as from those who insist on seeing the pre-industrial Cape in class terms. The interpretations, however, owe much to the stimulus provided by the Marxists, and this is one area in which the liberals have faced up to the challenges presented by class analysts.

Cape slavery has always had an image of mildness, mainly because the Cape economy differed from that of the New World. The impersonality, hugeness and regimentation of the West Indian sugar plantations were absent from the Cape, where slavery was a face-to-face institution and the paternalistic attitude portrayed by traditional histories seemed correct. Robert Ross's researches, however, based largely on the court testimonies of slaves, led him to the conclusion that Cape slavery, "far from being some benevolent paternalism, was harsh, brutal and bloody . . . Moreover, from the point of view of the masters, it had to be so, since slave resistance to their oppression was continual if unorganised and individualistic." The fact that the resistance of Cape slaves was individual and uncoordinated he explains in terms of the different areas from which they originated, the fact that slaves were held over a wide area in small homestead units, and there was a constant influx of new arrivals – all this prevented the slave community from becoming a close-knit one. Further research seems to confirm "the old horror stories of Barrow, of Van der Kemp and of James Read."[134]

After the debunking of MacCrone's views about the formation of white racist attitudes on the Cape frontier, the radicals placed the emphasis in the search for these attitudes on an industrialising South Africa. But others have made an attempt to shift the search for the origins of racial stratification and racism back into the pre-industrial era, and in 1981 George Fredrickson (*White supremacy: A comparative study of American and South African history*) identified slavery as the basis of white attitudes.[135] But his view that it was the frontier and the conflict with the Africans, that was responsible for bringing about a *rigid* racial division has come under attack. His characterisation of the western Cape as primarily a class society "in which race mattered in the determination of status but was not all-important", has in particular been singled out for criticism.[136]

Fredrickson argued that blacks were enslaved not because they were blacks and were thus considered inferior, but because legally they were captives and culturally they were heathens. He maintained that in America slavery was initially based on heathen status, but that by the end of the seventeenth century heathenness had come to be associated with blackness, after which time racial differences became the basis for slavery. He argued that the situation in the Cape was different, that slavery was based on heathenness, for the Synod of Dort in 1618 laid down that baptised slaves should not be sold but should have equal rights with other Christians.

Although Fredrickson can probably best be classified as a liberal, if indeed it is necessary to categorise him at all, like historical materialists such as William Freund, he also sees late eighteenth century society as very fluid. Freund argued that Cape slavery had social fluidity like that of Brazil, and was not like the American South with its rigid caste system. He believed that the vaguely defined line between European and black was often crossed by intermarriage, arguing that this blurring of the colour line meant that race (ethnic origin) was not the factor that determined one's legal and social status.[137]

It is in the same area that the radicals launched their first attacks on the liberals, namely on the question of the roots of South African racial attitudes and policies, that those who contest the primacy of the class explanation, have taken a stand.

Even before the appearance of Fredrickson's book, in *The shaping of South African society*, edited by Hermann Giliomee and Richard Elphick, and published in 1979, Elphick and Robert Shell had characterised the eighteenth century Cape slave society as "one of the most closed and rigid", and had made the point that there were marked regional differences; it was necessary to differentiate between Cape Town itself, which was much more open as regards manumission and intermarriage, and the rest of the south-western Cape, where about 75% of the slaves were held, and which was far more rigid.[138]

Their views, and those of Giliomee, who contested Fredrickson's thesis, place the foundations of South African society in the period of the Dutch East India Company. Slavery came to the Cape because the government imported slaves, so there was no debate about its legality or whether it should be based on colour or heathenness. The Synod of Dort was never seriously debated. Until a 1770 regulation confirmed the Synod of Dort very few of the slaves baptised were manumitted. In this respect Cape slavery was very much like the more rigid North American plantations.

Speaking of this south-western Cape, Hermann Giliomee was quite emphatic that "social stratification" was above all determined by racial slavery. The divide between the free and the slaves almost completely corresponded with the racial divide."[139] On the frontier some free blacks and Khoikhoi obtained intermediate positions like hunters, wagon drivers or barterers and there was a degree of intermarriage between them and some of the poorer whites. But when land on the frontier was no longer plentiful and the frontier closed, these "bastards" were pushed out, and not only because they were poor and powerless, but because of their colour. In his penetrating analysis of Fredrickson's work, Giliomee wrote that the frontier thus "tended to turn steadily into a society that was rigidly stratified along the lines of race, leaving only Cape Town to fit, in a limited sense, Fredrickson's characterisation of the Cape as a class society".[140]

If one looks at the situation of the so-called "free blacks" to see whether race determined their position in the social structure, both Nigel Worden and Leon Hattingh have taken issue with aspects of the class interpretation, and maintain that in the Cape and Stellenbosch districts there were few economic opportunities for free blacks in the rural areas. Even in Cape Town, where there was far more opportunity for free blacks to accumulate possessions, their position deteriorated in the second half of the eighteenth century as they became subject to increasing discriminatory restrictions and laws.[141] "It was not enough to be free – one had to be white as well", Giliomee concludes.[142]

Giliomee does not believe that there was much intermarriage at the Cape. He acknowledges that there were a fair number of such marriages in the early days after the introduction of slaves, but denies that this pattern continued later. It is also, he argues, not fair to take Cape Town with its seaport mores as typical of the colony as a whole, and there were not many marriages of this nature in Stellenbosch, Malmesbury and Graaff-Reinet. Nor does Giliomee believe that there is much evidence for the view that the children of mixed marriages were often accepted into Cape society. Giliomee, citing Schermerhorn,[143] pointed out that inter-racial mixing itself cannot be used as a yardstick of racial tolerance, since miscegenation occurred in any society as the sexual exploitation by dominant-group men of subordinate-group women. He argued that racial tolerance should rather be gauged in terms of the incidence of mixed marriages. Although inter-racial marriage was permitted at the Cape, he did not believe that many such marriages took place – apart from any other considerations, slaves were not allowed to marry and since so few slaves were manumitted, not many of them had an opportunity of marrying across the colour line.

The shaping of South African society, 1652-1820, has since its publication in 1979 rapidly become widely recognised as the best recent work on the period. It also makes a contribution to the debate on the frontier theme, on which the book concentrates fairly heavily. Not all the contributors adhere to a liberal point of view, but the liberal element is certainly the most prominent. Hermann Giliomee has attempted to find his way to a compromise between the cooperation and conflict theme of the liberals and the class analysis of the radicals, seeing different options operating during what he defines as the open and closed stages in the development of the frontier.

Although Martin Legassick has a chapter on the northern frontier to 1820 and the emergence of the Griquas, this is not as heavily Marxist as one might have expected. He provides a largely empirical account, with a preliminary section expounding Marxist thinking on the significance of trade, or commodity exchange as he calls it. The liberals had seen the expansion of the social relationships of trade between Cape Town and indigenous communities as harmonious, as establishing cooperative relationships; this was the way in which a new society was created. They had tried to explain how this harmony had turned into racial enmity and conflict. To Legassick, this was only one level at which trade could be regarded. For him, as for Marx, "commodity exchange was not a universal mode of social relationship, but a historical mode. Its appearance progressively disguised and fetished the social relationships of class which it expressed. Its appearance, indeed, could be said to have created the potential for relations of class exploitation and domination to take on 'racial' forms." But in the body of the chapter, Legassick was unable to explore this theme. The reason why the introduction to his chapter does not have a close connection with the main body of what he has to say, is explained by the fact that the contribution comes from his doctoral thesis, and that when he did the research for it, as well as when he agreed to revise it for the book, "he was not yet equipped to re-present the material to illustrate this theme adequately".[144]

A CRITICAL VIEW OF RADICAL HISTORIOGRAPHY

The advent on the historical scene of the radicals has led in the last 15 years to a sometimes heated debate about South African history. In the late 1970s Jeff Peires wrote with only slight exaggeration that "the very fierceness of the debate – with all its fouls, low blows and cunning misrepresentations – is a tribute to the vigour and relevance of South African historiography today."[1977][145] There are some who would argue that the use of the word "debate" is a misnomer, that the radicals were not prepared to debate, but only to assert the superiority of their own views and attack liberal history, and that even those prepared to debate had, in the light of more recent liberal work that differed from earlier liberal studies, to refer to liberal histories that were 20 to 30 years old in order to make their point.[146] John Wright put forward the view that radicals were "not interested in being drawn into a debate whose terms have been formulated by liberals. To do so would be to accept the liberals' own frame of reference, which is precisely what the radicals want to avoid."[147]

Be that as it may, loosely employed, the word "debate" seems acceptable. The debate which at times gave out more heat than light is no longer so fierce, and at various levels there is a coming together of radicals and liberals and a tendency to make an attempt to stop labelling and categorising historians. The debate was probably at its most acrimonious when the influence of Louis Althusser and Nicos Poulantzas was particularly strong on the radicals.

The debate has been largely between so-called liberals and radicals, and conservative South African historians have tended to stand aside from the debate and level vituperative criticisms from the sidelines.

The radicals have been criticised on various levels. The first person to articulate his criticism in a comprehensive way was Harrison Wright.[148] He wrote his essay in Cape Town late in 1975. More than a decade has since passed. When he wrote, the radicals had not published very much. Most of what they had done was in the form of seminar papers delivered at the Institute of Commonwealth Studies of London University, and Wright based his evaluation on a handful of examples. He believed that much of the radical criticism of liberal history had been unfounded or taken out of historical context, and in this regard he came down rather sharply on the review of the *Oxford History* by Nancy Westlake and Anthony Atmore.[149] He maintained that much of what the radicals were saying had been said before by the liberal historians, although it had not been couched in the same theoretical framework. He argued that a good deal of their work had been foreshadowed by de Kiewiet in the 1930s and Sheila van der Horst in the 1940s.[150]

Some of the faults of the radicals, Wright maintained, were the same ones of which he had accused the liberals. Thus the liberals had put no blame on the blacks who were seen as victims in the histories that they wrote. The fault of the radicals was that they "spend a considerable amount of time demonstrating the existence ... of the 'rationality' and the effectiveness of the African response. They are in fact so committed to African 'rationality' that on occasion they have nineteenth and early twentieth-century Africans thinking just as they would have done had they themselves been there". They had done this because they could not bear to see the Africans once again portrayed as "inferior" and "backward". "But surely", Wright went on to say, contesting the attempts by Bundy to demonstrate that blacks had responded effectively to change, "it does not necessarily imply cultural 'inferiority' even to suggest the existence of other cultural impediments to effective economic response."[151]

Jeff Peires took Wright to task for his views about African initiatives and motives, arguing that the view that "Africans are economically rational originated well outside South Africa and well before the beginning of the current debate."[152]

Peires was referring here to the well-known work of A. G. Hopkins. In *An economic history of West Africa*, published in 1973, an important part of Hopkins's task was to examine the place occupied by Africa "in the mythology of underdevelopment". "Pre-colonial Africa", he wrote, "is popularly regarded as forming an economic Plimsoll Line drawn to mark subsistence activities. Above this line are placed the supposedly more advanced economies of other pre-industrial regions, with the loftiest quarters being reserved for European countries." Hopkins demonstrated very effectively that allegations about the inefficiency of the indigenous labour force are for the most part without foundation. Africans did act rationally: "Where new plants and seeds were adopted, it was not because they caught the fancy of a primitive people, but because they were seen as useful additions to the existing range of foods, being worth more than the extra cost of producing them; or alternatively because they were regarded as good substitutes, yielding a higher return for the same input than the crops they displaced." Hopkins was in no doubt that "agricultural history in the pre-colonial period is a story of innovation rather than stagnation. The assumption that the economy was static, having been frozen at the very dawn of African history, is untenable, and the timeless concept of the 'traditional' society needs to be used with care, or, better still, not used at all."[153]

An article by Colin Bundy is written off by Harrison Wright as resting "on too narrow a base of theory and of fact". In Wright's opinion, Bundy failed to consider that the positive response of Africans might have been a result of European education and technology. Wright complains that Bundy places the blame for the decline of African peasantry only on the shoulders of capitalism, and does not consider sufficiently things like horse-sickness and droughts.[154]

Wright examined Legassick's article on the South African frontier in depth, and criticises him for saying that MacCrone was the pioneer in establishing the traditional frontier theory. He also maintains that Legassick had misunderstood Genovese and his work *The world the slaveholders made* to make out a case for the primacy of class and not race relations. These flaws, he believed, rendered the credibility of Legassick's article as a whole doubtful.[155] When Legassick's paper was later published in the collection of Marks and Atmore, the points raised by Wright were taken up.[156] At least one of the American reviewers of *The burden of the present*, agreed with Legassick's interpretation of Genovese, and implied that Wright had misread Genovese.[157] Although some of the points raised by Wright had a measure of validity, they did not alter the fact that Legassick had made a major contribution towards a reassessment of the frontier. By focusing on small items Wright attempted to damn the article without in any way challenging Legassick's conclusions.

Wright also criticised both the liberals and the radicals of excessive present-mindedness, of using the present in an unacceptable way. He was widely criticised for his views on presentism, and in replying to these critics he took a more cautious stand, writing that "the issue of present-mindedness is always difficult because it involves questions of balance and proportion." He maintained that the point he had wished to make in his essay about both liberal and radical historians "is that the particular weaknesses of their history does suggest a preoccupation with the present that diminishes to some extent the value of their history as an instrument of effective social analysis." Although this was natural and understandable in the South African context, historians should guard against the tendency "to use their histories 'directly' to promote social purposes".[158]

This is an endless debate, and does not properly belong to a study of South African historical writing. A few remarks, however, may seem necessary within this framework. Thomas Hodgkin a few years back said that "the purpose of understanding society should be to change it, and in this sense knowledge of the past could be 'usable' ".[159] More recently this sentiment has been implicit in criticism of academic historians writing about the struggles of the working class. It has been maintained that their studies should be "usable" and reflect the needs and aims of this working class.[160]

Donald Denoon and Balam Nyeko in the preface to the 1984 edition of their book, *Southern Africa since 1800*, wrote as follows: "It is our belief that the living conditions of the majority of the people must be transformed as soon as humanly possible; and that a reasonable understanding is the necessary first step towards achieving that change."[161]

This only appeared after Professor van Jaarsveld's book, which deals with the question of guilt and blame in South African history, but from what he writes about the study of history and presentism or present-mindedness, it seems likely that van Jaarsveld would not endorse this statement. Van Jaarsveld repeats many of Harrison Wright's criticisms and adds other charges of his own. He maintains that the radical school of historical materialists aims to rewrite South African history from the point of the black working classes in order, in the wake of the Soweto riots of 1976, to awaken black consciousness and spur blacks to action. He later repeats the charge, saying that Shula Marks wanted to reinterpret the past with the aim of helping to bring colonialism in South Africa to an end, and that in 1982 she admitted that the group of scholars of which she was at the centre, had two motives for publication, political and intellectual. The political motive was linked to the 1976 Soweto riots.[162]

An examination of his source fails to substantiate the activistic connotations that van Jaarsveld wished to give it. In the introduction to the work edited by Shula Marks and Richard Rathbone, *Industrialisation and social change in South Africa: African class formation, culture and consciousness, 1870–1930* (London, 1982) the editors do indeed state that "at its inception, there were two spurs to this project, political and intellectual." But they immediately go on to say that "in retrospect it seems no coincidence that it was conceived in the mid-seventies as African workers and students made their voices heard again after the long silence of the sixties. The 1972–1973 strikes which began in Namibia and Natal, at opposite ends of the subcontinent, and spread rapidly through the Republic, together with the revitalisation of the African trade union movement, had a profound effect both politically and intellectually." The authors describe the essays in the book as one of the "beginnings of a new literature which tries to unravel the historical complexities which have shaped this resurgent working class . . . It was the reawakening of the African working class in the early seventies which also in many ways brought to a head the limitations of the existing literature."[163]

It is these statements linking the study of African class formation and consciousness with political unrest in South Africa, that are regarded by van Jaarsveld as proof of the unacceptable use of the past to serve purposes in the present. An objective reading of these passages shows nothing untoward or sinister in Shula Marks and Richard Rathbone's statements. It would indeed have been strange if in the light of evidence of a "resurgent" black working class, historians did not delve into the past to throw light on the emergence of this phenomenon. It is ironic that van Jaarsveld, as mentioned earlier, has himself been accused of encouraging the search of the past to justify present political practices.[164]

While some radical literature undoubtedly has a revolutionary aim and is seen by their authors as contributing to the "liberation struggle",[165] the principal object was to develop an explanatory model which would prove superior to any other models that have been devised to account for the South African situation.[166]

Whether they really do offer a superior explanatory model has been queried by many people on different grounds. To take one example, Rob Davies, universally classified as a neo-Marxist or radical, wrote as follows: "Contrary to the assertion of certain critics, the purpose of this analysis is not to deny the existence and importance of racist ideology and racial prejudice but rather to see these as phenomena arising in the class struggle and therefore themselves requiring analysis and explanation instead of, as in the liberal problematic, the 'self-evident' starting point of all 'analysis' and 'explanation'."[167] To the radicals there is only one correct starting point, and this is the relationships of production in a specific mode of production.[168] By making this shift they do not, so they maintain, fall into the same trap as the liberals, of taking something for granted (the primacy of racial attitudes) which needs to be explained.

Philip Nel has examined their claims, and comes to the conclusion that "the very same critique so confidently developed by Marxists may be levelled against their own approach". He goes on to write that "no attempt, to my mind, has so far been undertaken by Marxists to supply an *a priori* justification of their assertion that the conceptual apparatus of historical materialism do indeed provide the only correct point of departure and point of no regression for the adequate explanation of South African reality. No explanation is offered why certain environmental factors can be considered as the 'primary social categories' and others not. Marxists have so far, it seems, missed the crucial issue that their 'starting point' may also be in need of explanation and justification; that they also break off the explanatory *regressum* at an arbitrary point; that they also presuppose that which is in need of explanation; that their explanatory method is as circular as the one they accuse other approaches of using; and finally, that in terms of their own criteria, their analyses may claim no explanatory superiority."[169]

Some other criticisms of the theoretical basis of radical literature have been noted in various parts of this chapter. Mention has been made of Geoffrey Kay's observations regarding the inability of merchant capital, as opposed to industrial capital, to restructure productive relations, since it meets the producer only in the market place.[170] The usefulness or validity of this observation has not been convincingly demonstrated by radical writers; it thus falls into the category of an "accepted truth" rather than a proposition which has been subjected to historical analysis.

There may have been too much theory in recent historical analyses, but this is partly an understandable reaction against those histories in which the nature of the research focus is determined by what is readily available in archives, and which lacks any recognisable interpretative framework. There is little doubt that much of the liberal and conservative work produced until the mid-1970s was, in the words of Frederick Johnstone "highly empiricist: a little bit of this, a little bit of that, a little bit of constitutions, a little bit of laws, a little bit of politics. The student would, as often as not, emerge from this labyrinth of 'facts' with little clear understanding of *what it was all about. What, in the midst of all these laws and constitutions and elections and events, was actually going on?*"[171]

Although the Marxists ask different questions from those posed by the liberals, the extent to which they offer a different methodology is a matter of controversy, and depends to a large extent on how one defines "methodology". Robin Law argues that "a set of ill-defined concepts such as 'mode of production' and 'class' and a highly qualified commitment to economic determination, . . . seem hardly to amount to a distinctive methodology." One should perhaps, he writes, think of Marx as not providing new methodology but rather "a plausible interpretaion of specific historical data which suggests the general advisability of directing attention to the economic 'base' of society: 'the content is different, not the nature of the method'."[172]

The workmanship of some radicals has been singled out for criticism. Hughes, for example, believed that "the revisionists have brought in a slackening of standards of what passes for evidence and what is accounted explanation".[173] Rodney Davenport has observed that in analysing recent works on the political economy of South Africa "we are faced with a number of premature, evidently flawed castings, so that one needs to ask of any new venture in political analysis whether it is yet another inadequately researched hypothetical construct, or whether it is thought out and tested with sufficient care to take us further along the road of rational understanding."[174]

Badly or inadequately researched histories are not confined to radical works, and every tradition of historical writing abounds with examples of its own, but where the radicals have been particularly open to criticism is that some of them make statements or generalisations with a confidence which all too often is not borne out by the evidence. It is true that their refreshing insights "sensitise" other historians to the possibilities inherent in their own material, and that a new way of looking at a subject or of approaching it, may stimulate other historians to climb out of the ruts into which their thinking has got them, but this does not alter the fact that certain of the claims made by the radicals have not been backed by thorough research into all main sources. Even Colin Bundy's excellent study of the Cape peasantry is based largely on the reports of the civil commissioners printed in *The Blue Book for the Colony of the Cape of Good Hope*. While he has substantiated his assertions, and in the process made good use of missionary material, he has had recourse to the Cape archives only "to test a hypothesis or to seek data known to exist in a specific file".[175] A glaring example of a "flawed casting" is the work of Dan O'Meara.[176]

Johannes de Bruyn in examining pre-colonial historiography stated that "although the use of Marxist concepts in recent work has added important dimensions to our understanding of precolonial societies, it has in some cases produced 'abstract' history, strangely devoid of sentiment, ideas and feeling. The impression is that some historians are more concerned with their concepts than with precolonial man: he produces and reproduces, he seldom lives. So far most recent works on precolonial South African history lack the essential connection between the world of ideas and feelings, and the economic base."[177]

This weakness did not only apply to radical writing on pre-colonial societies, and as indicated in a number of places in discussing specific radical works, this has probably been the major criticism of radical historical writing in general: that it has failed to take into account the independent role played by men's beliefs, their ideologies, their cultural equipage.

Professor B. J. Liebenberg said that, as an Afrikaner, he only wished it were true that O'Meara and his ilk could really demonstrate that the Afrikaners were not responsible for having created apartheid. But unfortunately he did not believe that they could do so: "The Afrikaner is the principal inventor and the principal maintainer of apartheid", he declared, "and all the attempts of O'Meara and his kindred spirits to place the guilt on the English and Jewish capitalists, are doomed to failure. The Afrikaner will simply have to take the blame for apartheid."[178]

By adopting a historical materialist approach the radicals have opened up new vistas, but by concentrating on this exclusively, and insisting on the primacy of class, some of the radical work has undoubtedly led to a distorted or one-sided picture of the past. But by the mid-1980s this had largely changed.

There was a realisation that class did not have all the answers, or even necessarily the most important ones.

THE MID-1980s

The controversy between the radicals and the liberals started out as a disagreement about whether "race" or "class" were the determining factors in South African history. This "race-class" debate "put a new sort of question onto the agenda of South African historiography". Deborah Posel writes that what began as an emphasis "on the class functions and determinants of apartheid and segregation, expanded and solidified into a theoretical and methodological approach, or problematic, which imposed a functionalist and reductionist perspective on the study of South African history . . . As a result, having opened up a new ground for historical inquiry, such revisionist theory has also tended to close it off to further expansion. For, the price paid for this approach is a foreclosing of inquiry into other sorts of questions concerning the tensions and contradictions in the relationship between racial policy and capitalism, on the one hand, and the irreducible importance of political and ideological factors, on the other."[179]

Deborah Posel developed her argument further by saying that "the very terms in which the 'race-class' debate is set up thus preclude a different mode of enquiry, oriented by a different question, which does not seek a uniform ranking of one variable over another, but rather their concrete interrelationships, in the ways in which racial cleavages and practices themselves structure class relations."[180]

There are signs that the attitude of "either race or class" is changing. A number of those who have been widely categorised as belonging to the radical school, have expressed views similar to Posel. Belinda Bozzoli echoed Deborah Posel's objections to the "either race or class" approach. She wrote that reality "does not fit into the interpretive straitjackets demanded by specific political movements, and one of the purposes of the researcher must be to reflect the ambiguities that reality contains . . . Thus while the trade unionist might wish 'class' to be the fundamental category within which all explanation should fit, and the nationalist might want 'race' or 'internal colonialism' to prevail as the major category, in truth . . . the realities of South African history were never clear-cut enough for either of these frameworks to hold true for all situations over the *whole* of the past." She goes on to say that "neither class nor the supposed alternatives to it are timeless. To a historical materialist these, and all similar concepts, are to be understood as historical and social categories rather than reified universals. At some historical moments social groups may well appear to be driven by ideological forces, or cultural ones, which have come to gain a certain relative autonomy; and at others, the crude realities of economic necessity and process seem to prevail. And at all times we need to be alert to the interplay between these dimensions rather than regarding them as polar opposites."[181]

While it was undoubtedly true that in the 1970s radical history was strongly theoretical and that consideration of ideological factors was scant, by the 1980s this position had begun to change and practitioners of South African history were making it clear that attention was now due to these non-material factors as well.

Thus, Tom Lodge as editor, writes of the papers gathered together under the title *Resistance and ideology in settler societies* (Johannesburg, 1986), and which deal with subjects such as popular resistance in Namibia in the 1920s, the social nature of I.C.U. leadership, also in the 1920s, black passengers on the South African Railways in the early twentieth century, and the Poqo insurrection of the 1960s, that they share an aversion "towards rigid forms of social classification. The sociology of the communities under discussion is commonly portrayed as fluid, emergent, fragile, and historically hybrid. Class concepts are employed with a consciousness of their ambiguity and the blurred nature of their boundaries. Reflecting the subtle and qualified deployment of class analysis, much of the argument in this volume ascribes to ideology an important function in shaping and determining historical action and political behaviour. The power of ideas to take on fresh meanings and outgrow the significance and content attached to them by their original advocates is a recurrent theme throughout the collection."[182] This examination of the changing meaning attached to ideas and the words 'in which they are given expression, is a theme that was also explored by O'Meara and seems likely to enjoy greater prominence in the future.

Shula Marks in the introduction to her recent study of Solomon ka Dinuzulu, John Dube and George Champion, describes the three essays as an attempt to "bring together in some sense the insights we have gained from both the new social history and the structural marxism of the seventies, by looking at both individual agency and social constraints."[183]

Frederick Johnstone has also made a plea for a pluralistic approach. In an article published in 1982, he wrote that when we move away from political economy to political sociology and social psychology, to discuss culture and identity, subjectivity and meaning, we are "faced with the paradigmatic weaknesses of an essentially materialist approach confronted by the role of non-economic factors in history and society. And regardless of how much of a paradigmatic problem this actually is, this is still an area in need of more attention, because the fact is that the new work has tended to prefer the secure ground of political economy, and focused its energies there. The very strengths of Marxist political economy have perhaps discouraged a greater concern for and sensitivity to this whole issue of the non-economic." Johnstone warned Marxists against adopting a superior attitude, saying that they should reject "the idea that any one approach alone can completely do justice to it all, and to accept some degree of epistemological and paradigmatic pluralism; to reject the fashionable assumption, favoured on the left, that only one paradigm can be valid, that different ones are completely incompatible, and that you just pick your paradigm and do your work; and, of course, to reject, as rather foolish, any glib ideas or implications to the effect that no other approach in the world besides Marxism understands anything. A more pluralistic Marxist approach would argue instead that inquiry can fruitfully proceed within a variety of paradigms; that there may be some measure of complementarity besides incompatibility; and that the fact of paradigmatic incommensurability does not in itself mean that only one paradigm can arrive at truth and knowledge and should be used to the exclusion of all others. This viewpoint does not mean that you cannot still insist on the relative superiority of one approach over another, and proceed to demonstrate that; it simply means you are not entitled to imply that because it is very powerful no other approach is worthy of attention."[184]

John Lonsdale, in a penetrating article written in the early 1980s, believed that in the fluid, economic and political situation prevailing in South Africa, he saw signs "that the liberal-Marxist dichotomy has begun to fade sufficiently for both sides to see more clearly the common ground on which they may fruitfully disagree . . . Among liberals there seems to be an increasing awareness of the need to study the material necessities of production and its contradictory social relations. Among some Marxists there has been a complementary realization that this material level is not so much determinant of as fundamental to all other human relations . . . It is clearly essential to analyse what appear to be the material necessities of any given mode of production, their internal structure and its corresponding social relations; class does have a strong structural component. But to stop there is to risk an ahistorical functionalism, to mistake consequences for causes. It is vital to consider the political level as well. The material level decides only what classes or nations cannot do, the political determines what they can . . . Mature capitalism has enormously complicated the relations of men and women to the means of production. The simplifying alliances within which classes of people are able to play some part in making their own history are formed not by material structures but by creative politics. Political coalitions and oppositions, with their accumulating myths of loyalty and betrayal, can indeed determine what materially productive strategies will or will not be attempted, and how effectively." He concludes "that liberal and Marxist historians of South Africa are often less divided than some of them suppose".[185]

Mention has been made at various points of presentism, and preoccupation with the present. Whether a liberal or Marxist approach to South African society is adopted, makes a considerable difference to an appreciation of the present, and also of the road from the present to the future. It vitally affects thinking, for example, on the whole question of disinvestment. Radicals define a person's class according to his position in the network of ownership relations. "On this view, the perpetuation of economic inequality between

214

working class and bourgeoisie is thus not simply a reflection of personal failings or wholly political constraints on workers, but illustrates the objective economic constraints on the possibilities for their acquiring and accumulating capital, individual effort and determination notwithstanding."[186]

Even those liberals who do give due attention to the economic determinants of racial policy, see matters differently from the radicals. They do not take much notice of the existence of objective class forces which determine what can and what cannot be done. They view the situation in terms of the intentions, actions and motives of various individuals and groups – they do not consider that there are *structural* limitations acting on classes that are beyond the ability of individuals or groups to control. They account for economic inequality in South Africa by referring to institutionalised racial discrimination, and in their view, what is needed to set the situation right is the removal of racial discrimination. Liberal reform by the state of existing institutions will eventually eliminate the injustices and inequalities of the system of apartheid. The liberals remain confident that the pressures of economic "reality" are inexorably forcing the government to move towards reform. They see recent reform tendencies as confirmation for their viewpoint. The radicals regard the situation as far more complex. They believe that the liberals underestimate the degree to which apartheid and capitalism are at home with one another, and that the political framework of the country is pretty resilient and resistant to genuine political reform. They regard the sort of reforms brought about in the early 1980s in the political sphere "as adaptive, rather than liberalising".[187] They do not believe that they have stemmed from liberalising tendencies in capitalism or industrialism. They argue that they have their origin in the changes that came about in the 1970s in both the international sphere and in South Africa, and in a new appreciation by capitalism of the costs of maintaining a system of capitalism that was based on race. As political and economic pressures on South Africa by the outside world increased, so did racial exploitation begin to become something of a political liability for capital. Up to the late 1970s, the benefits of racial exploitation were far greater than its costs. Although the attacks on white supremacy had gathered momentum in the 1960s in the wake of decolonisation in the rest of Africa, the attacks had not been on capital itself. This situation changed in the course of the 1970s, with the result that for capital, white supremacy now became a liability. Capital's attitude towards black labour became more "liberal" and capital moved away from reliance on a racially structured capitalism.[188] Capitalism was helped in this shift by the fact that for some time its structural dependence on racial exploitation had been declining.

Apart from the fact that the radicals were sceptical about whether the moves were genuinely reformist, they believe that "the class underpinnings of racial injustices in South Africa are such as to mitigate the possibility of a just distribution of resources by the changeover to liberal democratic institutions alone".[189] Because of the class dimensions of racial injustice, liberalisation means "a basic liberalisation of class relations, basic changes to South Africa's racially structured capitalism, a radical restructuring of wealth and power, for example of land rights, labour rights and more general civil and political rights". Believing that such fundamental changes alone could bring about genuine reform, they began to question the investment of the western world in helping to maintain the *status quo*. "No longer was it possible to portray this foreign investment as essentially beneficial." In this view, disinvestment will help to bring about change. Frederick Johnstone believes that "the new, more radical and class-oriented way of looking at South African history and society, which emerged at the beginning of the decade, definitely influenced the shape and thrust of political opposition to, and pressures upon, white domination in South Africa during the 1970s and into the present."[190]

* * *

The radicals have made a contribution by calling attention to very important areas which have thus far been overlooked but they have failed to establish a new alternative interpretation of South African history as a whole. Part of the reason undoubtedly is that it is not easy to marry theory and history, and even in Britain where there has been a lively debate for some time, K. Neild wrote in 1975 that "with a handful of honourable exceptions, history and theory in British Marxist historiography enjoy only a separate development".[191] Belinda Bozzoli explained the fact that "the growth of an alternative conception of history within this country has turned out to be a painfully slow and difficult one", as partly due to the impatience of radicals for "results". "The search for immediate relevance in every intellectual enterprise has led all too many aspiring radicals into undertaking quick but perhaps sometimes shallow examinations of current issues rather than the slower, more painful historically-based analyses of major processes of class formation, struggle and interaction." She warned that "placing those current issues in any sort of historical and structural context remains, and will remain, immensely difficult in the absence of longer-term, more ambitious, and perhaps less instantly gratifying work".[192]

It could be argued that before anything like a meaningful synthesis is possible, the sort of detailed study undertaken by Charles van Onselen will have to be duplicated many times at various levels. This painstaking research is time-consuming in the extreme, and has no appeal to students looking for instant results that will be "relevant" to their present situation. A number of researchers *are* throwing light on other small areas in order to arrive at a broader understanding, examining aspects of life in places like Herschel, Potchefstroom and Brakpan, focusing on the implications of soccer within a particular social framework, on Indian flower-sellers in Johannesburg, on job

216

protection in the Ironmoulders' Society, tenant production on the Vereeniging Estates.[193] But as the number of such studies proliferate, processes like urbanisation and proletarianisation are seen in all their intricate complexity, with each case study presenting subtle variations, so that a synthesis appears all the more difficult and unlikely.

A noteworthy attempt to include the results of much of the new writing in a general history of South Africa is *Southern Africa since 1800* by Donald Denoon and Balam Nyeko. The first edition was published in 1972. The second edition appeared in 1984. In the period between the appearance of the two editions so much new work had appeared that the authors "could not simply make the small changes which are often introduced into the second edition of a book". They re-wrote it, incorporating conclusions reached by both liberals and radicals. The emphasis given to the struggle between social classes as the motor of history, had obliged the liberals "to do more research and better analysis in defence of their belief that it is conflict between races which mainly inspires events". In their debate the radical and liberal scholars "have taken much more interest in ordinary people than they used to – black as well as white, poor as well as rich, women as well as men."[194]

The above statements in the preface to the book, are an indication of the direction of the changes made to the second edition. The new influences are immediately obvious from the chapter headings, starting off with a chapter entitled "The environment and the strategies of pre-capitalist production". Radical influences are also evident in the title of chapter 11, "Agricultural development and rural underdevelopment", and chapter 13, "Entrenching the post-colonial state". Denoon and Nyeko have also moved further away from the traditional periodisation in the second edition. The years 1910 and 1948 are no longer highlighted in chapter headings. This trend of changing the periodisation as established by writers like Theal at the turn of the century, was a feature of the *Oxford History*, which did not have separate chapters, for example, on the Great Trek and the Anglo-Boer War. Periodisation seems likely to become more of an issue in the future as white historians are increasingly confronted with views of the past as seen by blacks. The greater emphasis on social history will also tend to place more pressure on the "traditionalists" to defend their key dates in white history as being valid for a study of South Africa as a whole. There can be no doubt that while 1910, for example, represents a major constitutional landmark in the history of South Africa, and cannot be consigned to the scrapheap, it may be that 1910 makes no sense at all as a date of major significance for the majority of the working class, white and black, on the Witwatersrand, or in the rural areas. It could be that of the Native Land Act of 1913 is more relevant.

Denoon and Nyeko's book has largely replaced the use of books like that of de Kiewiet and Keppel-Jones as introductory surveys to South African history, particularly among students of African history abroad.

But for South African students who study South African history in greater detail and require more than a broad interpretative analysis for assignments, Rodney Davenport's *South Africa: A modern history* (Johannesburg, 1987) has filled the place held by Eric Walker's history in earlier decades. Like Walker's revisions, the third edition of Davenport's work has produced a much bulkier text, and one that is heavily focused on the twentieth century, even more so than was Walker's work. For the study of Dutch East India Company rule Elphick and Giliomee's *The shaping of South African society* at present has a monopoly. For a brief period, D. W. Krüger's *The making of a nation: A history of the Union of South Africa, 1910-1961,* (Johannesburg, 1969) replaced the rather unsatisfactory post-Union chapters in Walker, but since the first appearance of his work in 1977, Davenport's history has progressively gained greater acceptance for the study of twentieth century South African history. This is particularly true of the third edition. Whereas the first edition of 1977 handled post-1910 developments in some 200 pages, in the third edition more than 320 pages are required to deal with events since Union. Davenport has taken cognisance of recent developments, discussing new interpretations at the appropriate place in his largely narrative approach. But dispersed as it is throughout the book, the force and impact of the new research is somewhat diluted. To overcome this Davenport has added a section called the political economy. Although the two accounts do not lie easily together, and the constant references to authors and cross-references do not make for easy reading, it is a compromise that allows a narrative and largely political approach to incorporate a number of interpretative analyses that have widely divergent starting points.

A recent general history that enters into the historical debate, rather than dividing the new work into small and separate contributions to specific issues, is Merle Lipton's *Capitalism and apartheid: South Africa, 1910-1986* (London, 1986). Lipton attempts to add another dimension to the debate, and while agreeing that "a classical Marxist interpretation goes quite far in explaining some aspects of South African development", in her synthesis she makes particular use of what she refers to as "liberalism's superior insight into the behaviour of individuals and of firms".[195] She argues that capitalists in South Africa have never been unanimous in their support for apartheid, that segregation was functional for certain types of capitalist development but not for others. She thus believes that the question about whether economic growth bolsters or undermines apartheid is too crude a formulation. We should rather concentrate on different types of economic growth. Thus white agriculture up to the 1960s, and mining up to the 1970s, required a cheap, unskilled labour force for its growth and could thus live quite happily with apartheid. But manufacturing and commerce, for example, wanted skilled labour and a large domestic market, which higher wages would bring, and for them apartheid was less beneficial.

218

She also analyses the ability of the capitalists to obtain what they wanted. Until the mid-1960s, agricultural capital was more likely to get its own way, partly because of the tendency for ethnicity to play such a major role in political affiliation. But since the 1960s there has been a rapid shift from dependence upon mining and agriculture to greater dependence upon the manufacturing and service industries, which needed skilled labour. Even the mines and agriculture required greater numbers of skilled workers. They thus wanted a change in apartheid labour policies: "No longer so dependent upon a large mass of cheap, unskilled black workers, they wanted a free, mobile, competitive labour market, with large numbers of blacks entering skilled and semi-skilled jobs."[196] The power of agriculture declined, while with the preference given by the government to Afrikaner business since 1948, the growth of Afrikaner capital meant a group of new capitalists who also wanted to see apartheid eroded. As hostility gathered momentum abroad, the costs of apartheid mounted. Afrikaner business interests set their faces against apartheid because of its stifling effect on the growth of the domestic market, its threat to the growth of export markets, access to foreign capital and technology. There was a split in the ranks of the Afrikaner, but "the power of the declining classes and sectors had been institutionalised and entrenched, and as the challenge to them grew, they shored up their power by authoritarian measures. The ruling NP, and the vast bureaucracy it spawned, had a vested interest in controlling the rate of change, and in slowing and preventing some changes, particularly in the political sphere, which threatened their power and jobs."[197]

Having demonstrated the close interaction between class and ethnicity, Lipton concludes that "neither the broad class categories of capital and labour . . . nor ethnic/racial categories such as Whites, Blacks, English, Afrikaners, provide an adequate means of comprehending the behaviour of individuals and groups. In the competition for resources, class conflicts often took an ethnic form; the lines of cleavage between groups, and the alliances constructed in the political struggle, were usually along ethnic not class lines . . . Both ethnic/racial and class factors are therefore essential for understanding and predicting political behaviour. The fact that political mobilization took place along ethnic rather than class lines helps to explain, for example, why capitalists in SA were less powerful than expected."[198]

An attempt to make authoritative historical insights more readily available in an accessible form to a general intellectual public is the "coffee-table" *An illustrated history of South Africa*, edited by Trewhella Cameron and S. B. Spies (Johannesburg, 1986), which was published simultaneously in English and Afrikaans. A number of specialists in their own fields, both English and Afrikaans, have incorporated their research findings into a book that is remarkably free of specialist terminology and concepts. What is new to many South African readers, as opposed to historians, is the realisation it has brought of the multi-faceted role played by blacks in South African history. This book has been criticised for its periodisation, which is strongly white-centred and political. Thus the Great Trek, the Anglo-Boer War, Union in 1910, 1924 and 1948 remain its central lines of division. But any account that gives greater prominence to political factors than it does to social and economic determinants, is likely to be confronted by the same problem in a country where whites have called the political tune. Rodney Davenport's account is also largely divided into the components of major events in the history of white South Africa, having as his points of division the Great Trek, 1902, 1924, 1939, 1948 and 1960. Only the work of Denoon and Nyeko to a certain extent escapes this traditional white centred division.

*　*　*

In the early 1950s Professor Z. K. Matthews said: "I do not know if it is possible to approach history without bias. But if it is necessary to accept that all history is biased, the important thing is that all biases are represented, and it is high time that African history, written from the African point of view, takes its place on library shelves."[199] Over 30 years later such histories still do not take up very much space on library shelves. It is difficult to predict whether this is likely to change in the near future, or what direction the major trend in the writing of history by blacks will take. But there can be little doubt that what is at present missing in the study of South African history is a significant black input. An informed African perspective is long overdue.

It seems likely that continued involvement by black intellectuals in the struggle for political rights will keep the attention of black writers on the theme of white exploitation, and direct their focus to black nationalism. Perhaps some of the directions taken by historians in Africa north of the Limpopo in the first two decades of the era of political independence will apply here. Considering that the nationalist movements had played such a large role in wresting independence from the colonial governments, it was perhaps natural that African historians in the 1960s in the immediate aftermath of independence should give so much attention to African nationalism and its origins. They focused on the tradition of resistance in the early years of colonial rule, and attempted to draw a continuous line of resistance leading through to independence. They searched the past for continuities between the pre-colonial and post-independent eras in a bid to demonstrate that African society had not been destroyed by white rule, that underneath it all genuine indigenous African values had survived intact to give the new states their own special African character.

In the first decade after independence, in a reaction against the colonial myth that Africans were inferior and that it was the Europeans who had brought "progress" to Africa, African historians concentrated on portraying European explorers, missionaries, traders and governors as exploiters of the African people. This interpretation, which saw Africans as innocent victims, putty in the hands of European manipulators, was not a balanced view, and more recent research, which is being undertaken in terms of what are considered to be Africa's own values, and not simply a reaction to the European way of thinking, indicates that in general Africans had a good deal of latitude in deciding how to accommodate themselves to the newcomers in their midst, and in using new situations to further their own ends. In short, to a large extent they were agents of their own destiny.

The concentration on "nationalism" in the 1960s was unbalanced also in the sense that it tended to judge African history in terms of alien values. African historians were approaching history on the same basis as European historians, for although matters were changing in the European scene, much European history in the 1960s was still concerned with political systems and empires, with "national" history, with the affairs of governments, politicians and the elite. European historians who regarded these themes as the "proper" subject matter of history, were in the van of those asserting that Africa had no history. The new generation of indigenous African historians argued on their opponent's terms, and were at pains to show that Africa did in fact have sizeable kingdoms and empires comparable with those in Europe before the arrival on the scene of Europeans. They focused, therefore, on Ethiopia, Samory and the ancient empires of Ghana and Mali. They looked at those aspects of African history which resembled European history. But Professor Curtin has argued that in doing so they missed the point that more recent historical works are beginning to make more effectively, which is that "Africa's great achievement in law and politics was probably the stateless society, based on cooperation rather than coercion, not to mention the fact that the African states had been so organized as to preserve genuine local autonomy."[200]

Perhaps some of these trends will come to the fore in black historical writing in South Africa, but in the forseeable future it is likely that black historians will concentrate on the "exploitation" and "nationalist" themes.

NOTES

1 Tom Lodge, *Black politics in South Africa since 1945*, Johannesburg, 1983.
2 A second edition was published in 1964 by Wisconsin University Press, Madison.
3 Donald Denoon, "Synthesising South African history", *Transafrican Journal of History*, 2(1), 1972, p. 104.
4 K. R. Hughes, "Challenges from the past: Reflections on liberalism and radicalism in the writing of Southern African history", *Social Dynamics*, 3(1), 1977, p. 47.
5 I. B. Tabata, *The awakening of a people*, Nottingham 1974, pp. 97–98. (First published in 1950 by the All-African Convention in South Africa).
6 Lodge, p. 29.
7 Ibid., quoted by Lodge, p. 33.
8 Some of the works of relevance in this new tendency include J. K. Ngubane, *An African explains apartheid*, London, 1963; Tabata, *The awakening of a people*; W. M. Tsotsi, *From chattel to wage slavery: A new approach to South African history*, Maseru, 1981; N. Majeke, *The role of the missionaries in conquest*, Cape Town, 1952; "Mnguni", *Three hundred years:*

A history of South Africa, Cape Town, 1952; David Dube, The rise of Azania, the fall of South Africa, Lusaka, 1983.

9 Christopher Saunders, " 'Mnguni' and 'Three hundred years' revisited", Kronos, 11, 1986, pp. 74–76.

10 Ibid.

11 Ibid., quoted by Saunders, p. 75.

12 Majeke, pp. 10, 19.

13 Anthony Atmore and Shula Marks, "The imperial factor in South Africa in the nineteenth century: Towards a reassessment", Journal of Imperial and Commonwealth History, 3(1), 1974; Susan Newton-King, "The labour market of the Cape Colony, 1807–28" in Shula Marks and Anthony Atmore (eds), Economy and society in pre-industrial South Africa, London, 1980.

14 Majeke, pp. 16–17.

15 Ibid., pp. 79–86, 95. See also Atmore and Marks, "The imperial factor in South Africa" for the development of this theme.

16 Luthuli, Let my people go: An autobiography, London, 1962, p. 44.

17 See F. A. van Jaarsveld, Omstrede Suid-Afrikaanse verlede: Geskiedenisideologie en die historiese skuldvraagstuk, Johannesburg and Cape Town, 1984, pp. 144–163.

18 S. M. Molema, "A historical parallel and warning", Bantu World, 4, 11 October 1952.

19 Quoted by van Jaarsveld, Omstrede verlede, pp. 154–155. It seems likely that the words quoted are an adulterated version of those contained in F. W. Reitz (issued by) A century of wrong, published in London in 1900 and which read as follows: "As in 1880, we now submit our cause with perfect confidence to the whole world. Whether the result be Victory or Death, Liberty will assuredly rise in South Africa like the sun from out the mists of the morning, just as Freedom dawned over the United States of America a little more than a century ago. Then from the Zambesi to Simon's Bay it will be 'Africa for the Africander' " (p. 98). These words were in fact written by Jan Smuts, who apparently took them from a non-official manifesto written by Dr (later judge) E. J. P. Jorissen at the time of the First Anglo-Boer War in 1880–1881: The original read as follows: "Hetzij wij overwinnen, hetzij wij sterven: de Vrijheid zal in Zuid-Afrika rijzen als de zon uit de morgen wolken, als de Vrijheid rees in de Vereenigde State van Noord-Amerika. Dan zal het zijn van Zambezie tot aan Simonsbaai: Afrika voor den Afrikaner". See 'n Eeu van onreg, Afrikaans translation by F. J. le Roux with a preface by D. J. van Zyl, Cape Town and Pretoria, 1985.

20 Star, 29 April 1982, p. 30.

21 Magubane, p. xin.

22 Frederick Johnstone, " 'Most painful to our hearts': South Africa through the eyes of the new school", Canadian Journal of African Studies, 16(1), 1982, p. 5.

23 Ibid.

24 Robert Kubicek says that it was Harrison Wright who gave the name "radical" to the new school. See R. O. Collins, "Synthesis and reflections: African history is a precarious profession" in D. I. Ray, P. Shinnie and D. Williams (eds), Into the 80's: The proceedings of the eleventh annual conference of the Canadian Association of African Studies, 2 vols, vol. 1, Vancouver, 1981, p. 245.

25 Jeff Peires, "On the burden of the present", Social Dynamics, 3(1), 1977, p. 65.

26 Robin Law, "In search of a Marxist perspective on pre-colonial tropical Africa", Journal of African History, 19(3), 1978, p. 451.

27 The full title is The burden of the present: Liberal – radical controversy over Southern African history, Cape Town and London, 1977.

28 Wright, The burden of the present, pp. 72–82; Jeff Peires, "On the burden of the present", p. 64.

29 Harrison M. Wright, "The burden of the present and its critics", Social Dynamics, 6(1), 1980, p. 42. See also Barry A. Kosmin, "The Inyoka tobacco industry of the Shangwe

people: A case study of the displacement of a pre-colonial economy in Southern Rhodesia, 1898–1938", *African Social Research*, 17, 1974, pp. 554–577 and Giovanni Arrighi, "Labour supplies in historical perspective: A study of the proletarianization of the African peasantry in Rhodesia", *Journal of Development Studies*, 1, 1970, pp. 197–234. This article is also reproduced in G. Arrighi and J. S. Saul, *Essays on the political economy of Africa*, New York, 1973. This is not the only work of Arrighi but it is the one principally used by Wright. When Wright wrote, Bundy's work, *The rise and fall of the South African peasantry*, London, 1979, had not yet appeared, and Wright based his argument mainly on the article by Bundy, "The emergence and decline of a South African peasantry", *African Affairs*, 71(285), 1972, pp. 369–388.

30 David Yudelman, "Dan O'Meara's Afrikaner nationalism", *Social Dynamics*, 9(1), 1983, pp. 102–103.

31 See "Let the academics think; the rest can dance or sing", letter by Karl van Holdt, *Weekly Mail*, 3(7), 20–26 February, 1987, p. 12. Some of the papers given at the first History Workshop were published in Belinda Bozzoli (ed.), *Labour, townships and protest*, Johannesburg, 1978. Contributions from the second workshop appeared in Bozzoli (ed.), *Town and countryside in the Transvaal: Capitalist penetration and popular response*, Johannesburg, 1983, while the third History Workshop gave rise to Bozzoli, (ed.), *Class, community and conflict: South African perspectives*, Johannesburg, 1987.

32 Van Jaarsveld, *Omstrede Verlede*, pp. 87–122.

33 Jeff Peires, "The legend of Fenner-Solomon" in Bozzoli, *Class, community and conflict*, pp. 66–67.

34 Ted Matsetela, "The life story of Nkgono Mma-Pooe: Aspects of sharecropping and proletarianisation in the northern Orange Free State, 1890–1930" in Shula Marks and Richard Rathbone (eds), *Industrialisation and social change in South Africa: African class formation, culture, and consciousness, 1870–1930*, London, 1982, p. 212.

35 G. A. Cohen, *Karl Marx's theory of history: A defence*, Princeton, 1978, p. 73. See also Marks and Rathbone, *Industrialisation and social change in South Africa*, p. 8.

36 Deborah Posel, "Rethinking the 'race-class debate' in South African historiography", *Social Dynamics*, 9(1), 1983, p. 60.

37 M. Legassick, "Capital accumulation and violence", *Economy and Society*, 3(3), 1974, p. 255.

38 Johnstone, " 'Most painful to our hearts' ", p. 8.

39 L. Althusser, *Reading capital*, London, 1979; N. Geras, "Althusser's Marxism: An account and an assessment", *New Left Review*, 71, 1972; N. Poulantzas, *Political power and social classes*, London, 1973 and "Internationalisation of capitalist relations and the Nation-State", *Economy and Society*, 3(2), 1974; M. Godelier, *Perspectives in Marxist anthropology*, Cambridge, 1977; C. Meillassoux, "From reproduction to production: A Marxist approach to economic anthropology", *Economy and Society*, 1, 1972, pp. 93–105 and *Maidens, meal and money: Capitalism and the domestic community*, Cambridge, 1981 (This is a translation of *Femmes, greniers et capitaux*, which appeared in 1975); E. Terray, *Marxism and 'primitive' societies*, New York and London, 1972.

40 E. D. Genovese, *The world the slaveholders made: Two essays in interpretation*, London, 1969. See also E. D. Genovese, *In red and black: Marxian explorations in Southern and Afro-American history*, London, 1971.

41 Van Jaarsveld, *Omstrede verlede* is a good source for historical trends abroad, particularly in West Germany.

42 André Gunder Frank, *Capitalism and underdevelopment in Latin America: Historical studies of Chile and Brazil*, New York, 1967 and *Latin America: Underdevelopment or revolution*, New York, 1969; Harvey J. Kaye, *The British Marxist historians: An introductory analysis*, Cambridge and Oxford, 1984, pp. 50–53.

43 E. Laclau, "Feudalism and capitalism in Latin America", *New Left Review*, 67, 1971, pp. 19–38, reprinted in E. Laclau, *Politics and ideology in Marxist theory*, London, 1977, pp. 15–50; Kaye, pp. 51–53.

44 *How Europe underdeveloped Africa*, London, 1972; Wright, *The burden of the present*, pp. 15–16.

45 *Ivory and slaves in East Central Africa: Changing patterns of international trade to the later nineteenth century*, London, 1975.

46 Bundy, *The rise and fall of the South African peasantry*; Harold Wolpe, "Capitalism and cheap labour power: From segregation to apartheid", *Economy and Society*, 1, 1972, pp. 425–456; William Beinart, *The political economy of Pondoland 1860–1930*, Johannesburg, 1982.

47 E. P. Thompson, *The poverty of theory and other essays*, London, 1978 is largely an attack on structural Marxism.

48 Quoted by Kaye, *The British Marxist historians*, p. 209.

49 R. H. Davies, *Capital, state and white labour in South Africa 1900–1960*, Brighton, 1979; Dan O'Meara, *Volkskapitalisme: Class, capital and ideology in the development of Afrikaner nationalism, 1934–1948*, Johannesburg, 1983; Duncan Innes, *Anglo: Anglo-American and the rise of modern South Africa*, Johannesburg, 1984.

50 R. Law, "How not to be a Marxist historian: The Althusserian threat to African history" in R. Samuel (ed.), *People's history and socialist theory*, London, 1981, p. 315.

51 Bozzoli, "History, experience and culture" in Bozzoli, *Town and countryside*, pp. 27–28.

52 Hindess and Hirst, p. 321.

53 Saul Dubow, *Land, labour and capital in the pre-industrial rural economy of the Cape: The experience of the Graaff-Reinet district (1852–72)*, Centre for African Studies, Communications of the University of Cape Town, no. 6, 1982, pp. ii, 5.

54 Robert Ross, "The first two centuries of colonial agriculture in the Cape Colony: A historiographical review", *Social Dynamics*, 9(1), p. 44, n. 11.

55 Johannes du Bruyn, "The 'Forgotten Factor' sixteen years later: Some trends in historical writing on precolonial South Africa", *Kleio*, 16, 1984, p. 40.

56 Kaye, *The British Marxist historians*, pp. 148–149.

57 Charles van Onselen, "The Regiment of the Hills – Umkosi Wezintaba: The Witwatersrand's lumpenproletarian army, 1890–1920" in *Studies in the social and economic history of the Witwatersrand, 1886–1914*, vol. 2, Johannesburg, 1982 and *The small matter of a horse: The life of 'Nongoloza' Mathebula, 1867–1948*, Johannesburg, 1984; Don Pinnock, "Stone's Boys and the making of a Cape Flats Mafia" in Bozzoli (ed.), *Class, community and conflict*. In this above volume, see also Jeff Guy and Motlatsi Thabane, "The Ma-Rashea: A participant's perspective".

58 H. C. Bredekamp, *Marxist historiography on South Africa before the 1970s*, Centre for Research on Africa, University of the Western Cape, Occasional Paper 1, 1983.

59 J. Lonsdale, "From colony to industrial state: South African historiography as seen from England", *Social Dynamics*, 9(1), 1983, p. 69.

60 H. Adam, *Modernising racial domination*, Berkeley, 1971.

61 D. Yudelman, *The emergence of modern South Africa: State, capital, and the incorporation of organized labor on the South African gold fields, 1902–1939*, Cape Town, 1984, p. 14.

62 Reprinted with additional footnotes in Marks and Atmore, *Economy and society*, pp. 44–79.

63 Ibid., p. 51. See also Genovese, *The world the slaveholders made*, p. 7.

64 I. D. MacCrone, *Race attitudes in South Africa: Historical, experimental and psychological studies*, Johannesburg, 1937; Legassick, "The frontier tradition", p. 60.

65 Legassick, "The frontier tradition", p. 62.

66 Ibid., p. 67.

67 Shula Marks, "South African studies since World War Two" in C. Fyfe (ed.), *African studies since 1945: A tribute to Basil Davidson*, London, 1976, p. 194.

68 "The imperial factor in South Africa in the nineteenth century: Towards a reassessment", *Journal of Imperial and Commonwealth History*, 3(1), 1974.

69 Monica Wilson and Leonard Thompson (eds), *The Oxford History of South Africa*, 2, South Africa 1870–1966, Oxford, 1971, p. 364.

70 Marks and Atmore, "The imperial factor", p. 132.

71 Ibid., p. 116.

72 Susan Newton-King, "The labour market of the Cape Colony, 1807–28" in Marks and Atmore, *Economy and society*, pp. 197, 200.

73 "The imperial factor", p. 125.

74 Ibid., p. 109.

75 J. A. Hobson, *Imperialism: A study*, London, 1902.

76 J. S. Marais, *The fall of Kruger's republic*, Oxford, 1961; G. D. Scholtz, *Die oorsake van die Tweede Vryheidsoorlog 1899–1902*, 2 vols, Johannesburg, 1947.

77 See for example, Stanley Trapido, "Landlord and tenant in a colonial economy: The Transvaal 1880–1910", *Journal of Southern African Studies*, 5(1), 1978 and "Reflections on land, office and wealth in the South African Republic, 1850–1900" in Marks and Atmore, *Economy and society*, pp. 350–368; Donald Denoon and Balam Nyeko, *Southern Africa since 1800*, new ed., London and New York, 1984, pp. 104–105.

78 Patrick Harries, "Capital, state, and labour on the nineteenth century Witwatersrand: A reassessment", *South African Historical Journal*, 18, 1986, pp. 27–28.

79 C. van Onselen, *Studies in the social and economic history of the Witwatersrand*, vol. 1, p. 94.

80 Ibid., p. 95.

81 Harries, p. 41.

82 See pp. 107–108.

83 Martin Legassick, "The making of South African 'Native Policy', 1903–1923: The origins of segregation", Institute of Commonwealth Studies postgraduate seminar, 15 February 1972.

84 Van Onselen, vol. 1, p. xvi.

85 Denoon and Nyeko, p. 103.

86 See review of Yudelman by Noel Garson, *Social Dynamics*, 9(1), 1983, pp. 98–101.

87 O'Meara, *Volkskapitalisme*, p. 26.

88 Denoon and Nyeko, pp. 135–136.

89 O'Meara, *Volkskapitalisme*, pp. 27–30. See also Yudelman's review of O'Meara in *Social Dynamics*, 9(1), 1983, pp. 102–105.

90 See T. R. H. Davenport's review of Yudelman in *Social Dynamics*, 9(1), 1983, pp. 95–98.

91 M. Lacey, *Working for Boroko: The origins of a coercive labour system in South Africa*, Johannesburg, 1981.

92 For conflicting views among liberal historians about the turning point, see the reviews of T. R. H. Davenport and Noel Garson in *Social Dynamics*, 9(1), 1983, pp. 96, 101.

93 Innes, *Anglo*, pp. 42, 118–132.

94 Denoon and Nyeko, p. 157.

95 Marks and Rathbone, *Industrialisation and social change*, p. 11; G. Kay, *Development and underdevelopment*, London, 1979, p. 126.

96 O'Meara, pp. 176, 244. See also Stanley B. Greenberg's review of O'Meara, *Social Dynamics*, 9(1), 1983, pp. 105–107, and J. P. Brits, "Marxistiese geskiedskrywing en die opkoms van die 'Afrikaner-magnaat', 1934–1948", *Kleio*, 16, 1984, pp. 46–52.

97 Van Jaarsveld, *Omstrede verlede*, p. 107.

98 Moodie, p. xiv of the Introduction to the paperback edition, Berkeley and Los Angeles, 1980.

99 *Studies in the social and economic history of the Witwatersrand*, vol. 1, pp. xv–xvi.

100 N. Poulantzas, "Internationalisation of capitalist relations and the Nation–State", p. 164.

101 Yudelman, *The emergence of modern South Africa* pp. 17, 234–235. See Davenport's review of Yudelman, *Social Dynamics*, 9(1), 1983.

102 See reviews of *Volkskapitalisme* by David Yudelman and Stanley B. Greenberg in *Social Dynamics*, 9(1), 1983, pp. 102–107.

103 L. M. Thompson, *Survival in two worlds: Moshoeshoe of Lesotho 1786–1870*, Oxford, 1975; P. Sanders, *Moshoeshoe: Chief of the Sotho*, London and Cape Town, 1975.

104 Jeff Guy, *The destruction of the Zulu kingdom: The civil war in Zululand, 1879–1884*, London, 1979; Philip Bonner, *Kings, commoners and concessionaires: The evolution and dissolution of the nineteenth century Swazi state*, Johannesburg, 1983; William Beinart, *The political economy of Pondoland 1860–1930*, Johannesburg, 1982; Peter Delius, *The land belongs to us: The Pedi polity, the Boers and the British in the nineteenth century Transvaal*, Johannesburg, 1983; R. K. Rasmussen, *Migrant kingdom: Mzilikazi's Ndebele in South Africa*, London and Cape Town, 1978; J. Peires, *The House of Phalo: A history of the Xhosa people in the days of their independence*, Johannesburg, 1981; K. Shillington, *The colonisation of the southern Tswana 1870–1900*, Johannesburg, 1985.

105 For a good account of the contribution made in the sphere of pre-colonial history, see du Bruyn, "The 'Forgotten Factor' ".

106 Shula Marks, "South African studies since World War Two", p. 195.

107 Rob Turrell, "Kimberley: Labour and compounds, 1871–1888" in Marks and Rathbone, *Industrialisation and social change*, pp. 45–76.

108 Marks and Rathbone, p. 15.

109 Bozzoli, "Class, community and ideology in the evolution of South African society" in Bozzoli, *Class, community and conflict*, p. 23.

110 Marks and Atmore, *Economy and society*, pp. 2, 25.

111 Bundy, *The rise and fall of the South African peasantry*, p. 1.

112 Houghton, pp. 45–47.

113 Ernesto Laclau, *Politics and ideology in Marxist theory*, London, 1977, pp. 34–35.

114 Philip Nel, "Recent Marxist analyses of South Africa: The question concerning explanatory superiority", *South African Journal of Philosophy*, 2(3), 1983, pp. 146–147.

115 Dubow, *Land, labour and merchant capital*, pp. 20–22.

116 "Notes on the Southern Tswana social formation" in K. Gottschalk and C. C. Saunders (eds), *Africa seminar collected papers*, vol. 2, Centre for African Studies, University of Cape Town, 1981, pp. 167–194; " 'Beasts of burden': The subordination of Southern Tswana women, ca. 1800–1840", *Journal of Southern African Studies*, 10(1), 1983, pp. 39–54.

117 Du Bruyn, "The 'Forgotten Factor' ", p. 45.

118 J. D. Omer-Cooper, *The Zulu aftermath: A nineteenth century revolution in Bantu Africa*, London, 1966.

119 Jeff Guy, "Ecological factors in the rise of Shaka and the Zulu kingdom" in Marks and Atmore, *Economy and society*, pp. 102–119.

120 Beinart, *The political economy of Pondoland 1860–1930*.

121 Bonner, *Kings, commoners and concessionaires*.

122 Delius, *The land belongs to us*, p. 191.

123 Bundy, *The rise and fall of the South African peasantry*, p. 13.

124 Denoon and Nyeko, pp. 126–127.

125 Tim Keegan's latest and fullest handling of these and related issues is his *Rural transformations in industrializing South Africa: The southern highveld to 1914*, Johannesburg, 1987. See also Tim Keegan, "The sharecropping economy; African class formation and the Natives' Land Act of 1913 in the highveld maize belt", and Ted Matsetela, "The life story of Nkgono Mma-Pooe: Aspects of sharecropping and proletarianization in the northern Orange Free State 1890–1930" in Marks and Rathbone, pp. 195–237; Tim Keegan, "The restructuring of agrarian class relations in a colonial economy: The Orange River Colony, 1902–1910", *Journal of Southern African Studies*, 5, 1979, pp. 234–254.

126 Marks, "Towards a people's history of South Africa?", p. 306.

127 Wolpe, "Capitalism and cheap labour power," pp. 425–456.

128 Lacey, *Working for Boroko*.

129 M. Legassick, "Capitalist roots of apartheid", *Journal of African History*, 25(3), 1984, p. 358.

226

130 Stanley Trapido, " 'The friends of the natives': Merchants, peasants and the political and ideological structure of liberalism in the Cape, 1854–1910" in Marks and Atmore, *Economy and society*, p. 247.

131 T. R. H. Davenport, *South Africa: A modern history*, 3rd ed., Johannesburg, 1987, pp. 119–120. See also Rodney Davenport, "The Cape liberal tradition to 1910" in Jeffrey Butler, Richard Elphick and David Welsh (eds), *Democratic liberalism in South Africa: Its history and prospects*, Middletown (Connecticut), Cape Town and Johannesburg, 1987.

132 Ross, "The origins of capitalist agriculture in the Cape Colony: A survey", in William Beinart, Peter Delius and Stanley Trapido (eds), *Putting a plough to the ground: Accumulation and dispossession in rural South Africa*, Johannesburg, 1986, pp. 56–58.

133 Robert Ross, *Cape of torments: Slavery and resistance in South Africa*, London, 1983; Nigel Worden, *Slavery in Dutch South Africa*, Cambridge, 1985.

134 Ross, "The first two centuries of colonial agriculture in the Cape Colony", pp. 38–39.

135 G. Fredrickson, *White supremacy: A comparative study of American and South African history*, New York, etc., 1981.

136 Hermann Giliomee gives a penetrating analysis of Fredrickson in "Eighteenth century Cape society and its historiography: Culture, race and class", *Social Dynamics*, 9(1), 1983, pp. 18–29.

137 W. M. Freund, "Race in the social structure of South Africa, 1652–1836", *Race and Class*, 38, 1976, pp. 53–67.

138 Richard Elphick and Robert Shell, "Intergroup relations: Khoikhoi, settlers, slaves and free blacks, 1652–1795", pp. 116–123, 145, 160–162.

139 Giliomee, "Eighteenth century Cape society", p. 22.

140 Ibid., p. 23.

141 Worden, *Slavery in Dutch South Africa* and "Violence, crime and slavery on Cape farmsteads in the eighteenth century", *Kronos*, 5, 1982; J. L. Hattingh, *Die eerste vryswartes van Stellenbosch, 1679–1720*, Bellville, 1981.

142 Giliomee, "Eighteenth century Cape society", p. 23.

143 R. A. Schermerhorn, *Comparative ethnic relations*, Chicago, 1978, p. 114.

144 Elphick and Giliomee, pp. 244–245.

145 Jeff Peires, "On the burden of the present", p. 65.

146 Yudelman, "Dan O'Meara's Afrikaner nationalism", p. 104n.

147 John Wright, "Clash of paradigms" in B. J. Liebenberg (comp.), *Trends in the South African historiography*, Unisa, Pretoria, 1986, p. 143.

148 Wright, *The burden of the present*.

149 Anthony Atmore and Nancy Westlake, "A liberal dilemma: A critique of the Oxford History of South Africa", *Race* 14(2), 1972, pp. 107–136.

150 S. T. van der Horst, *Native labour in South Africa*, London, 1942; for de Kiewiet see pp. 113–119.

151 Wright, *The burden of the present*, pp. 85–88.

152 Peires, "On the burden of the present", p. 64.

153 Hopkins, pp. 4, 31.

154 Wright, *The burden of the present*, pp. 77–82.

155 Ibid., pp. 63–67.

156 Marks and Atmore, *Economy and society*, pp. 44–79.

157 R. Hunt Davis, Jr, "The burden of the present", *International Journal of African Historical Studies*, 12(2), 1979, p. 280.

158 Harrison Wright, "The burden of the present and its critics", *Social Dynamics*, 6(1), 1980, p. 46.

159 Fyfe, *African studies since 1945*, p. 15.

160 See p. 165.

161 Denoon and Nyeko, p. x.

162 Van Jaarsveld, *Omstrede verlede*, pp. 73, 83.

163 Marks and Rathbone, *Industrialisation and social change*, p. 3.

164 See pp. 91–93.

165 Wolpe, "Capitalism and cheap labour–power" pp. 425–456; Martin Legassick, "Legislation, ideology and economy in post-1948 South Africa", *Journal of Southern African Studies*, 1(1), 1974, pp. 5–35; Legassick, "South Africa: Forced labour, industrialization, and racial differentiation" in R. Harris, *The political economy of Africa*, New York, 1975, pp. 229–270; Legassick, "South Africa: Capital accumulation and violence", *Economy and Society*, 3(3), 1974, pp. 253–291.

166 Nel, "Recent Marxist analyses", p. 144.

167 Davies, *Capital, state and white labour in South Africa*, p. 3.

168 See H. Wolpe, "Industrialism and race in South Africa", in S. Zubaida, *Race and racialism*, London, 1970, p. 170 and "Ideology, policy and capitalism in South Africa" in R. Benewick et al, *Knowledge and belief in politics – the problem of ideology*, London, 1973, p. 284; F. A. Johnstone, *Class, race and gold: A study of class relations and racial discrimination in South Africa*, London, 1976, p. 2.

169 Nel, "Recent Marxist analyses", p. 150.

170 See p. 192.

171 " 'Most painful to our hearts' ", p. 6.

172 "In search of a Marxist perspective", p. 451.

173 Hughes, "Challenges from the past", p. 58.

174 Davenport's review of Yudelman, *Social Dynamics*, 9(1), 1983, p. 95.

175 Bundy, *The rise and fall of the South African peasantry*, preface.

176 O'Meara, *Volkskapitalisme*.

177 Du Bruyn, "The 'Forgotten Factor' ", p. 45.

178 B. J. Liebenberg, "Omstrede Suid-Afrikaanse verlede – 'n omstrede boek deur 'n omstrede skrywer", *Kleio*, 17, 1985, p. 110.

179 Deborah Posel, "Rethinking the 'race-class debate' in South African historiography", *Social Dynamics*, 9(1), 1983, p. 50.

180 Ibid., p. 52.

181 Bozzoli, "Class, community and ideology", pp. xvii–xviii, 2.

182 Lodge, p. 5.

183 Marks, *The ambiguities of dependence*, p. 8.

184 " 'Most painful to our hearts' " pp. 23, 25.

185 Lonsdale, "From colony to industrial state", p. 71.

186 Posel, p. 60.

187 Ibid., p. 63.

188 Johnstone, " 'Most painful to our hearts' ", pp. 20–21.

189 Posel, p. 63.

190 " 'Most painful to our hearts' ", pp. 19–20.

191 Quoted by Yudelman in his review of O'Meara, *Social Dynamics*, 9(1), 1983, p. 102.

192 Bozzoli, *Town and countryside*, pp. 2–3.

193 See inter alia, Bozzoli, *Town and countryside* and Beinart, Delius and Trapido, *Putting a plough to the ground*.

194 Denoon and Nyeko, p. x.

195 See *Weekly Mail*, 20–26 February 1987, p. 12.

196 Lipton, p. 7.

197 Ibid., p. 9.

198 Ibid., pp. 10–11.

199 Z. K. Matthews, *Freedom for my people: The autobiography of Z. K. Matthews: Southern Africa 1901–1968*, Cape Town, 1981, p. 59.

200 P. Curtin, "Recent trends in African historiography and their contribution to history in general" in J. Ki-Zerbo (ed.), Unesco *General history of Africa*, vol. 1, *Methodology and African prehistory*, London, 1981, p. 58.

Index

229

Annals of the Cape of Good Hope (J.C. Chase) 23

Anthropology 10, 14, 139–140, 145, 166, 188

Apartheid (Separate Development) 92–93, 97–98, 118, 136, 138, 144, 172–174, 184, 211–212, 215, 218–219

Apartheid and economic development 118–119, 143, 158, 167, 172, 215, 218

Archaeology 10–11, 139–141, 145, 166, 187–188

Archives 12, 14, 21–22, 24, 33, 35–36, 45–47, 58, 67–68, 70–71, 73, 78–79, 88, 114, 120, 166, 211

Archives Commission 77, 79

Archives Yearbook for S.A. History 45, 70, 77

Arrighi, G. 163

Aryans 67

Atmore, Anthony 114, 170, 175–178, 191, 206–207

Azania 160

Babrow, Merle 3, 31, 42–43

See also Lipton, Merle

Bantjes, Jan 75

Bantu, Boer, and Briton, the making of the South African Native problem (W.M. Macmillan) 42, 110–111, 127

Bantu Education Act of 1954 159

Bantu Studies 134

Barnard, S.L. 88

Barrow, John 13, 33, 202

Basutoland 25, 33, 35

Basutoland Records 33, 35–36, 58

Batavian rule 13

Beinart, William 107, 164, 170, 188, 193–195, 198

Beit, Alfred 45

Belangrijke Historische Dokumenten over Zuid-Afrika 12 34

Benians, E.A. 130

Bergh, J.S. 88

Bergh, Olof 12

Berlin Missionary Society 195

Bethelsdorp 158

Beutler, A.F. 13

Bezuidenhout, C.P. 61

Biography 66–67, 71–72, 82–83, 88, 123, 125

Bird, J. 58

Blaauwkrans 124

Black Circuit 105

Black Consciousness Movement 4

Blacks

contribution to S.A. historiography 4–6, 131–133, 155, 157, 159–162, 220–221

education 4–5, 96, 159–160

as farmers 178, 191–192, 196–197

in historical writing 19, 22–24, 26, 28, 36–42, 47–49, 71–72, 84, 87, 103–104, 111–112, 122, 129, 131–133, 138, 144, 157–162,

173–177, 189–190, 206–208, 219–221

view of whites 133–134, 156–157

Bloch, Marc 168

Bloemfontein Convention 25

Blommaert, W. 46, 69, 76–77

Blood River 46, 71, 74, 76, 85, 124

Boers and Bantu (G.M. Theal) 33

Boëseken, A.J. 42, 89

Bonner, Philip 188, 193–194

Bosman, I.D. 3, 69

Botha, Louis 86, 88, 181

Boyce, W.B. 15

Bozzoli, Belinda 171, 212, 216

Bradford, Helen 199

Braudel, Fernand 168

Brazil 95–96, 203

Bredell, H.C. 63

Bristol University 123

Britain's title in South Africa (J. Cappon) 40

British colonial policy and the South African republics, 1848–1872 (C.W. de Kiewiet) 113

British Empire 29, 104, 116, 125

British Marxist historiography 168, 170, 216

British school of history 18–31, 39–40, 49, 122–129

British Settlers (1820) 15, 44–45, 47

Brits, J.P. 88

Broederbond 183–184

Bronnelys en voetnote (P.J. van der Merwe) 77

Brookes, Edgar 31

Brownlee, Charles 88

Brugmans, H. 69, 81

Bundy, Colin 109, 163, 170, 191, 196–197, 200, 207, 211

Burchell, W.J. 13, 33

Bushmen

See San

Buthelezi, Chief Mangosuthu 5, 133

Butler, General 121

Butler, Jeffrey 121

Buys, Coenraad 174

Bywoners 178, 197–198

Cambridge University 44, 46, 125–126, 128, 141

Cambridge History of the British Empire (E.A. Walker) 122, 124–125, 130

Camdebo 13

Cameron, Trewhella 219

Campbell, John 14

Cana, Frank R. 48

Cape liberalism 144, 155, 157, 200–201

Capital

agriculture 181, 183, 219

industrial 189, 196

mercantile 189, 192, 194, 196, 210

mining 177, 182, 199–200

230

231

Muslim 11–12
Myths and demythologising 21, 41, 73–76, 78, 85, 89–90, 97–98, 139, 173, 200, 206, 220
Mzilikazi 79, 144

Naidoo, Jayaraman 3
Narrative history 91, 188, 218
Natal (annexation) 59
Natal sugar fields 194
National Convention of 1908–1909 123
National Party 64, 90, 97–98, 137–138, 155, 158, 161, 183–184, 199, 219
National Socialism 67, 86
National University of Lesotho 171
Native Land Act of 1913 133, 217
Native labour in South Africa (S.T. van der Horst) 137
Ndebele 79, 176
Ndlambe 159
Neild, K. 216
Nel, Philip 209
Neo-colonialism 189
New Era Fellowship 157
New Imperialism 25
Newton, A.P. 113, 130
Newton-King, Susan 159, 177
Ngubane, Jordan K. 133–134
Nguni 140, 193
Ninth Frontier War 32
Nixon, John 26
Nkomo, Joshua 133
Nkrumah, Kwame 160
Nobel Peace Prize 133, 159
Noble, John 18, 24–25
Nog verder noord, die Potgieterkommissie se besoek aan die gebied van die teenswoordige Suid-Rhodesië, 1836 (P.J. van der Merwe) 76, 79–80
Nordic peoples 67
North American plantations 203
Notes on South African affairs from 1834 to 1838 (W. B. Boyce) 15
Nyeko, Balam 208, 217, 220

O'Meara, Dan 164, 170, 181, 183–185, 187, 211, 213
Oberholster, J.J. 79
Okoye, Felix 5
Omer-Cooper, John (J.D.) 145, 193
Omstrede Suid-Afrikaanse verlede: geskiedenis-ideologie en die historiese skuldvraagstuk (F.A. van Jaarsveld) 3
Ons Vaderland 66
Oral evidence, oral history, tradition 4, 11, 134, 141–142, 166–167, 188
Orange River Sovereignty 22
Ordinance 50 of 1828 110, 159, 177
Oud en nieuw Oost-Indiën (F. Valentyn) 13
Owen, Rev Francis 20, 46

Oxford University 10, 107, 122, 126, 155
Oxford University Press 115–117, 122
Pact government 181–183, 199
Pan-African Congress (P.A.C.) 160
Paravicini di Capelli, W.B.E. 13
Pass laws 93, 110, 179, 199
Past and Present 168
Pastoralism 197, 201
Paterson, William 13
Patriot movement 71, 73
Pedi 26, 176, 193, 195–196
Peires, Jeff 111, 163, 166, 188, 193, 205–206
People's history 165
Periodisation in historical writing 69, 217, 220
Philip, Dr John 14, 20, 38, 88, 109–111, 133–135, 159, 177
Piet Retief se lewe in die Kolonie (J.L.M. Franken) 71
Piet Retief, Lewensgeskiedenis van die Grote Voortrekker (G.S. Preller) 66
Piet Uys (C.W.H. van der Post) 66
Pinnock, Don 172
Pioniers van die Dorsland (P.J. van der Merwe) 76
Pirow, Oswald 127
Plaatjie, Sol T. 132
Plant, Arnold 124
Political economy 167, 210, 213, 218
Politieke groepering in die wording van die Afrikanernasie (J.A. Coetzee) 86
Poor whites, white poverty 67, 78, 103–104, 106, 108, 182, 197
Poqo 213
Portuguese 12, 34
Portugese ontdekkers om die Kaap (W.J. de Kock) 89
Posel, Deborah 212
Potchefstroom University for Christian Higher Education 86
Potgieter, Carl 71
Potgieter, Hendrik (A.H.) 16, 24, 71
Potgieter, Hermanus 24
Poulantzas, N. 164, 170, 184, 186–187, 206
Poverty 94, 103, 105–106, 108, 119, 124, 145, 169, 194, 204
Pre-capitalist modes of production 171
Pre-colonial African societies 118, 138–140, 143–144, 164, 166–167, 171, 188, 190, 192, 211
Précis of the Archives of the Cape of Good Hope (H.C.V. Leibbrandt) 35, 58
Preller, G.S. 46, 48, 66–68, 70–74
Preller Collection 68
Presentism (present-mindedness) 2, 92, 143, 207–209, 214
Pretorius, Andries (A.W.J.) 16, 46, 66–67, 73–75
Primer of South African history (G.M.Theal) 34
Proletarianisation 124, 165–166, 176, 188, 190–192, 197–201, 217

236

238